Constructivism and the Technology of Instruction: A Conversation

Constructivism and the Technology of Instruction: A Conversation

Edited by
Thomas M. Duffy
Indiana University

David H. Jonassen
University of Colorado

LEA LAWRENCE ERLBAUM ASSOCIATES, PUBLISHERS
1992 Hillsdale, New Jersey Hove and London

With special assistance from Peggy Cole.

Lawrence Erlbaum Associates, Inc., Publishers
365 Broadway
Hillsdale, New Jersey 07642

Library of Congress Cataloging-in-Publication Data

Constructivism and the technology of instruction: a conversation
edited by Thomas M. Duffy, David H. Jonassen
p. cm.
Includes bibliographical references and index.
ISBN 0-8058-1272-5
1. Instructional systems--Design. 2. Constructivism (Education)
I. Duffy, Thomas M. II. Jonassen, David H., 1947-
LB1028.38.C66 1992
370.15'23—dc20
92-22781
CIP

Books published by Lawrence Erlbaum Associates are printed on acid-free paper, and their bindings are chosen for strength and durability.

Printed in the United States of America

10 9 8 7 6 5

Contents

V. Reflections on the Conversation

Acknowledgments

We would like to express a special thanks to Larry Lipsitz of Educational Technology Publications for his support in this project. Larry was the initial stimulus for developing the conversation, and he was most encouraging and cooperative in supporting the extension of the conversations to this book. We thank him and Educational Technology Publications for permission to reprint chapters 3 through 15 and chapters 17 and 19, all of which originally appeared in *Educational Technology* (May and September, 1991).

We also wish to thank David Loertscher and Libraries Unlimited for permission to reprint chapter 2, which originally appeared in G. Anglin (Ed.) (1991). *Instructional technology: Past, present, and future*. Denver, CO: Libraries Unlimited. Finally, we would like to thank Hollis Heimbouch, of Lawrence Erlbaum Associates, for her help and cooperation in making this effort flow smoothly.

Preface

This book is about the implications of constructivism for instructional-design practice. However, more importantly, it is a dialogue between instructional developers and learning theorists. We have been involved in both the theory of learning and the practice of instructional design. As we work with colleagues in each discipline, we have been amazed to find a general lack of familiarity with each other's work. Indeed, most often there is even a lack of interest in the work of the other. Even the leading publishers in the two fields, Lawrence Erlbaum Associates and Educational Technology Publications, had never met until conferring for the preparation of this book. Just as the preparation of this book served as a vehicle for the publishers to exchange ideas, so too we hope that the book itself will serve as a vehicle for the exchange of ideas between learning theory and instructional practice.

We find the lack of communication between these fields extremely surprising and puzzling. From an instructional-design perspective, it seems to us that the practice of instructional design must be based on some conception of how people learn and on what it means to learn. From a learning-theory perspective, it also seems quite obvious that the value of learning theory rests in the ability to predict the impact of alternative learning environments or instructional practices on what is learned. Thus, the interchange of ideas between these disciplines is essential.

Constructivism provided a very important vehicle for establishing the dialogue. It is not that constructivism is a new perspective. Rather, we think that two changes in our society—the volume of information we must manage and the new opportunities provided through technology—have caused us to revisit constructivism. The effect has been indirect. The information age and the technological capabilities have caused us to reconceptualize the learning process and to design new instructional approaches. Both the learning theories and the instructional approaches are consistent with the constructivist epistemology.

The information age has resulted in rapidly increasing and changing information while at the same time making it more available. Traditional models of learning and instruction emphasized forms of mastering the information in a content domain. Storing information and being able to recall it was central to the missions of both schools and business training. However, it simply is no longer possible (there is too much) or even reasonable (it changes too rapidly) to master most content domains.

Numerous technological advances have permitted us (perhaps required us) to move away from instructional strategies that focus on the presentation of abstract information to the individual to master. Computer network systems enable collaboration which business and industry are demanding. Video provides the opportunity to work in more concrete and stimulus-rich environments and to capture and analyze performances. Advances in hypermedia technology enable individuals to manage information, to begin to generate their own issues, and to test alternative hypotheses.

As a consequence of both the information-rich environment and the technological capability, we see business moving away from presenting a fixed curriculum, toward providing information and instruction when it is needed. In "just in time" training the individual seeks information and instruction as particular job requirements demand it. The goal is not to master the content, but rather to understand and use information to solve a real-world problem. Instructional goals and mastery are determined by the individual—they are not externally imposed. Similarly, in the schools we see calls for theme-based instruction in which the students work on real problems using (and learning) information across disciplines in working on that theme. While topics are specified, the instructional sequence and the details of what is learned arise out of the work rather than being designed a priori. In both cases, learning is seen to be situated in the work context, with the meaning derived from that context.

The first editor initially discussed these changes in a paper with Ann Bednar, Don Cunningham, and David Perry, which was originally published as a chapter in Anglin (1991). As a consequence of these changes, the editors see a window of opportunity for establishing a dialogue that will provide for a richer or more meaningful understanding of both learning and the instructional environment required to achieve that learning. To begin the dialogue we first went to some of the key learning theorists and researchers whose work, we felt, reflected the constructivist perspective. We asked them to describe their theoretical perspective and to consider the implication of their views for the instructional-design process, including front-end analysis, instructional strategies, and assessment. In essence, we wanted them to discuss the link, as they saw it, between constructivist theory of learning and instructional-design practices.

We then went to two of the leading instructional-design researchers and asked them to reflect on the constructivist views presented from the perspective of the practice of instructional design. We wanted to understand, from their perspective, if the constructivist perspective offered new opportunities or challenges to the practice of designing instruction. These chapters originally appeared in the May, 1991 issue of *Educational Technology* magazine.

To provide a conversation, we returned to our original authors and asked them—given the critique from instructional designers—to reexamine the implications of their work for instructional design. We also invited other leading instructional designers and learning theorists to enter into the conversation. Some were asked to offer their comments on the critique of the constructivist perspective, while others were asked to step back and reflect on the implications to be derived from the conversation. Most of these chapters originally appeared in the September, 1991 issue of *Educational Technology* magazine.

We hope that this conversation is simply the beginning of an expanding and thoroughly engaging conversation between those involved in learning theory and those involved in the design of instruction. In coming to understand the different perspectives, we hope that all of us emerge with an enriched understanding of learning and instruction.

REFERENCES

Anglin, G. (Ed.). (1991). *Instructional technology: Past, present, and future* (pp. 88-101). Denver, CO: Libraries Unlimited.

I INTRODUCTION

1

Constructivism: New Implications for Instructional Technology

Thomas M. Duffy
Indiana University

David H. Jonassen
University of Colorado

OBJECTIVIST AND CONSTRUCTIVIST CONCEPTIONS OF LEARNING AND INSTRUCTION

This book is about the design of instructional materials. In particular, it is about the assumptions that we make about the learner and the learning process when we identify learning goals, when we design instructional materials relevant to those goals, and when we select or develop an approach to delivering those materials.

Like all designers, instructional designers call on prior knowledge and experience when developing instruction. They call to mind previous instruction they have designed, have experienced, or have seen that fits the particular constraints of the current situation (Rowland, 1991). These previous experiences play a central role in specifying content and determining instructional strategies.

The models derived from those experiences do not simply reflect instructional strategies and methods—simple behavioral activities. They also reflect an underlying conceptualization of what it means to learn, to understand, and to instruct. Carroll and Campbell (1988) argue that the things we build (computer interfaces in their case) provide a rich basis for studying and understanding the theory that underlies our design. That is, our theory of learning is implicit in our design, and hence one can come to a reasonable understanding of our beliefs about learning from an analysis of that design. While instructional designers typically may not have the time or support to explicitly apply a theory of learning during a design or development task, the theory is nonetheless an integral part of the instruction that is produced.

The integration of learning theory and product design contrasts Reigeluth's distinction between descriptive learning theory and prescriptive instructional theory. Reigeluth (1983) suggests that instructional designers require prescriptive instructional theory—a set of specific methods for manipulating the instructional environment along with the conditions under which each specific set of manipulations should be used to produce a desired learning outcome. More importantly, he argues that a prescriptive instructional theory may be independent of learning theory—the descriptive theories do not need to consider the assumptions we are making about the learning process and what it means to learn and understand.

As Carroll and Campbell have noted, our artifacts clearly reflect our theory. Our designs are not just objective descriptions of the instructional sequence, but rather they are also an implicit expression of our theory of learning. Theories of learning and prescriptions for practice must go hand in hand. Indeed, instructional designers often report that they have difficulty getting the instructor to follow the instructional plan. We would suggest that one of the reasons for this is that the instructor very likely will have different goals for learning and a different concept of what it means to "understand" the subject matter. That is, the instructor will have a different theory of learning and will modify the instructional prescriptions to accommodate that theory. Hence the instructor will seek to supplement or replace content and strategies with approaches that he or she feels will lead to the "appropriate" understanding of the subject matter by the student.

Our commitment to theory-based instruction does not dispute the need for prescriptions as frameworks for thinking about instruction. Nor are we disputing the need for learning theories to provide a better description of the instructional strategies or tactics implied by the theory. Indeed, one of our goals in organizing this book has been to provide a firmer link between learning theories and instructional practices. We firmly believe that prescriptions, along with a rich array of examples, form a foundation for instructional design practices. They provide the base of ideas from which designers can begin to develop their own plan for instruction in the particular situation (Duffy, 1990; Rowland, 1991).

THE OBJECTIVIST TRADITION

Instructional design, and indeed instruction in general in the United States, emerged from an objectivist tradition. Objectivism holds that the world is completely and correctly structured in terms of entities, properties, and relations (Lakoff, 1987, p. 159). Experience plays an insignificant role in the structuring of the world; meaning is something that exists in the world quite aside from experience. Hence, the goal of understanding is coming to know the entities, attributes, and relations that exist. The objectivist view acknowledges that people have different understandings based on differing experiences. Indeed, because of prior experience it is unlikely that two people will have identical understandings. However, the impact of prior experience and human interpretation is seen as leading to partial understandings and biased understandings. The goal is to strive for the complete and correct understanding.

This very basic assumption has significant implications for instruction. The world, according to this view, can be described by set theoretic models (e.g., the propositional models of many current cognitive theories). The goal of instruction is to help the learner acquire the entities and relations and the attributes of each—to build "the" correct propositional structure. An objectivist approach to front end analysis focuses on identifying the entities, relations, and attributes that the learner must "know." An objectivist view of instruction may call for an active student learner, but the purpose of that activity is to cause the student to pay closer attention to the stimulus events, to practice, and to demonstrate mastery of the knowledge. At issue, in the design of the objectivist instruction, is the depth and amount of processing of the stimulus events.

Since knowledge is believed to exist independently of instruction, an objectivist need not look at the instructional activities to see what is learned. Rather, designers produce a test that stands separate from the instruction and is designed to probe the knowledge acquired in an objective way. Furthermore, we can look for mastery of learning; an assumption that everyone has acquired the same basic information and now has it available to use.

Behaviorism is not the only objectivist class of theories. An objectivist epistemology also underlies much of the information-processing-based cognitive psychology (Bednar, Cunningham, Duffy, & Perry, chapter 2; Bruner, 1990). Indeed, the objectivist cognitive psychology is even more explicit about the independent existence of information and the acquisition of that information. Understanding is seen as being composed of a knowledge base in the form of an "expert" model (which consists of production rules, frames, slots, etc.). Particular stimulus events (either internal or external) trigger particular productions. Hence, learning simply involves acquiring the information frames or production rules. A person's understanding can be fully specified by these exogenous descriptions.

CONSTRUCTIVISM

Constructivism provides an alternative epistemological base to the objectivist tradition. Constructivism, like objectivism, holds that there is a real world that we experience. However, the argument is that meaning is imposed on the world by us, rather than existing in the world independently of us. There are many ways to structure the world, and there are many meanings or perspectives for any event or concept. Thus there is not a correct meaning that we are striving for.

While the philosophical roots of constructivism antedate modern learning psychology, there is only enough space to deal with current conceptions. The current interest in constructivism can be marked by a number of works and specific theoretical positions. In this book we have chapters from four groups involved in constructivist theory development. Before turning to those chapters, let us briefly consider some related perspectives on constructivism.

Meaning is seen as rooted in, and *indexed* by, experience (Brown, Collins, & Duguid, 1989a). Each experience with an idea—and the environment of which that idea is a part—becomes part of the meaning of that idea. The experience in which an idea is embedded is critical to the individual's understanding of and ability to use that idea. Therefore, that experience must be examined to understand the learning that occurs. Most of us agree that the experience with concepts and relations in school typically is quite different from the experience with them in the real world. Resnick (1987); Brown, Collins, and Duguid (1989a); and Sherwood, Kinzer, Hasselbring, and Bransford (1987) all point to these differences as a major factor underlying the failure of transfer from school-based learning.

Therefore, constructivists (see Brown et al., 1989a) emphasize "situating" cognitive experiences in authentic activities. For example, cognitive apprenticeship is an instructional strategy that is particularly appropriate to providing authentic experiences (see Collins, Brown, & Newman, 1988 for an excellent discussion and examples of cognitive apprenticeship). Resnick (1987) amplifies many of these same themes, but pays particular attention to the distinction between in-school and out-of-school learning and behavior. She notes the lack of transfer between the two environments and argues that it results from the decontextualization of learning, a theme that runs throughout the chapters in this book. Bednar, Cunningham, Duffy, and Perry (chapter 2); Streibel (1991); and Kember and Murphy (1990) all extend these issues to instructional technology.

If we accept that understanding is indexed by experience and that it is constructed, then what is the role of "plans"? We see many examples of successful performance where the individual talks about the plan that guided behavior. Much of current instructional design is based on the presumption that we can give individuals plans of action, and success is simply a matter of following the plans. Suchman (1987) argues that plans are simply projective or retrospective accounts of action. While an individual enters a situation with a plan, the critical aspect of performance is the ability to respond to the situational constraints—to be able to construct new plans based on the changing demands and constraints of the situation. In this view, then, plans (the principles, rules, procedures we teach) are *"part of the subject matter of purposeful action, not something to be improved upon or transformed into axiomatic theories of action."* Instruction, we believe, should not focus on transmitting plans to the learner but rather on developing the skills of the learner to construct (and reconstruct) plans in response to situational demands and opportunities.

Instruction should provide contexts and assistance that will aid the individual in making sense of the environment as it is encountered. A plan is one part of that sense making, but plans must be constructed, tested, and revised as a function of the particular encounters in the environment.

A critical component of constructivism that is explicit in Suchman's arguments is that there is no ultimate, shared reality, but rather, reality that is the outcome of constructive processes. Thus when two people are carrying on a discussion concerning some issue, there is always uncertainty on the part of Person *B* as to whether Person *A* "really" understands the point being made. No matter how much *A* says "I understand" there is still uncertainty on the part of *B* as to whether he "really" did fully get the point. According to Suchman (1987), there should be uncertainty. *A* is constructing an understanding that cannot be identical to *B*'s. Each has constructed an understanding and revised it as necessary to permit them to come to certain agreements (the discussion), but this does not suggest that their understandings are identical. On a larger scale, Suchman presents the example of two people walking into a room. Each constructs a plan for functioning in that room. This plan is basically an attempt to impose order (rather than to "find" order) in the mass of stimuli and events. Each revises his or her plan as it fails to help in negotiating the environment (which includes physical and social negotiation). The important point is that each has their own construction, their own understanding, rather than some common reality.

Winograd and Flores (1986) argue that because behavior is situationally determined, "One cannot construct machines that either exhibit or successfully model intelligent behavior" (p. 11). Thus they present a strong indictment of the computer models of mind. The reasoning rests largely on the argument that behavior is situationally determined. "Every action is an interpretation of the current situation based on an entire history of our interactions" (Clancy, 1986, p. 5). There are not representations stored in the head, but rather the representation is constructed *in situ* based on an unformalized (unstructured) prior history.

Computer models of mind rely on a formalization of knowledge. Experiences must be represented in some propositional form. However, any propositionalization is simply one representation of that prior experience. The individual, but not the computer or the computer model of mind, can reconceptualize, reconstruct, and repropositionalize that experience in many different ways. It is the storage of experiences (unformalized background) that the computer systems and models cannot achieve, and it is this unformalized background that gives the individual the ability to construct new understandings and representations based on that experience.

Teaching for Winograd and Flores (1986) involves providing the student with the means of experiencing the history of interactions—building the "unformalized" background that can be used to create representations in the future. In providing these histories the goal is to support the constructive activities of the learner so that efforts at constructing understanding—using our cognitive tools—become transparent or "ready-at-hand."

Clancy (1986), who created classic, propositional representations of thinking such as Mycin and Guidon, concluded from his review of Winograd and Flores that "After reading the book twice and after much consideration, I believe Winograd and Flores are mostly right.... At its heart, the world is not as we thought."

INTRODUCTION TO THE BOOK

PART II. CONSTRUCTIVIST PERSPECTIVES

What are the implications of constructivism for instructional design? The authors of the chapters in Part II of this book, Constructivist Perspectives, examine the implications of constructivism for instructional theory and practice. For those chapters, we asked researchers who have contributed substantially to the enunciation of constructivist theory of instructional design to describe their theories and relate them to issues in instructional design: front-end analysis, selection and design of instructional strategies, and assessment. Each emphasizes, appropriately enough, a different issue in the constructivist epistemology and may, in fact, disagree with portions of what we have attributed to constructivism. Nonetheless, there is, in our minds, something different from traditional instructional design in their theories and in the artifacts of instruction they describe. We see constructivism as the common thread between them. Each of the authors presents their theoretical position and then discusses the implications of that view for front-end analysis, instructional strategies, and assessment. Hence our hope is that this discussion will help to establish an important link between prescriptive instructional theory and descriptive learning theory.

• **Bednar** and her colleagues (chapter 2) expand the foundations for a discussion of constructivism laid in this chapter by arguing that abstracting concepts and strategies from their theoretical position, as instructional systems theory has done, strips them of their meaning, so it is necessary to deliberately apply some particular theory of learning (preferably constructivist, cognitive theory) to the design and development of instructional materials. The implications of constructivist theory for instructional developers are that specific content and outcomes cannot be prespecified although a core knowledge domain may be specified; types of learning cannot be identified independent of the content and the context of learning; learning outcomes should focus on the process of knowledge construction and the development of reflexive awareness of that process; learning goals should be determined from authentic tasks with more specific objectives resulting from the process of solving the real-world task; the processes of learning should be modeled and coached for students with unscripted teacher responses; and learners should be able to construct multiple perspectives on an issue, that is, see an issue from different viewpoints. This chapter elaborates the constructivist framework which this chapter begins and the following chapters instantiate.

• **Cunningham** (chapter 3) argues that the goal of instruction is not to assure that individuals know particular things (e.g., as argued by Hirsch, 1987) but rather to show them how to construct plausible interpretations of those things, using the tools that we have provided or developed in collaboration with them. Part of assuring that it is "plausible" includes assuming alternative perspectives (alternative goals, emphases) and developing or soliciting alternative interpretations from those other perspectives. Thus, while all interpretations or constructions are not equal, it cannot be presumed that there is one correct perspective or one correct interpretation.

Cunningham explicitly rejects the notion that he is simply discussing higher order learning—one of the many possible categories of learning. This is a view that is rather consistently expressed by the contributors. Skills cannot be considered independently of the problems to which they are applied. Learning a particular subskill means using it effectively in solving problems. Consistent with this, Cunningham rejects traditional tests, suggesting that we look at the learning activity itself and look at the child's ability to reflect upon or discuss that activity. Cunningham argues that assessment emerges quite naturally from task performance if we have authentic tasks of some substance (e.g., beyond doing word problems at the end of a chapter).

• **Perkins** (chapter 4) emphasizes the "active learner" component of constructivism. By this he means not just that the learner is an active processor of information but more importantly that the learner elaborates upon and interprets the information. Perkins emphasizes that this is not just a phenomenon of higher order learning but occurs even with such simple tasks as learning a person's name (learning a name isn't simply verbal activity). Perkins notes that a constructivist approach need not be discovery learning (Without the Information Given, WIG) but can also focus on more direct instruction as long as the emphasis is ongoing "Beyond the Information Given" (BIG). Whether BIG or WIG, he emphasizes maintaining the integrity of the whole task with a focus on a "phenomenaria" environment rather than an "information bank" environment. He emphasizes testing through explanation, extrapolation, and evidence giving—eschewing the limitations of the typical CAI assessment process.

• **Spiro** and his colleagues (chapter 5) emphasize context in a different way. They adopt the views of Wittgenstein (Fogelin, 1987), emphasizing that context is an integral part of meaning. If we focus on only the critical features of a concept—even family resemblances across examples—we will have a limited, textbook understanding. This is because we are not working with the concept in the complex environment, experiencing (exploring, evaluating) the complex interrelationships in that environment that determine how and when the concept is used. We cannot simplify the context by removing the complex features, for example, as is done in forming an epitome (Reigeluth & Stein, 1983), for this changes the context and hence the understanding of the concept. Rather we must aid the individual in working with the concept in the complex environment, thus helping him or her to see the complex interrelationships and dependencies.

Like traditional instructional prescriptions, Spiro emphasizes working with the concept in a variety of contexts or examples. However, the underlying motivation and hence the implementation are different. We are not searching for critical features of the concept, but rather we are approaching the context from different points of view or purposes and focusing on how the concept might be understood differently for these different purposes. Spiro emphasizes criss-crossing the landscape of contexts, looking at the concept from a different point of view each time the context is revisited. The strategy of this traversal is critical to instruction.

• In the final chapter in Part II, the **Cognition and Technology Group at Vanderbilt** (chapter 6) emphasizes the importance of situating learning in a macrocontext in which the learner can engage in sustained exploration. They use video to provide a context rich in cues and in which the student can develop relevant pattern-recognition skills. In previous work, they have demonstrated that when learning occurs in isolation as separate topics, the learning remains inert. That is, the learner has the information available in memory, but simply never recognizes when it is relevant. Learning in context *can* facilitate the development of usable knowledge if the emphasis is on generative tasks and if the learner is immersed in the environment. The goal is to create an environment in which the student works for an extended time, in which subtasks take on meaning in a larger context rather than being ends in and of themselves, and in which new information is not seen as a new learning demand but rather as useful information or tools for effective functioning in that larger context.

Generative learning is a critical component of this environment. By this they mean that the students are given an overall problem for functioning in the environment (getting home safely) and generate subproblems or subgoals (to notice relevant information and to develop strategies) for achieving the larger task. A learner gauges his/her understanding of the subtasks (calculating the fuel required to get home) by the successful completion of the larger goal—not by a decontextualized standard. Earlier research by the group has demonstrated that this approach leads to a significant increase in transfer, that is, the development of more usable knowledge (Sherwood, Kinzer, Bransford, & Franks, 1987).

It is, of course, more valuable if these contexts are authentic. However, the context need not be the real world of work in order for it to be authentic. Rather the authenticity arises from engaging in the kinds of tasks using the kinds of tools that are authentic to that domain. Teachers and students need to be "genuinely engaged in and reflecting upon authentic exploration of the subject matter" (Brown, Collins, & Duguid, 1989b). This is accomplished using a travel theme, developing videos in which the learner solves problems required to successfully complete a trip.

PART III. INSTRUCTIONAL TECHNOLOGY PERSPECTIVES

The five chapters in Part II of this book, provide an epistemologically rich and consistent theory of instructional design and development that contrasts substantively with traditional practice in the field. In order to articulate that contrast, we asked two of the most prominent instructional designers, Walter Dick and David Merrill, to reflect on the chapters in Part II. Part III, Instructional Technology Perspectives, presents Dick's and Merrill's perspectives on those chapters as well as their views, in general, of the implications of constructivism for instructional technology. Are these ideas new? Does constructivism imply different prescriptions for instruction? Can descriptive learning theory adequately inform instructional prescriptive theory?

Walt Dick (chapter 7) reflects primarily on the chapters by Perkins, Bransford, Cunningham, and Spiro. Dick believes that Perkin's BIG constructivism is an instantiation of the discovery learning model of instruction, which remains valid. He claims that designers would have little problem with Bransford's principles as well, except for the problem complexity which may overwhelm learners without adequate entry-level skills. Dick agrees with Cunningham's belief about embedded assessment, claiming that it is a restatement of the consistent belief that the conditions of the test item reflect the conditions stated in the objective. His greatest concern is with how to assess both group learning and individual student learning and mastery using embedded knowledge construction outcomes. Additionally, Dick claims, such techniques would make formative evaluation of instructional materials very problematic. Spiro's chapter highlights perhaps the greatest difference between designers and constructivists, that designers focus on skills to be learned and constructivists focus on learning a "domain" of knowledge. Designers do not focus on facilitating knowledge as much as they identify and analyze skills that must be acquired for the prerequisite subskills.

Dick concludes his chapter by raising problems, such as the breadth of applicability of constructivist theory, the concern over whether it really is a theory, the efficiency and effectiveness of constructivist instruction because it tries to cover too much, the lack of concern with entry behaviors of students, the efficiency and reliability of their evaluation methods, and the lack of accountability for the learner control invested in the learners. The instructional designer's understanding of instruction as an intervention is inconsistent with constructivist notions because it does not intervene congruently.

Merrill (chapter 8) assumes a different tack by claiming that most of the principles of constructivism, excepting the more radical assumptions, are somewhat congruent not only with his ID_2 model but with most of instructional design theory. Merrill makes this claim by contrasting the fundamental ideas of his theory: that learning results in the organizing of memory into mental models; that performance results from an organized and elaborated cognitive structure; that the construction of a mental model by a learner is facilitated by instruction that explicitly organizes and elaborates the knowledge being taught; that there are different organizations and elaborations of knowledge required to promote different learning outcomes; that only the knowledge represented in a knowledge base external to the learner can be analyzed; that there is some correspondence between these and the representations in the mind; that complex mental models enable the learner to engage in complex human activity; and that instructional strategies are independent of the knowledge to be taught and that the same strategy can be used to teach different content with constructivist beliefs about constructed learning, personal interpretations, active, collaborative, and situated learning, and integrated testing. He takes specific issue with the constructivist concerns about prespecified knowledge and domain-specific learning outcomes and its emphasis on authentic tasks. The fundamental assumption that strategy and subject matter content are somewhat independent and that the learner need not always be in control are major points of difference. Like Dick (chapter 7), Merrill wonders how the consistent methodology implied by instructional design can be accomplished by constructivists, except that constructivists are systematic about the procedures for choosing relevant tasks.

PART IV. CLARIFYING THE RELATIONSHIP

In order to simulate a dialogue and further the dialectic on constructivism and instructional design, we invited the authors of the "constructivist" chapters from Part II to reflect on the comments provided by Dick and Merrill in Part III. In Part IV, Clarifying the Relationship, we also asked other members of the instructional design community to contribute to the dialogue on constructivistic beliefs and practice, especially as related to instructional design. The original authors tended to focus on clarifying and extending the ideas in their chapters, while the new authors reflected on the issues raised. Therefore, we will focus on the issues that are embedded in the chapters in Part IV which include:

Extremism. Reigeluth (chapter 13) takes the most critical view of constructivism, echoing many of the views expressed by Merrill (chapter 8), including the distinction between "extreme" and "moderate" approaches to constructivism. Reigeluth finds it useful to distinguish between curriculum theory and instruction theory and between performance technology and educational technology in analyzing what he characterizes as the "extreme" constructivist views. Reigeluth cannot find "a single point of disagreement" with Spiro et al. and apparently sees the view as fully consistent with elaboration theory and the notion of epitomes. Duffy and Bednar, Spiro et al., and CTGV raise issues, however, that question whether elaboration theory is consistent with their views. Similarly, Reigeluth agrees with Perkins' views and feels instructional designers have already incorporated or should incorporate all the CTGV principles into their repertoire. These notions of constructivism, he claims, do not represent extreme views. Cunningham retorts that the most distinguishing feature of constructivism is its emphasis on argument, discussion, and debate, because from that debate emerges some socially constructed meaning. Extremism is a part of all knowledge domains, and it positively contributes to our understanding of the domain. "There is no right or wrong here in any absolute sense." Different world views should contribute to the dialogue and to the individual's awareness of the assumptions underlying their chosen world view and of the assumptions underlying others. Each contributes, as they have in this book, to our (and hopefully your) understanding of instructional design.

Prespecification of Knowledge. Is knowledge an identifiable entity with some fixed truth value? Is the goal of instruction to acquire a knowledge base that is prespecified? The CTGV raises these questions and answers them by noting that they "contrast our view with one that holds that knowledge is an identifiable entity with some absolute truth value.... One of our major goals...is to encourage students to develop socially acceptable systems for exploring their ideas and their differences in opinion." Spiro et al. concur with this view and note that the rigid prespecification of knowledge is inconsistent with a theory of cognitive flexibility. Duffy and Bednar note that the content of the course is information; knowledge develops through, and is embedded in, the tasks or experiences of the learner. They provide two examples of instruction that reflect their view of constructivism.

Multiple Perspectives. Duffy and Bednar, the CTGV, Cunningham, and Spiro et al. all emphasize that individuals construct their own understanding of the world. As Spiro et al. note, "one must have available a diverse repertoire of ways of constructing situation-specific understandings."

Duffy and Bednar and CTGV further emphasize that these constructed understandings do not mean that any interpretation is as good as any other, but rather that there is a social negotiation of meaning. A critical component of learning and understanding is the ability to evaluate alternative understandings in terms of their usability. Finally, Cunningham points to philosophers of science in noting that even supposedly "standard objective views" arise through social negotiation and are in steady flux. Cunningham uses Merrill's examples of a heart surgeon to illustrate.

Complexity. Both Spiro et al. and the CTGV group emphasize that the real world is complex. Simplifying that world, for example, by providing an epitome, too often leads to a variety of misconceptions. The goal is to provide the complex environment and aid the learner in working in that environment. Both Spiro et al. and CTGV note that in this way the richness of conceptual understanding is developed and students construct important sets of ideas and beliefs.

Entry Skills. Perkins focused on the demands that a constructivist learning environment places on the learner, and acknowledges that much more systematic attention must be given to ways of supporting that learner. In particular he notes the demands that arise from the complexity of managing oneself in the complex learning environment, facing conflicts with one's intuitive models of the world, and adapting to the "new" approach to learning at the same time students are working in the content domain.

Perkins notes that this demand should not lead to a rejection of constructivism but rather to the systematic development of strategies for aiding the learner in managing the complexity. Jonassen suggests, however, that because of these demands, a constructivist learning environment may only be appropriate for advanced knowledge acquisition. He later retracts this position, noting that constructivist approaches may be even more appropriate for younger, novice learners. Spiro et al. also see the restriction on the applicability of constructivist environments. In particular they see the approach as appropriate only in complex and ill-structured domains. In contrast, the CTGV applies their complex environments to instruction of elementary-school children in what is generally considered to be a well-structured domain (math). Consistent with Perkins' argument, they work to develop strategies for aiding the students in working in the domain. Indeed, one might view the elementary-school students as faced with ill-structured problems in a complex domain when they are asked to solve real-world problems using arithmetic. If ill-structuredness and domain complexity are viewed from the perspective of the learner, rather than from the view of an expert analysis of the domain, then most learning that involves the authentic use of knowledge may in fact involve ill-structured problems in a complex domain.

Conditions of Learning. Cunningham notes that constructivism and objectivism are two alternative perspectives on learning and understanding. Any learning situation may be approached from either perspective. This is in contrast to the view of Merrill as well as several of the contributors in this book, that constructivism is an instructional strategy to be placed in the repertoire of strategies and called upon for specific conditions of learning. Viewed as an instructional strategy, the applicability of constructivism is limited to specific learning situations. Viewed as an alternative perspective that includes a wide range of instructional strategies, constructivism is a pedagogical view that can be applied to most if not all learning goals. It is perhaps this contrast of views that has led Cunningham (and the present authors) to be referred to as zealots by Merrill and Reigeluth.

Assessment. Jonassen focuses on issues of assessment. He reviews the critical concepts in constructivism and discusses the implications for assessment. He concludes that assessment in a constructivist environment should be more goal free, assess knowledge construction in real-world contexts, and require authentic learning tasks that represent multiple perspectives and viewpoints.

PART V. REFLECTIONS ON THE CONVERSATION

In this final part of the book, we asked "new" contributors to reflect on the conversations in the first four parts of the book in order to provide an even greater variety of viewpoints. As expected and desired, these four chapters provide four very different syntheses of the state of the art.

Both Winn (chapter 17) and Tobias (chapter 19) note that constructivism is not a new concept but rather one that is generally accepted. Winn goes on to reflect on why this "old concept" has generated so much recent discussion. He suggests that constructivism results in shifting instructional decisions to the time of delivery, consistent with the notion that thinking cannot be separated from doing. Thus, constructivism calls for dramatic rethinking of the role of the instructional designer. In this new view, Winn proposes that a significant instructional design effort is in the designing of the shells or learning environments and providing them with the ability to support students in their construction of meaning. He also seems to agree with Cunningham (chapter 3) that, "the instructional developer will work within the teacher's zone of proximal development, providing tools and techniques to help the teacher accomplish his/her goals."

Fosnot (chapter 16), who provides perhaps the most consistently and radically (Piagetian) constructivist perspective in the book, claims that constructivism is the latest bandwagon to affect education. While the constructivist epistemology is well understood, its implications for instruction are not. She claims that since cognitive research clearly shows that learners progress from concrete explorations in meaningful contexts to symbolic representations of these actions and then on to abstract models, the assumptions of "constructivistic" instructional models in this book are most consistent with this intellectual development pattern. She claims that the constructivist notion of assimilation, that requires that teachers focus on entry-level skills (a point raised by the objectivists as well) appears absent in most of the constructivist applications. Fosnot believes that many "constructivists" have a long way to go before they are truly constructivist.

Tobias sees constructivism as quite different from traditional instructional design models and sees that difference being realized most clearly in the consideration of transfer. While the objectivist and constructivist views are clearly distinguishable, he laments the emphasis on polemics and the dearth of research evidence on either side of the controversy. Tobias identifies some of those research questions. He also identifies some of the issues, including learner control and student entry levels, for which the constructivists must clarify their position relative to the research literature.

Clearly, the most self-reflective chapter in the book is provided by Brock Allen in his confessions of a born-again constructivist (chapter 18). He believes that constructivism and instructional design are not completely incongruent. In fact, many objectivist activities can be used in relatively constructivistic ways. It is the context ("domain-of-experience") and the intention of the designer—more than the methods used—that determine the effect. Allen argues that the authenticity in any learning environment or process results from presenting "a range of opportunities and challenges in which members of a community could assume different roles and learn through interaction and negotiation about how others perform *their* roles." It is the vestiges of "classical instructional design," such as mastery learning and "top-down bias," that bother him the most. Yet he warns that without appropriate expertise, constructivist enterprises may degenerate into meaningless and non-constructive activity. His understanding of the precepts of constructivism are especially acute as he seeks to replace the propositional, set-theoretic reality of objectivism with an experience-based, personalized understanding of things in the world. Allen is at once both a philosopher and a pragmatist which makes his perspectives acceptable to both camps. And he obviously practices what he preaches.

CONCLUSIONS

And with that, we can only note that the issues and implications of constructivism for instructional design are clearly not resolved. We can only hope that this book will lay the foundation for continued discussion so that we may all construct more meaningful interpretations of learning and instruction.

REFERENCES

Brown, J. S., Collins, A., & Duguid, P. (1989a). Situated cognition and the culture of learning. *Educational Researcher, 18*, 32-42.

Brown, J. S., Collins, A., & Duguid, P. (1989b). Debating the situation: A rejoinder to Palincsar and Wineburg. *Educational Researcher, 18*, 10-12.

Bruner, J. S. (1966). *Toward a theory of instruction*. Cambridge, MA: Harvard University Press.

Bruner, J. S. (1990). *Acts of meaning*. Cambridge, MA: Harvard University Press.

Carroll, J. M., & Campbell, R. L. (1988). *Artifacts as psychological theories: The case of human-computer interaction*. Technical Report RC 13454 (#60225). Yorktown Heights, NJ: IBM Research Division, T. J. Watson Research Center.

Clancy, W. J. (1986). *Review of Winograd and Flores' understanding computers and cognition: A favorable interpretation*. (STAN-CS-87-1173). Palo Alto, CA: Dept. of Computer Science, Stanford University.

Collins, A., Brown, J. S., & Newman, S. E. (1988). Cognitive apprenticeship: Teaching the craft of reading, writing, and mathematics. In L B. Resnick (Ed.), *Cognition and instruction: Issues and agendas*. Hillsdale, NJ: Lawrence Erlbaum Associates.

Duffy, T. M. (1990). *Toward aiding the text design process*. Paper presented at the annual meeting of the American Educational Research Association, San Francisco, CA.

Fogelin, R. J. (1987). *Wittgenstein*. New York: Routledge & Kagan Paul.

Hirsch, E. D., Jr. (1987). *Cultural literacy: What every American needs to know*. Boston: Houghton Mifflin.

Kember, D., & Murphy, D. (1990). Alternative new directions for instructional design. *Educational Technology, 30*, 42-47.

Lakoff, G. (1987). *Women, fire, and dangerous things*. Chicago, IL: University of Chicago Press.

Reigeluth, C. M. (1983). Instructional design: What is it and why is it? In C. M. Reigeluth (Ed.), *Instructional-design theories and models* (pp. 3-36). Hillsdale, NJ: Lawrence Erlbaum Associates.

Reigeluth, C. M., & Stein, F. S. (1983). The elaboration theory of instruction. In C. M. Reigeluth (Ed.), *Instructional-design theories and models* (pp. 338-381). Hillsdale, NJ: Lawrence Erlbaum Associates.

Resnick, L. (1987). Learning in school and out. *Educational Researcher, 16*, 13-20.

Rowland, G. (1991). *Problem solving in instructional design*. Unpublished doctoral dissertation, Bloomington, IN: Instructional Systems Technology, Indiana University.

Sherwood, R. D., Kinzer, C., Bransford, J., & Franks, J. J. (1987). Some benefits of creating macro-contexts for science instruction: Initial findings. *Journal of Research in Science Teaching, 24,* 417-435.

Sherwood, R. D., Kinzer, C., Hasselbring, T., & Bransford, J. (1987). Macro contexts for learning: Initial findings and issues. *Journal of Applied Cognition, 1,* 93-108.

Streibel, M. J. (1991). Instructional plans and situated learning: The challenge of Suchman's theory of situated actions for instructional designers and instructional systems. In G. Anglin (Ed.), *Instructional technology: Past, present, and future* (pp. 117-132). Denver, CO: Libraries Unlimited.

Suchman, L. A. (1987). *Plans and situated actions*. New York: Cambridge University Press.

Winograd, T., & Flores, F. (1986). *Understanding computers and cognition: A new foundation for design*. Norwood, NJ: Ablex Publishing Co.

II CONSTRUCTIVIST PERSPECTIVES

2

Theory into Practice: How Do We Link?

Anne K. Bednar
Donald Cunningham
Thomas M. Duffy
J. David Perry
Indiana University

The field of Instructional Systems Technology (IST) prides itself on being an eclectic field, Dewey's proverbial "linking science" between theories of the behavioral and cognitive sciences and instructional practice. This view of the relationship between theory and the field of IST takes the perspective that it is appropriate to select principles and techniques from the many theoretical perspectives in much the same way we might select international dishes from a smorgasbord, choosing those we like best and ending up with a meal which represents no nationality exclusively and a design technology based on no single theoretical base.

That is, the primary strategy for providing this "link" between theory and practice has been to collect concepts and strategies suggested by the theories and make them available to the practitioners. The concepts and strategies are abstracted out of their theoretical framework, placed within a practitioner's framework, and grouped based on their relevance to a particular instructional design task (i.e., positioned in some form of a general systems model). In the case of instructional concepts and strategies, these are grouped based on their relevance to the particular learning goal, category of learning, or performance objective.

An eclectic approach is clearly preferred by the field of IST. Practitioners, it is argued, need the best guidance possible for their design and development efforts, and that guidance should be sought from the widest array of research and theory on human learning and cognition (Fleming & Levie, 1978). It seems unreasonable to presume that each individual could continually maintain an awareness of all of the research (empirical and theoretical) that is potentially relevant and synthesize that research to arrive at its practical implications. Thus, abstracting the techniques from the theories is a practical mechanism for providing the guidance that practitioners require. While one might be concerned with mixing techniques from different theoretical perspectives, advocates of this strategy simply point to the fact that the instructional moves derived from one learning theory are often very similar to those derived from another learning theory even when the theoretical explanations of those moves may differ (Bonner, 1988; Fleming & Levie, 1978; Reigeluth, 1987). The techniques that lead to instruction seem separable from their theoretical framework.

The field of instructional systems technology currently draws principles of instructional design and development from empirical studies conducted within the traditions of an incredible variety of paradigms and disciplines: behavioral learning theory, cybernetics, information-processing cognitive theory, media design/production, adult learning, systems theory, and so forth. As we acquire more and more tools with which to work, interesting mixtures of theories and practice begin to emerge. A striking example is Keller's (1987) ARCS theory which draws on theories based on a premise of free will as well as behavioral theories based on the premise of determinism. However, even more unified approaches, such as elaboration theory (Reigeluth & Stein, 1983), reflect this eclecticism in that while they may draw from theories which share common epistemological assumptions, they borrow from the wide array of alternative, and sometimes significantly different, theoretical representations.

Until recently the field of IST has tended to rely for a theory of learning most heavily on the field of behavioral learning theory. The overwhelming focus of IST on behavioral learning outcomes and on the design of maximally effective and efficient learning environments is incontrovertible evidence of this influence. But, as cognitive theory has moved to the forefront of learning theories, the question arises more and more frequently in the field as to whether and how instructional systems designers can add to their arsenal of concepts and strategies by integrating the ideas basic to current cognitive theory into professional practice (Bonner, 1988; DiVesta & Rieber, 1987; Gagné & Dick, 1983; Low, 1981). The perspectives expressed so far on this question suggest that theories and research on cognitive information processing (the currently most popular version of cognitive psychology), while not currently included as part of instructional design models, could be incorporated into those existing systems to improve their effectiveness. And so instructional designers are encouraged to learn techniques of protocol analysis and knowledge representation, to examine the literatures on expert/novice problem solving, metacognition, imagery processes and so on as they consider instructional problems within the context of a traditional instructional design model.

In this chapter we wish to challenge the concept that the eclectic nature of the field of IST is necessarily a strength. We will illustrate our argument by reference to the implications of various versions of cognitive science for the field of IST but we wish to emphasize that our argument applies to theories of all varieties which have been assumed to inform instructional design and development.

In brief, we will argue that abstracting concepts and strategies from the theoretical position that spawned them strips them of their meaning. Theoretical concepts emerge in the context of certain epistemological assumptions which underlie the theory. To use a concept like knowledge of results stripped from the assumption that learning is the strengthening of S-R bonds strips the concept of its fundamental basis. We propose that:

> *Instructional design and development must be based upon some theory of learning and/or cognition; effective design is possible only if the developer has developed reflexive awareness of the theoretical basis underlying the design.*

In other words, we will argue that effective instructional design emerges from the deliberate application of some particular theory of learning. While we certainly have our preferences for some theories as opposed to others, in this paper we simply wish to promote the idea that developers need to be aware of their personal beliefs about the nature of learning and select concepts and strategies from those theories which are consistent with those beliefs.

We will begin by presenting the basic characteristics of the information processing and constructivist viewpoints within cognitive psychology. We will then contrast the implications of these views for instruction and the instructional design process. Finally, we will reflect on the implications of the discussion for the future directions of the field. In general, the conclusion we will come to is that our instructional methods and our methods of analysis reflect a theory of learning and, more fundamentally, reflect an epistemology. The theory and methods simply cannot be separated. The epistemology gives meaning to the methods both globally and in any detailed implementation:

- Globally, theory reflects epistemology. Any theory must of necessity embody a perspective on what we mean by knowing. As we shall see, adoption of a particular epistemological view has far ranging implications. We think it is essential that a designer be aware of the epistemology her instruction embodies. We also think that it is inconceivable to mix epistemologies in an instructional program.

- In detailed implementation, the way in which a technique or concept is realized in its application is a reflection of the theoretical interpretation of that technique or concept. The theoretical framework from which that method or concept was abstracted is essential for guiding the designer in her decision making.

THE COGNITIVE SCIENCES

There are many approaches to the study of cognition and we will limit our discussion to two general ones: traditional (often referred to as the Turing, symbol-manipulation, or information-processing view) and constructivist (experiential, semiotic, etc.).

Traditional Cognitive Science. Howard Gardner (1987, p. 6) defines cognitive science as "a contemporary, empirically based effort to answer long-standing epistemological questions—particularly those concerned with the nature of knowledge, its components, its sources, its development, and its deployment." Gardner lists five features generally associated with cognitive science, three of which are relevant to our purposes here. First, cognitive science is explicitly multidisciplinary, drawing especially upon the disciplines of psychology, linguistics, anthropology, philosophy, neuroscience, and artificial intelligence. Second, a central issue for this discipline is cognitive representation, its form, structure, and embodiment at various levels (neurological, linguistic, sociological, etc.). And third is the faith that the electronic computer will prove central to the solution of problems of cognitive science, both in the conduct of research to investigate various cognitive representations and in providing viable models of the thought process itself.

While certainly interdisciplinary, it should be obvious that cognitive science as described above is unanimous in its agreement on certain fundamental assumptions underlying the discipline. And, we would argue that in spite of their many differences, this version of cognitive science shares many of these assumptions with behaviorism, making its uneasy alliance as a linking science for IST possible. The most crucial of these fundamental assumptions is labeled *objectivism* by George Lakoff (1987).

Objectivism is a view of the nature of knowledge and what it means to know something. In this view, the mind is an instantiation of a computer, manipulating symbols in the same way (or analogously, at least) as a computer. These symbols acquire meaning when an external and independent reality is "mapped" onto them in our interactions in the world. Knowledge, therefore, is some entity existing independently of the mind which is transferred "inside the mind." Cognition is the rule-based manipulation of these symbols via processes that will be ultimately describable through the language of mathematics and/or logic. Thus, this school of thought believes that the external world is mind independent (i.e., the same for everyone) and we can say things about it that are objectively, absolutely and unconditionally true or false. Of course, since we are human, we are subject to error (illusion, errors of perception, errors of judgment, emotions and personal and cultural biases). These subjective judgments can be avoided, however, if we rely on the methodologies of science and logical reasoning. The use of these will allow us to rise above such limitations so that we will eventually be able to achieve understanding from a universally valid and unbiased point of view. Science can ultimately give a correct, definitive, and general account of reality, and, through its methodology, it is progressing toward that goal. Objectivity is a goal we must constantly strive for.

Consistent with this view of knowledge, the goal of instruction, from both the behavioral and cognitive information-processing perspective, is to communicate or transfer knowledge to learners in the most efficient, effective manner possible. Knowledge can be completely characterized using the techniques of semantic analysis (or its second cousin, task analysis). One key to efficiency and effectiveness is simplification and regularization; that is, thought is atomistic in that it can be completely broken down into simple building blocks which form the basis for instruction. Thus, this transfer of knowledge is most efficient if the excess baggage of irrelevant content and context can be eliminated.

Because behaviorism and cognitive information processing share this objectivist epistemology, they are the source of insights for those in the field of IST who share their assumption. Behaviorist applications will focus on the design of learning environments which optimize knowledge transfer while cognitive information processing stresses efficient processing strategies.

However, in a process somewhat akin to religious conversion, we have come to question objectivist epistemology. We have adopted what we will call a constructivist view and begun to explore the implications of such a view for the field of IST. While we are very early in this process, there is one thing which is very clear: Constructivism is completely incompatible with objectivism. We cannot simply add constructivist theory to our smorgasbord of behaviorism and cognitive information processing.

Constructivist Cognitive Science. The constructivist view of cognition is not new but is receiving increasing attention because of an amazing convergence of disciplines which are coming to recognize it: connectionist approaches to cognitive science (Rummelhart & McClelland, 1986), semiotics (Cunningham, 1987), experientialism (Lakoff, 1987), intertextuality (Morgan, 1985), relativism (Perry, 1970), and so forth.

In this view, learning is a constructive process in which the learner is building an internal representation of knowledge, a personal interpretation of experience. This representation is constantly open to change, its structure and linkages forming the foundation to which other knowledge structures are appended. Learning is an active process in which meaning is developed on the basis of experience. This view of knowledge does not necessarily deny the existence of the real world and agrees that reality places constraints on the concepts that are knowable, but contends that all we know of the world are human interpretations of our experience of the world. Conceptual growth comes from the sharing of multiple perspectives and the simultaneous changing of our internal representations in response to those perspectives as well as through cumulative experience.

Consistent with this view of knowledge, learning must be situated in a rich context, reflective of real-world contexts for this constructive process to occur and transfer to environments beyond the school or training classroom. Learning through cognitive apprenticeship, reflecting the collaboration of real-world problem solving and using the tools available in problem-solving situations are key (Brown, Collins, & Duguid, 1989a, 1989b). How effective or instrumental the learner's knowledge structure is in facilitating thinking in the content field is the measure of learning.

IMPLICATIONS FOR THE INSTRUCTIONAL DESIGN PROCESS

Traditional behavioral theory and cognitive science contrast dramatically to the constructivist theories in terms of the underlying epistemological assumptions. As should be clear from the discussion thus far, these epistemological differences have significant consequences for our goals and strategies in the instructional design process. The objectivist approach to instructional design is well documented and thus we will not dwell on it here. The interested reader may see Dick and Carey (1985), Gagné and Briggs (1979), and Romiszowski (1981) for views of instructional design which emerge from the behaviorist tradition. The cognitive objectivist view is perhaps best described in Polson and Richardson (1988); Mumaw and Means (1988); Schlager, Means, and Roth (1988); and Lesgold, LaJoie, Bunzo, and Eggan (1992).

We will focus here on the implications for instructional design derived from a constructivist view. We see the view of learning as a constructive process having wide-ranging implications for virtually all aspects of the design process: the concept of the learning objective, the specification of goals outcomes, and methodologies for analysis, synthesis and evaluation. Indeed, it even calls into question the traditional separation of method from content.

Analysis

In the traditional approach to instructional design, the developer analyzes the conditions which bear on the instructional system (such as content, the learner, and the instructional setting) in preparation for the specification of intended learning outcomes.

Analysis of Content. The traditional approach to content analysis has two goals. First, there is an attempt to simplify and regularize, or systematize, the components to be learned, to translate them into process or method. This is done by identifying content components and classifying the components based on the nature of the content and the goals of the learner. For example, one system would see components as facts, principles, concepts, and procedures, while the goals would be to remember, use, or find. Second, the analysis specifies prerequisite learning. In essence the analysis prespecifies all of the relevant content and the logical dependencies between the components of the content.

The constructivist view is very different. Since the learner must construct an understanding or viewpoint, the content cannot be prespecified. Indeed, while a core knowledge domain may be specified, the student is encouraged to search for other knowledge domains that may be relevant to the issue. It is clear that knowledge domains are not readily separated in the world; information from many sources bears on the analysis of any issue. Further, it is often the case that the most successful individual in nonschool related environments is the one who can bring a new perspective, new data, to bear on an issue. In school, we must also encourage students to seek new points of view; to consider alternative data sources. Please note that we are not arguing that there can be no specification of relevant domains of information. We can and must define a central or core body of information; we simply cannot define the boundaries of what may be relevant (Lakoff, 1987; Wittgenstein, 1953). Indeed, we would argue strenuously that the traditional segregation of knowledge domains contributes to the development of much "inert" knowledge. Students simply do not see the use of information outside of the traditional limits of the domain or the setting in which it was learned (e.g., school).

The constructivist view also does not accept the assumption that types of learning can be identified independent of the content and the context of learning. Indeed, from a constructivist viewpoint it is not possible to isolate units of information or make a priori assumptions of how the information will be used. Facts are not simply facts to be remembered in isolation. Surely there is no reason to learn a fact by itself. Instead of dividing up the knowledge domain based on a logical analysis of dependencies, the constructivist view turns toward a consideration of what real people in a particular knowledge domain and real life context typically do (Brown et al., 1989a; Resnick, 1987). The overarching goal of such an approach is to move the learner into thinking in the knowledge domain as an expert user of that domain might think. Hence, designers operating under these assumptions must identify the variety of expert users and the tasks they do. For example, our goal should not be to teach students geography principles or geography facts, but to teach students to use the domain of geographic information as a geographer, navigator, or cartographer might do.

Of course, we may not be able to start the student with the authentic task. In some way, we must simplify the task while still maintaining its essence. Reigeluth and Stein's (1983) notion of an epitome seems to fit well here as a means of task definition. However, and most importantly, the goal is to portray tasks, not to define the structure of learning required to achieve that task. Just as the cartographer or geographer must bring new perspectives to bear and construct a particular understanding or an interpretation of a situation, so too must the student. And just as different geographers identify different relevant information and come to different conclusions, so too must we leave the identification of relevant information and "correct" solutions open in the instructional situation. It is the process of constructing a perspective or understanding that is essential to learning; no meaningful construction (nor authentic activity) is possible if all relevant information is prespecified.

Analysis of Learners. When designing instructional systems from a traditional instructional design perspective, the "learner" is most often the pool of learners, the average conditions and range under which the system must function. Certainly some adaptive models for instructional design measure individual progress toward learning goals as part of the system; however, those models are not the norm in instructional design. Further, even in adaptive models there is a concept of the general learner which guides the original design of the materials. Then the individuals are placed within the materials through pretest.

The constructivist approach will also identify the skills of the learner. However, just as we did not identify content units in the domain, we also do not seek a detailed accounting of deficiencies. The focus will be on skills of reflexivity, not remembering. Traditional approaches to learning skills stress the efficient processing of information—the accurate storage and retrieval of externally defined information. Constructivists focus on the process of knowledge construction and the development of reflexive awareness of that process: the possibility of alternative sign systems, the imaginative (e.g., metaphorical) aspects of much of our knowledge, the development of self-conscious manipulation of the constructive process, etc. Since every learner will have a unique perspective entering the learning experience and leaving the experience, the concept of global learner is not part of the constructivist perspective.

Specification of Objectives. In the traditional instructional design approach, the product of the analysis phase is the specification of intended learning outcomes. Throughout the analysis phase the developer classifies the characteristics of the content and learner so as to facilitate their translation in the synthesis phase to instructional method. The categories used by the developer are applied across contents, regardless of the nature of the domain. Similarly, in the synthesis phase the instructional process or methods which are drawn from to comprise the design are considered applicable across domains.

From the constructivist perspective, every field has its unique ways of knowing, and the function of analysis is to try to characterize this. If the field is history, for example, we are trying to discover ways that historians think about their world and provide means to promote such thinking in the learner. Our goal is to teach how to think like a historian, not to teach any particular version of history. Thus constructivists do not have learning and performance objectives that are internal to the content domain (e.g., apply the principle), but rather we search for authentic tasks and let the more specific objectives emerge and be realized as they are appropriate to the individual learner in solving the real-world task.

Synthesis

Traditionally, the design (or synthesis) phase of the instructional design process applies principles derived from psychology and media research to design an instructional sequence (macrolevel) and message (microlevel) which are optimal treatments to achieve a specified performance objective. The design principles are considered to be generally applicable across content and across context. The sequence of instruction is specified based on logical dependencies in the knowledge domain and on the hierarchy of learning objectives.

Examined from a perspective which views knowing as a constructive process, these design principles are called into question. Indeed, the approach is simply antithetical to the constructivist viewpoint. What is central, in our view, is the development of learning environments which encourage construction of understanding from multiple perspectives. "Effective" sequencing of the information or rigorous external control of instructional events simply precludes that constructive activity. Also precluded is the possibility of developing alternative perspectives since the relevant information and the proper conclusion are pre-defined in traditional instruction.

In the same way that macro design strategies are inappropriate, so too are design strategies at the microlevel. For example, it is inappropriate to control or focus the attention of the learner in a manner distinct from a real-world context. Instead, the instruction is based on techniques which are drawn from the constructivist's epistemological assumptions and which are consistent with their theory of learning, for example, situating cognition in real-world contexts, teaching through cognitive apprenticeship, and construction of multiple perspectives.

Situating Cognition. There is a need for the learning experience to be situated in real-world contexts (Brown et al. 1989a, 1989b; Resnick, 1987; Rogoff & Lave, 1984). By "real-world contexts" we mean that:

- The task is not isolated, but rather is part of a larger context (Bransford, Sherwood, Hasselbring, Kinzer, & Williams, 1990). We do not simply ask students to do word problems in the book. Rather we create projects, or create environments, that capture a larger context in which that problem is relevant.

- The "real worldness" of the context refers as much to the task of the learner as it does to the surrounding environment or information base (Brown et al., 1989a; Resnick, 1987). We are not simply talking about critical and incidental attributes of the environment. We also argue that the reason for solving the problem must be authentic to the context in which the learning is to be applied. Thus, we do not have learning and performance objectives that are internal to the content domain (e.g., apply the principle), but rather we search for authentic tasks and let the more specific objectives be realized as they are appropriate to that task.

- The environmental context is critical. An essential concept in the constructivist view is that the information cannot be remembered as independent, abstract entities. Learning always takes place in a context and the context forms an inexorable link with the knowledge embedded within it. Most simply stated, an abstract, simplified environment (school learning) is not just quantitatively different from the real-world environment but is also qualitatively different. The reason that so much of what is learned in school fails to transfer to nonschool environments or even from one subject matter to another is due, in part, to the fact that the school context is so different from the nonschool environment. Hence, Spiro (1988) argues that we must not simplify environments as we typically do in school settings, but rather we must *maintain* the complexity of the environment and help the student to understand the concept embedded in the multiple complex environments in which it is found. Salomon and Perkins (1989) make a similar point in their discussion of high-level transfer.

  Authentic learning environments may be expected to vary in complexity with the expertise of the learner. That is, the child would not be confronted with the complexity of the adult's world—indeed, the child's world is not that complex. Similarly, the economic world seen by the average citizen is far less complex than the world seen by the economist. Hence, when we propose an authentic environment and a complex environment, we are referring to authenticity and complexity within a proximal range of the learner's knowledge and prior experience.

A related issue is the tendency in traditional instructional design to separate the content from the use of the content. Hence we learn about something so that we can use that knowledge later. We believe, however, the learning of a content must be embedded in the use of that content. Sticht and Hickey (1988) have nicely demonstrated this approach in their design of basic electricity training. The traditional approach to this particular course was to prepare an electricity curriculum, based on an analysis of the facts, procedures, concepts, and procedures in the knowledge domain and taught in a traditional textbook fashion. Once learned, the thinking went, the students could go off to their particular specialties and apply the knowledge. This approach was taken by numerous experts in instructional design, in numerous revisions of this particular course.

Sticht and Hickey (1988), in contrast, focused on the functional context of the electricity knowledge. They identified authentic tasks and provided instruction in the context of those tasks. Thus, for example, students were asked to diagnose why a flashlight would not light. Then the class discussed how the various diagnoses might be represented in an overall picture (i.e., a functional analysis). From context to context, they moved the students to more complex and less familiar systems—but always maintaining the functional context of the task.

In a similar fashion, adult reading instruction has always been seen as a skill one acquires before using it. Thus, the reading curriculum for a job precedes job training, and the content of that reading curriculum is seen as independent of the use of reading on the job. Duffy (1985, 1990), Sticht (1975), and Mikulecky (1982), among others, have argued, consistent with the constructivist view, that the reading instruction, as well as the job knowledge, must be taught in the context of job tasks. The tasks and content combine qualitatively to provide an authentic context in which the learner can develop integrated skills.

Cognitive Apprenticeship. The constructivist teacher must model the process for students and coach the students toward expert performance. Collins, Brown, and Newman (1988) provide an excellent discussion of cognitive apprenticeship and summarize three approaches that are well documented in the literature. A critical feature of these approaches is that the teacher's responses are not scripted. The teacher cannot serve as an effective model if he has prepared responses and strategies ahead of time and only reveals an idealized path to the correct solution. Rather, students must come to understand the authentic ways in which the teacher (expert) attempts to represent an issue. For example, Schoenfeld (1985), in teaching university level mathematics, invites students to bring him word problems—brain teasers. The problems are given to him in class and he thinks outloud as he searches for a solution. Of course there are numerous blind alleys and errors in thinking. The class discussion afterward focuses on the strategies that were used, the ways in which the problem was represented, how various sources of information were called upon, and how errors were a natural occurrence of trying alternative representations or strategies.

Multiple Perspectives. The constructivist view emphasizes that students should learn to construct multiple perspectives on an issue. They must attempt to see an issue from different vantage points. It is essential that students make the best case possible from each perspective; that is, that they truly try to understand the alternative views. If we focus on constructing an understanding and if we are providing authentic contexts, then these multiple perspectives can even be applied to content domains that seem very well structured, such as arithmetic (Bransford et al., 1990; Schoenfeld, 1985). Of course, the students must also evaluate those perspectives, identifying the shortcomings as well as the strengths. Finally, they adopt the perspective that is most useful, meaningful, or relevant to them in the particular context.

A central strategy for achieving these perspectives is to create a collaborative learning environment. Note that while cooperative learning has a long history, the focus in that literature has been on the behavioral principles of learning that can be realized in the group environment. We wish to emphasize, instead, the use of collaboration to develop and share alternative views. It is from the views of other group members that alternative perspectives most often are to be realized. Thus, sharing a workload or coming to a consensus is not the goal of collaboration; rather, it is to develop, compare, and understand multiple perspectives on an issue. This is not meant to be simply a "sharing" experience, though respect for other views is important. Rather, the goal is to search for and evaluate the evidence for the viewpoint. Different sorts of evidence and different arguments will support the differing views. It is the rigorous process of developing and evaluating the arguments that is the goal. Further, this is not a competitive endeavor, where groups debate each other to see who is "right." Rather, it is a cooperative effort in which each student is seen as coming to understand each perspective and even contributing to the development of each perspective.

A second important strategy for achieving multiple perspectives and a rich understanding has to do with the use of examples. In traditional instructional approaches the examples are carefully chosen to highlight critical attributes and systematically manipulate the complex of irrelevant attributes. Like word problems at the end of a chapter, there is little that is authentic about the examples: There is a clear correct answer and it is the student's job to find that answer. Of course that is not the nature of the real world—there is little in real life in the way of clear cut examples with only one correct solution. As an alternative to that approach, we would explore the use of real "slices of life." For example, to support teacher education, we would consider recording entire class periods to provide rich contexts for developing perspectives on teaching. The traditional approach to instructional design might instead select clips that represented correct or incorrect examples of a particular concept or principle. We prefer, as students are exposed to the perspectives of experts and peers, to permit the students to select particular instances and bring to bear whatever perspective is useful rather than learn to classify according to some archetypal, decontextualized categories. Our goal, then, is to have students see the alternative views of how a concept is seen in actual instruction. Most importantly, students must learn to develop and evaluate the evidence to support each contention. Note that this task supports a construction of understanding and provides authenticity to the instruction as well as supporting the development of multiple perspectives.

From the traditional instructional design perspective it may be tempting to equate learning in a constructivist sense as pure discovery learning and to criticize that approach for its lack of efficiency. It should be apparent, however, from the previous discussions of situated cognition and cognitive apprenticeship that we are not espousing an unstructured discovery environment devoid of learning goals or learning events. In contrast to discovery learning, there is considerable guidance. It is simply not guidance on mastering a particular content element.

Evaluation

In traditional instructional design, evaluation assumes a universal goal or objective for the instruction. An exam measures progress toward the goal and the data across many students indicate the relative effectiveness of the system in terms of achievement of the goal. With a constructive view of knowledge, the goal is to improve the ability to use the content domain in authentic tasks (Brown et al., 1989a). Instruction is the act of providing students with these tasks and providing them with the tools needed to develop the skills of constructing an informed response and for evaluating alternative responses.

Evaluation in the constructivist perspective must examine the thinking process. This is not to suggest, however, that the issue of thinking is independent of the content domain—quite the contrary. As the extensive research on expert and novice strategies indicates, effective problem-solving strategies are intimately tied to the content domain. Experts are experts because of their understanding of the content domain.

One possible type of student evaluation activity would ask learners to address a problem in the field of content and then defend their decisions. Another might ask the learners to reflect on their own learning and document the process through which they have constructed their view of the content. The strategies common to the problem-solving approach in writing (Hayes & Flower, 1986) clearly reflect this constructivist view and the important blending of content and process.

Two elements seem to be important: (a) that the perspective that each student develops in the content area is effective in working in that area and (b) that the student can defend his/her judgments. The first element might be referred to as instrumentality: To what degree does the learner's constructed knowledge of the field permit him/her to function effectively in the discipline? The most obvious application of the concept of instrumentality might be in problem solving. Can the learner arrive at reasoned solutions to problems in the field? But the concept equally applies in contents which are not traditionally considered to be problem-solving fields; for example, a literature student analyzing a body of literature, an art student critiquing a painting, or an elementary school student learning how different cultures in the world share universal concerns from differing perspectives.

The second element, the ability to explain and defend decisions, is related to the development of metacognitive skills, thinking about thinking. Reflexive awareness of one's own thinking implies monitoring both the development of the structure of knowledge being studied and the process of constructing that knowledge representation.

While either of these student evaluation mechanisms might suggest a viable system evaluation method, that method would certainly contrast to instructional design's traditional mastery model. One of the issues would be how to operationalize the concept of instrumentality, given that no two students would be expected to make the same interpretations of learning experiences nor to apply their learning in exactly the same way to real-world problems which do not have one best answer.

CONCLUSIONS

From our perspective, it appears that the implications of constructivism for instructional design are revolutionary rather than evolutionary. Viewed from contrasting epistemologies, the findings of constructivism replace rather than add to our current understanding of learning. With a new view of what it means to know, it is imperative to reexamine all of the assumptions of any field and particularly one which purports to improve the human condition.

One of the basic assumptions underlying the professional practice of instructional design is the separation of instructional process from content, a belief that general principles of learning apply across contents to a significant enough degree that basic principles of instruction can be successfully applied regardless of content. From a view of knowledge as constructed, the process emerges from the content. In-depth understanding of the content arises from, and is essential to, understanding disciplinary thinking. Since influencing how learners think in a content domain is the goal of instruction, the learning process must reflect those thought processes.

One of the most far reaching implications of constructivism for instructional design is that designers must attach themselves to content domains in much the same way secondary teachers specialize in a content area or the way faculty at the university refer to pedagogy in their discipline. The next generation of instructional designers may be specialists in the design of instruction for teaching reading, or language, or biology. Certainly the relationship between instructional consultant and subject matter expert must be reexamined.

Many issues remain. Is critical thinking the goal of all learning? Do the contexts in which learning is to be applied relate to the nature of the learning experience? Are there contexts where it is appropriate to apply traditional instructional development models and others where it is not? Does a distinction exist between training and education such that a training environment is more appropriate for instruction based on traditional instructional design principles than a school? At what level of schooling is critical thinking a reasonable goal? Is it reasonable to differentiate levels of learning—for example, introductory learning from advanced knowledge acquisition (Spiro, 1988) or memory from problem solving—and to apply different instructional techniques based on different theories, or does that imply that you must believe the nature of knowing, what it means to know, changes between introductory and advanced levels?

Where must we go now as a field? First, we must examine the assumptions which underlie the theories upon which our field is based. Turning toward a view of knowledge as constructed requires a major reconceptualization of our assumptions and practices. But even if such a view is ultimately rejected, we must not delay a full analysis of the assumptions which support our field. In those situations where the assumptions lack consistency, we must adopt a consistent set of assumptions and reject the findings of research and the development of theory based on different assumptions. We must constantly reexamine our assumptions in light of new findings about learning.

As a field we must ground ourselves in theory. One of the practices which requires scrutiny is the practice of drawing from fields with different theoretical bases without examining the conflict between the basic assumptions of those theories. Optimally, we would tie our prescriptions for learning to a specific theoretical position—the prescriptions would be the realization of a particular understanding of how people learn. Minimally, we must be aware of the epistemological underpinnings of our instructional design and we must be aware of the consequences of that epistemology on our goals for instruction, our design of instruction, and on the very process of design.

NOTE

This chapter appeared in Anglin (1991). This work was funded in part by AT&T through a grant to the Center for Excellence in Education, Indiana University.

REFERENCES

Anglin, G. (Ed.). (1991). *Instructional technology: Past, present, and future.* Denver, CO: Libraries Unlimited.

Bonner, J. (1988). Implications of cognitive theory for instructional design: Revisited. *Educational Communication and Technology Journal, 36,* 3-14.

Bransford, J. D., Sherwood, R .D., Hasselbring, T. S., Kinzer, C. K., & Williams, S. M. (1990). Anchored instruction: Why we need it and how technology can help. In D. Nix & R. Spiro (Eds.), *Cognition, education, and multimedia: Exploring ideas in high technology* (pp. 115-139). Hillsdale, NJ: Lawrence Erlbaum Associates.

Brown, J. S., Collins, A., & Duguid, P. (1989a). Situated cognition and the culture of learning. *Educational Researcher, 18,* 32-42.

Brown, J. S., Collins, A., & Duguid, P. (1989b). Debating the situation: A rejoinder to Palincsar and Wineburg. *Educational Researcher, 18,* 10-12.

Collins, A., Brown, J. S., & Newman, S. E. (1988). Cognitive apprenticeship: Teaching the craft of reading, writing, and mathematics. In L B. Resnick (Ed.), *Knowing, learning and instruction: Essays in honor of Robert Glaser* (pp. 453-494). Hillsdale, NJ: Lawrence Erlbaum Associates.

Cunningham, D. (1987). Outline of an educational semiotic. *The American Journal of Semiotics, 5,* 201-216.

Dick, W., & Carey, L. (1985). *The systematic design of instruction.* Glenview, IL: Scott, Foresman.

DiVesta, F. J., & Rieber, L. P. (1987). The next generation of instructional systems. *Educational Communications and Technology Journal, 35,* 213-230.

Duffy, T. M. (1985). Literacy instruction in the armed forces. *Armed Forces and Society, 11,* 437-467.

Duffy, T. M. (1990). What makes a difference in instruction? In T. G. Sticht, B. McDonald, & M. Beeler (Eds.), *The intergenerational transfer of cognitive skills.* Norwood, NJ: Ablex.

Fleming, M., & Levie, W. H. (1978). *Instructional design: Principles from the behavioral sciences.* Englewood Cliffs, NJ: Educational Technology Publications.

Gagné, R. M., & Briggs, L. J. (1979). *Principles of instructional design.* New York: Holt, Rinehart & Winston.

Gagné, R. M., & Dick, W. (1983). Instructional psychology. *Annual Review of Psychology, 34,* 261-295.

Gardner, H. (1987). *The mind's new science.* New York: Basic Books.

Hayes, J. R., & Flower, L. S. (1986). Writing research and the writer. *American Psychologist, 41,* 1106-1103.

Keller, J. M. (1987). Development and use of the ARCS model of motivational design. *Journal of Instructional Development, 10,* 2-10.

Lakoff, G. (1987). *Women, fire and dangerous things.* Chicago: University of Chicago Press.

Lesgold, A., LaJoie, S., Bunzo, M., & Eggan, G. (1992). Sherlock: A coached practice environment for an electronics troubleshooting job. In J. Larkin & R. Chebay (Eds.), *Computer assisted instruction and intelligent tutoring systems: Shared goals and complementary approaches* (pp. 201-238). Hillsdale, NJ: Lawrence Erlbaum Associates.

Low, W. C. (1981). Changes in instructional development: The aftermath of an information processing takeover in psychology. *Journal of Instructional Development, 4*(2), 10-18.

Mikulecky, L. (1982). Job literacy: The relationship between school preparation and workplace actuality. *Reading Research Quarterly, 17*, 400-419.

Morgan, T. (1985). Is there an intertext in this text?: Literary and inter-disciplinary approaches to intertextuality. *The American Journal of Semiotics, 3*, 1-40.

Mumaw, R., & Means, B. (1988). *Cognitive analysis of expert knowledge: Input to test design.* Paper presented at the annual meeting of the American Educational Research Association, New Orleans, LA.

Perry, W. (1970). *Forms of intellectual and ethical development in the college years: A scheme.* New York: Holt, Rinehart & Winston.

Polson, M. C., & Richardson, J. J. (Eds.). (1988). *Foundations of intelligent tutoring systems.* Hillsdale, NJ: Lawrence Erlbaum Associates.

Reigeluth, C. M. (1987). Educational technology at the crossroads: New mindsets and new directions. *Educational Technology Research and Development, 37*, 67-80.

Reigeluth, C. M., & Stein, F. S. (1983). The elaboration theory of instruction. In C. Reigeluth (Ed.), *Instructional-design theories and models.* Hillsdale, NJ: Lawrence Erlbaum Associates.

Resnick, L. (1987) Learning in school and out. *Educational Researcher*, 16, 13-20.

Rogoff, B., & Lave, J. (Eds.). (1984). *Everyday cognition: Its development in social context.* Cambridge, MA: Harvard University Press.

Romiszowski, A. J. (1981). *Designing instructional systems.* New York: Nichols Publishing.

Rummelhart, D., & McClelland, J. (1986). *Parallel distributed processing.* Cambridge, MA: MIT Press.

Salomon, G., & Perkins, D. (1989). Rocky road to transfer: Rethinking mechanisms of a neglected phenomenon. *Educational Psychologist, 24*, 113-142.

Schlager, M., Means, B., & Roth, C. (1988). *Cognitive analysis of expert knowledge: Input into design of training.* Paper presented at the annual meeting of the American Educational Research Association, New Orleans, LA.

Schoenfeld, A. H. (1985). *Mathematical problem solving.* New York: Academic Press.

Spiro, R. (1988). *Cognitive flexibility theory: Advanced knowledge acquisition in ill-structured domains* (Tech. Rep. No. 441). Champaign, IL: Center for the Study of Reading.

Sticht, T. G. (1975). *Reading for working: A functional literacy anthology.* Alexandria VA: Human Resources Research Organization.

Sticht, T. G., & Hickey, D. T. (1988). Functional context theory, literacy, and electronics training. In R. Dillon & J. Pellegrino (Eds.), *Instruction: Theoretical and applied perspectives.* New York: Praeger Publishers.

Wittgenstein, L. (1953). *Philosophical investigations.* New York: Macmillan.

3

Assessing Constructions and Constructing Assessments: A Dialogue

Donald J. Cunningham
Indiana University, Bloomington

What follows is my attempt to explore some of the issues that emerge out of the constructivist perspective related to the issue of assessment. I have chosen the form of a "Galilean Dialogue," modeled after Galileo's famous "Two Major Systems of the World" (see Jauch, 1973, for a more recent incarnation of this format). The topic of Galileo's dialogue was the comparison of the Ptolemaic and Copernican views of the universe. To some, a discussion of objectivist and constructivist views of assessment may seem trivial in comparison, but I would disagree. The issues raised here go to the heart of our world view, to the heart of what we believe it means to be human. I have retained the names of the original participants (Salviati, Sagredo, and Simplicio), although their role in the dialogue is transformed to accommodate the issue at hand.

SALVIATI. I am pleased, my friends, that we could meet again after so long a time. As I remember, we last met during the year 1973 to debate quantum versus classical views of physics. Much has happened since then in the world of scholarship generally that could occupy us here today. But I propose that we focus our discussion on the emerging issues surrounding the constructivist view of learning and instruction that seems to have attracted more and more advocates recently. But perhaps we should begin with a brief summary of the views. Please interrupt me if you feel that I have misrepresented a position or made an error. The first position, that I will call objectivism, conceives of learning and instruction as phenomena amenable to scientific analysis. I believe it was Edward Thorndike (1905) who said something to the effect "If something exists, it exists in some quantity, and if it exists in some quantity it can be measured and submitted to scientific analysis." (I may have that wrong, my memory is not what it used to be.) If the methods of science can be applied to learning and instruction, then we will have a powerful means of understanding these phenomena and maximizing them for the betterment of our world. Through our efforts we will inevitably approach an account of the true nature of learning processes and discover completely valid and reliable means of assessing them. Knowledge, those things we wish our students to know or be able to do, must be concretely specified and the means discovered to effectively and efficiently instill those capabilities in our students. If we are clear about what it is we want our students to know, then and only then can we determine if we have been successful.

SIMPLICIO. Yes, Salviati, I think you have represented the position well, although I think you should stress that instruction is a question of engineering, not simply science. In the same sense that you couldn't possibly build a skyscraper without a set of plans showing the details of the structure, how then can we decide if learning has taken place without a clear and objective indication?

SALVIATI. Thank you for your observation. It is certainly the case that instructional developers take the engineering analogy to heart in their methods and procedures. But let us turn to constructivism. Sagredo, I know you favor this view so please help me if I am not clear.

SAGREDO. Please continue.

SALVIATI. Constructivism holds that learning is a process of building up structures of experience. Learners do not transfer knowledge from the external world into their memories; rather, they create interpretations of the world based upon their past experiences and their interactions in the world. How someone construes the world, their existing metaphors, is at least as powerful a factor influencing what is learned as any characteristic of that world. Some would even argue that knowledge that is incompatible with or unaccounted for in an individual's interpretation cannot be learned. I believe it was Umberto Eco (1984) who said that "A world view can conceive of anything except an alternative world view." As I understand it, this view holds that learning is infinite and not subject to the sorts of analyses favored by objectivists except in the most trivial cases. Things can be known from a variety of sign systems (verbal, mathematical, visual, musical, gestural, etc.), a variety of metaphors (UP IS GOOD, LIFE IS A JOURNEY, LEARNING IS A JOB, etc.), and with varying degrees of self-awareness of the processes by means of which constructions are made. The role of education in a constructivist view is to show students how to construct knowledge, to promote collaboration with others to show the multiple perspectives that can be brought to bear on a particular problem, and to arrive at self-chosen positions to which they can commit themselves, while realizing the basis of other views with which they may disagree.

SIMPLICIO. I have heard these views before and never fail to be puzzled by them. Is it the belief of these constructivists that nothing exists except that which the mind creates? That the chair that I am sitting in exists only because I will it to? What utter nonsense! I thought that such solipsism had faded away long ago!

SAGREDO. I agree, Simplicio, that solipsism is a potential danger to constructivism and must be avoided. But constructivism need not lead inevitably to utter subjectivism. The biologist Humberto Maturana (Maturana & Varela, 1987), who has proposed a view of human understanding very compatible with constructivism, speaks of walking the "razor's edge" between objectivism and solipsism.

SIMPLICIO. But to what end? Does my chair exist or not?

SAGREDO. I hope so, for I would hate to see my valued colleague sprawled on the floor. The point, however, is that our knowledge of chairs is determined by our experience of them in many and varied way: We sit on them, feel the support, move them around if they are not too heavy, stand on them to reach the light bulb, hide behind them in our childhood games, draw them in pictures, use them as metaphors, talk about them as we are doing now, etc. The sense of chair that is "correct" cannot be determined independent of the context in which it appears.

SALVIATI. But I take Simplicio's point, Sagredo. If the chair exists in some context, then it should be possible to determine if someone knew what a chair was in that context.

SIMPLICIO. And we can simply design contexts, or engineer learning environments, to efficiently and effectively communicate that information to the learner. If we want someone to know that a chair is a handy thing to stand on to change a light bulb, then we tell him/her that, and check later on to see if they remember. Seems perfectly straightforward to me.

SAGREDO. But why would a student need to know that?

SIMPLICIO. Obviously, if they need to change a light bulb, the information would come in very handy.

SAGREDO. Thank you Simplicio. You have made one of the points that lies at the very heart of constructivism. Knowledge emerges in contexts to which it is relevant. To engineer a learning environment that communicates all of the possible interpretations of chair that we (and many others) could imagine would be a very complex job indeed. Some have used the words "situated" or "anchored" instruction to convey the idea that learning should occur in realistic settings, aimed toward the solution of problems that actually confront the students in their lives.

SALVIATI. But surely those settings have to be planned and specified in advance. It seems to me that the activities of an instructional developer would be quite similar under both an objectivist and a constructivist framework.

SAGREDO. Perhaps, but I don't think so. Under objectivism, someone decides what it is the student should know, constructs a task analysis of that knowledge, analyzes the learner's existing capabilities, designs a strategy to communicate the required information to the learner, then tests to see if the communication process has been successful. Commonly this is carried out within the artificial setting of the classroom or learning laboratory since distractions to the learning process are minimized. All of these are seen as somewhat independent stages in an ongoing process. The constructivist would proceed by selecting tasks that are relevant to the child's lived experience. This is an important characteristic since Paulo Freire (1970) has shown dramatically that learners must see the relevance of the knowledge and skill to their lives, how such knowledge can help them do things that are embedded in the concerns that they have. The teacher or instructional developer then provides access to tools that can be used to better understand or construct solutions to the problem. Sometimes this can be accomplished by an individual learner, but more often is better approached with a collaborative group, as are most of life's problems. No separate test is required. The "proof," if you will, of the success of the learning is the successful completion of the task.

SIMPLICIO. Who is to decide if the task is successfully completed? And if the task is completed by a group, how do we know if any more than one member of the group has learned? The literature on group work is full of cases where one member of the group dominates and the rest learn very little. It seems to me that the only fair way to assess learning is to construct a test that is given to all members of the group, with demonstrated validity and reliability, and that unambiguously discriminates between those who have learned and those who have not. I find myself agreeing with the sentiment of Thorndike that was referred to by Salviati. If constructions exist, they can be measured. If they don't exist, then you are wasting my time.

SALVIATI. Ah! My dear Simplicio. I implore you to bear with the discussion, for your questions are penetrating and insightful. I am reminded that there are two systems of jurisprudence in the world: one where you are innocent until proven guilty, the other where you are guilty until proven innocent. It appears that you are applying the second to Sagredo.

SIMPLICIO. My apologies to both of you. I meant no offense. Of course I will remain, since I am anxious to hear Sagredo's response to my concerns.

SAGREDO. And they are concerns that I share and to which I do not have answers that are completely satisfactory to me. Let me see if I can remember all of the issues you raised. Who is to judge if a task has been successfully completed? My answer is the teacher. The teacher should bring to bear a variety of evidence and be able to clearly defend his/her assessment, but the final judgment must be a human one.

SIMPLICIO. But then you are saying that assessment is subjective? That objective measurement is of no value?

SAGREDO. I am saying that objective measurement is a fiction or at best a degenerative case where knowledge is so decontextualized that only one context (the school context) is relevant.

SALVIATI. And the teacher should base his or her assessment simply on private opinion?

SAGREDO. Not at all. The teacher should gather as much information as possible. Observe the students. Talk to them. Talk to other teachers. Read the children's class diaries. Videotape the children and show the tapes to others. Give them many tasks to do both as individuals and in groups. Even look at the ubiquitous standardized test scores. Use all of these sources of information. But the point I want to stress is that all of these, save perhaps the standardized test, are part and parcel of the educative process. Assessment is not a separate activity carried out after instruction, using some pseudo-scientific instrument purported to reveal the truth of the student's accomplishment (within the limits of the standard error of measurement, of course).

SIMPLICIO. How can you call objective tests pseudo-scientific? Over 100 years of solid scientific work has gone into the development of test technology, including performance tests of the sort you seem to be advocating. Tests have proven of great value in diagnosis and remediation of learning difficulties, personality disorders, personnel selection, and many other areas.

SALVIATI. Your point, Sagredo, reminds me of another remark I once heard (I can't remember who said it): When we have experts in an area, the rest of us are relieved of the responsibility for concern about it. If, for example, we appoint an officer in charge of affirmative action in our university, we can personally ignore the issue.

SAGREDO. Thank you, Salviati, for that wonderful comment. It captures beautifully much of what I was trying to say. Simplicio, I am not protesting against tests per se. I am simply trying to point out that assessment, at its roots, is a human matter and when instruction is embedded in situations where students are involved in realistic or actual tasks, assessment arises naturally from those situations, not from an instrument designed to be as uncontaminated by context as possible.

SIMPLICIO. But it seems to me that you are placing additional burdens on our already overworked teachers. Must they all become experts in assessment as well as teaching methods? To be sure, the informal observations of teachers may provide valuable insights into children's learning and development. But they can't substitute for more psychometrically sound techniques.

SAGREDO. On the contrary, I would say that your psychometrically sound instruments cannot substitute for teacher judgment. Such instruments could contribute to teacher judgment, but I am reluctant to give them more credence simply because they were developed using procedures that psychologists have decreed to be sound. I don't feel this position places additional burden on the teachers. As I said earlier, assessment emerges naturally from the task. Traditional tests can be part (but only part) of an arsenal of tools that we can provide for teachers to help them make judgments.

SALVIATI. Your arguments, Sagredo, remind me very much of the writings of Lev Vygotsky (1978). He proposed that each child has a Zone of Proximal Development where, with the assistance of a more mature partner (a teacher or more advanced student) the child can accomplish more, solve more advanced problems than he/she could alone. Such assistance would be disallowed in traditional assessment because each child might be treated differently, require different types or amounts of assistance.

SAGREDO. Vygotsky's views are basic to the constructivist position. The role of the teacher, under such a view, changes from authority figure who presents knowledge to students, to one of senior partner, or master in a master/apprentice relationship. The teacher moves the student from the point of completing tasks with help, to independence in an ever increasing cycle. That is what I mean when I say that assessment arises naturally. The "test" of whether someone can complete a task, is the task completion itself.

SIMPLICIO. And can this sequence from novice to expert be specified?

SAGREDO. In a general sense, yes.

SIMPLICIO. Then in principle, I see little difference between constructivism and what you call objectivism. The objective of the task can be specified, analyzed, and measures constructed to test its attainment. I see no reason why the traditional methods of instructional design and development cannot be applied in the sort of tasks you describe.

SAGREDO. The difference lies in the intent of the instruction. In more traditional instruction, where the intent is the communication of knowledge, then it seems reasonable to break the knowledge into its components and systematically present that material to the learner. If you want the students to understand better the unemployment problem in Detroit, for example, then you could proceed by identifying five factors responsible and communicating that to the learner. But if your intent is to provide students with the means for constructing their own interpretation of that problem, then your task is to provide them with tools for inquiring into it. Show them the tools that various groups use to understand unemployment: economists (economic indices, trade balances, etc.), sociologists (social class, education level, race, etc.), political scientists (national policy, partisan issues, etc.), and so forth. Show them the various means by which information about the problem could be collected (interview, questionnaire, library research, etc.) and represented (text, graphics, numerical tables, photographs, etc.). Help the children see that each source of information provides a different perspective on the problem, how the various representations of the data reveal certain aspects of the issue, but conceal or ignore other aspects. You see, we are not so much interested in whether the children know specific things. There is so much knowledge in the world it would be impossible to teach them everything, in any event. What we are after is showing the children how to construct plausible interpretations of their own, using the tools that we have provided.

SIMPLICIO. You are simply talking about higher level skills, problem-solving strategies, that again I insist are amenable to the same sort of analyses that we have always done. No one has ever seriously considered the communication of knowledge the primary purpose of instruction. The higher level cognitive strategies like analysis, synthesis, and evaluation have always been our ultimate goal.

SAGREDO. Yet you speak of these "skills" as if they can be conceived independent of the problems to which they are applied. Here is another area of disagreement between us. I would claim that the skill of analysis, for example, does not exist in some pure form waiting to be to applied to some problem or other. That's how a computer works, not a mind.

SALVIATI. You reject the computer analogy of mind? How interesting! I thought that it was widely accepted.

SAGREDO. Indeed I do reject it. The mind does not "process" information, it constructs it based upon past experience and ongoing interactions in the world. It is this construction process we must nurture, not the acquisition and processing of information. For too long we have assumed that learning is brought about by instruction. Instruction does not cause learning. At best it can support and nurture it.

SALVIATI. And the "constructions" you speak of. What is their nature?

SIMPLICIO. And how can we assess them?

SAGREDO. We assess them, as I indicated earlier, by seeing if the students can successfully construct plausible solutions to the tasks they are presented, a kind of instrumentality criterion. And we check to see if the student is developing self-awareness of the constructive process: the context-specific nature of interpretations, the value of multiple perspectives, the relativity of positions, etc. All of these, I repeat again, arise naturally in the course of instruction as the constructivist sees it. As to the nature of constructions, I am less sure. I do not see strong parallels between constructivism and neural network models as I once did.

SALVIATI. You are both aware, I believe, of my strong interest in semiotics, the study of sign process. It seems to me that the concept of semiosis has much to offer in conceptualizing constructive process. Umberto Eco's (1984) work should be of particular value to you.

SAGREDO. Thank you. I shall certainly look at his work.

SIMPLICIO. It still seems to me that you are placing far too much responsibility on the teacher. What of instructional development? Will the teacher have to assume that role as well?

SAGREDO. I think the role of instructional developer will turn to more of one of consultant. The instructional developer will work within the teacher's zone of proximal development, providing tools and techniques to help the teacher accomplish his/her goals. Use of computers, videos, particular strategies, etc., to nurture or monitor the constructive process can be developed in a collaboration between the teacher and instructional developer. The teacher will likewise be working in the instructional developer's zone of proximal development, nurturing a better understanding of the children and the kind of tasks they are capable of working on.

SIMPLICIO. All this talk of collaboration reminds me that you have not yet answered a question I raised earlier. Not everyone in a group learns the same thing. Some members could easily solve the problem on their own without the group, hence learn nothing. Some don't participate and learn very little. How can you defend the use of collaborative techniques such as this when the effects are so unpredictable?

SAGREDO. If the purpose of the group is to promote the attainment of the same objective by every member, then your criticism may be justified. In such case, the group must be well managed so that everyone participates, some do not dominate, and the work is shared on some equitable basis. If, however, the objective of the group is a collective one—that is, to solve the problem at hand—then these matters are less of a concern. Management is still required, but now it is pursuit of a joint goal, say, a better understanding of the causes of unemployment in Detroit. The contributions and attainments of each of the members are likely to vary widely in both amount and type, as is typically the case in real life.

SALVIATI. I take your point. Consider the discussion we've had here today. I believe that I have developed a better understanding of the views that each of you represent.

SAGREDO. And expressing my thoughts and responding to your questions has clarified many issues about which I was unsure.

SIMPLICIO. And I have become convinced more than ever that constructivism is simply a label for fuzzy, unscientific thinking. The logic underlying what we have here been calling objectivism is simply so compelling in my mind, despite your wonderful arguments, that I cannot seriously consider constructivism as a viable alternative.

SALVIATI. Then I declare that we have collectively reached the objective of a stimulating afternoon of conversation and individually achieved results with which we are satisfied. There is only one reward for such a felicitous result, and I propose to buy the first round. Gentlemen will you join me please? Orange juice for you Simplicio?

REFERENCES

Eco, U. (1984). *Semiotics and the philosophy of language.* Bloomington, IN: Indiana University Press.

Freire, P. (1970). *The pedagogy of the oppressed.* New York: Herder & Herder.

Jauch, J. (1973). *Are quanta real?* Bloomington, IN: Indiana University Press.

Maturana, H., & Varela, F. (1987). *The tree of knowledge.* Boston: New Science Library.

Thorndike, E. (1905). *The elements of psychology.* New York: A. G. Seiler.

Vygotsky, L. (1978). *Mind in society.* Cambridge, MA: Harvard University.

4

Technology Meets Constructivism: Do They Make a Marriage?

D. N. Perkins
Harvard Graduate School of Education

The basic goals of education are deceptively simple. To mention three, education strives for the *retention, understanding,* and *active use* of knowledge and skills. Surely we want what is taught retained, else why teach it? Unless knowledge is understood, to what purposes can it be put? Finally, having and understanding knowledge and skills comes to naught unless the learner actually makes active use of them later in life—in studying other subjects, shopping in the supermarket, getting a better job, casting a vote, or whatever other context. Although other *desiderata* can be added to *retention, understanding,* and *active use,* it is difficult to discard any one of these.

The trouble with this trio of simple-sounding aspirations is that they have proven remarkably difficult to achieve. Surveys of contemporary education endlessly trumpet the gaps in youngsters' basic knowledge of mathematics, geography, or history (Boyer, 1983; Goodlad, 1984; Ravitch & Finn, 1987). Research on students' understanding of science post instruction routinely discloses profound misunderstandings of key concepts such as heat and motion (e.g., Clement, 1982, 1983; McCloskey, 1983; Perkins & Simmons, 1988). John Bransford and his colleagues, among others, have drawn attention to the massive problem of "inert knowledge" (Bransford, Franks, Vye, & Sherwood, 1989). Learners commonly know far more in a passive sense than they ever muster in realistic contexts of application. Although "there for the quiz," the knowledge otherwise disappears into the attic of unused memories.

The challenges of retention, understanding, and active use of knowledge and skills confront education and educators today on a massive scale, exacerbated by problems of at-risk learners, the underfunding of education, an aging population of teachers less familiar with new techniques, and so on. Amidst these troublesome signs, however, some positive notes can be heard. Two of these are information processing technologies, and the diversity of educational practices surrounding the idea of "constructivism." These two provide the focus of this chapter.

Then, what do information-processing technologies offer educational practice? What do constructivist perspectives offer? And what to the two afford in combination? In particular, is there more to be looked for than the usual "sum of the parts"?

FIVE FACETS OF A LEARNING ENVIRONMENT

Consider the classroom, with its books, blackboards, notebooks, pencils, teachers, students, desks, wall charts, and so on—a bewildering collection of paraphernalia. Complex as this or any learning environment is, one can roughly parse such an environment into five facets, not all of which are always present: *information banks, symbol pads, construction kits, phenomenaria,* and *task managers.* The five taken together offer a perspective on the general structure and style of the environment and its underlying assumptions about the nature of teaching and learning. They also provide a grid for describing how information processing technologies can figure in the instructional process.

Information Banks

The classic information bank in the classroom setting is, of course, the text. An information bank is any resource that, more than anything else, serves as a source of explicit information about topics. Other familiar information banks in the classroom include dictionaries and encyclopedias, and we must not forget the human information bank who stands at center stage much of the time—the teacher.

Information-processing technologies expand the kinds and amount of information accessible and shorten the access paths to the information. For example, telecommunications permits access to vast databases of current popular and technical literature. Videodisc and rapid computer lookup procedures can afford almost instant access to anything from the spelling of a word to views of a painting from the National Gallery of Art.

Symbol Pads

A basic function of educational environments for a long time has been to provide surfaces for the construction and manipulation of symbols. From the handheld slate to the student's notebook to the laptop computer, diverse resources have served to support learners' short term memories as they record ideas, develop outlines, formulate and manipulate equations, and so on.

Technology expands the power of such symbol pads in a number of ways. Devices such as word processors allow the easy editing and rearranging of large chunks of text. Drawing programs permit carefully controlled composition of drawings with flexible editing.

Construction Kits

Construction kits of one sort or another are a classic part of settings for learning. Both in the home and in primary school, such favorite examples as Legos, TinkerToys, Lincoln Logs, and Erector Sets come to mind. Laboratory apparatus provides a construction kit for a variety of different experiments in physics, chemistry, and biology, experiments that are, however, highly "canned."

The advent of information processing technologies has dramatically expanded the kinds of construction kits possible in the classroom. Now learners can assemble not just *things*, such as TinkerToys, but more abstract entities such as commands in a programming language, creatures in a simulated ecology, or equations in an environment supporting mathematical manipulations.

Construction kits may sound rather similar to symbol pads, and so they are. But there is a difference in emphasis. Construction kits include a fund of prefabricated parts and processes with emphasis falling on molar things and actions. Symbol pads—such as the classic blank sheet of paper—leave it more to the user to put down whatever structures are wanted. But the two blur into one another: A spreadsheet arguably is somewhere in between.

Phenomenaria

Part of many learning environments is what might be called a "phenomenarium," an area for the specific purpose of presenting phenomena and making them accessible to scrutiny and manipulation. Although the term is coined, it has legitimate precedent in the familiar aquarium and terrarium, microcosms of the aquatic and terrestrial biological worlds found in many classrooms.

Other phenomenaria in the classroom include those created by various experimental apparatus around questions in physics and chemistry, and simulation games, that seek to capture in miniature complex dynamics of, for example, war or negotiation among nations. Information-processing technologies offer a flexible resource for creating complex phenomenaria to explore. Examples include the several physics "microworlds" that allow students to observe and manipulate Newtonian motion (e.g., White, 1984; White & Horwitz, 1987) and programs that model other sorts of environments, for example the popular SimCity.

Task Managers

A final element in any learning setting might be called "task managers." These are elements of the environment that set tasks to be undertaken in the course of learning, guide and sometimes help with the execution of those tasks, and provide feedback regarding process and/or product. The classic task manager is, of course, the teacher, who proposes exercises and circulates around the class troubleshooting. Texts also do considerable task managing by way of exercises at the ends of chapters and answer lists at the ends of books. And, of course, learners are expected to undertake a certain amount of their own task managing, with considerable variation in how much depending on the style of instruction.

With information-processing technologies comes the possibility of electronic task managers. This is very much the case with the early teaching machines and classic computer-aided instruction (CAI) and equally but in a different way the case with the more contemporary "intelligent tutors" that have been developed for areas such as learning the computer language LISP or Euclidean Geometry (Anderson, Farrell, & Sauers, 1984; Anderson & Thompson, 1989).

MINIMALIST AND RICHER LEARNING ENVIRONMENTS

With these categories in mind, it's worth returning to the earlier remark that not all learning environments display all five. Indeed, the typical somewhat dry environment of ordinary classroom instruction features principally information banks (the teacher, the text), symbol pads (notebooks, scratch paper, worksheets), and task managers (the teacher, written instructions). A number of premises lie tacit in this profile of facets, for instance, that learning occurs through telling students about things (information banks rather than phenomenaria); that students cannot manage much of their own learning (little task management left to them); that working out problems rather than constructing entities is primary (symbol pads rather than construction kits).

In contrast, many more progressive learning environments give center stage to phenomenaria and construction kits. Instruction in, and through, Logo is a notable example of instruction centered on a construction kit—the Logo language (Papert, 1980). Environments for science learning commonly highlight phenomenaria, such as the well-known *ThinkerTools*, which simulates Newtonian motion on computer (White & Horwitz, 1987). In both cases, learners bear much more responsibility for their own task management than in more conventional settings, and the role of the teacher shifts to something more like that of a coach.

While these are technological examples, they should not be taken to imply that learning environments highlighting phenomenaria and construction kits are characteristic only of modern times. Apprenticeship settings, for example, inherently present learners with the very phenomena they are learning about—milking cows, making bricks, and crafting paintings. And they typically involve the construction of things abetted by modularity in the parts with which the learner is working—boards, thread, and sheet metal. Phenomenaria and construction kits are characteristic of learning "situated" in authentically complex and meaningful contexts (Brown, Collins, & Duguid, 1989).

THE CONSTRUCTIVIST OFFERING

Constructivism has multiple roots in the psychology and philosophy of this century: the developmental perspective of Jean Piaget, the emergence of cognitive psychology under the guidance of such figures as Jerome Bruner and Ulric Neisser, the constructivist perspective of philosophers such as Nelson Goodman. Central to the vision of constructivism is the notion of the organism as "active"—not just responding to stimuli, as in the behaviorist rubric, but engaging, grappling, and seeking to make sense of things.

In particular, learners do not just take in and store up given information. They make tentative interpretations of experience and go on to elaborate and test those interpretations. Even when the learning process appears to be relatively straightforward, say a matter of learning a new friend's name or a term in a foreign language, constructive processes operate: Candidate mental structures are formed, elaborated, and tested, until a satisfactory structure emerges.

If learning has this constructive character inherently, it follows that teaching practices need to be supportive of the construction that must occur. The constructivist critique of much conventional educational practice is that it is not especially supportive of the work of construction that needs to be done in the minds of the learners.

BIG versus WIG constructivism

Almost all educators and psychologists are constructivists of some stripe these days. But battles rage concerning just how constructive one should be. A way to catch the sense of the issues is to draw a contrast between what we might call BIG constructivism and WIG constructivism. These are acronyms. BIG stands for "beyond the information given," Jerome Bruner's (1973) classic phrase that characterizes how human cognition reaches beyond a reflexive reaction to the "input." WIG, in contrast, stands for "without the information given."

What this contrast really means becomes clearer in the context of an example. Suppose, for instance, that we are teaching seventh graders about the distinction between heat and temperature, one of the subtle contrasts in physics that troubles many students. A "beyond the information given" approach might rather directly introduce the contrast, using imagistic mental models, perhaps computer based, to clarify it. Of course, as a brand of constructivism, this approach would recognize that mere exposure to certain ideas and experiences would not suffice. The learners would need the opportunity to work through their understandings in various ways. Accordingly, while presenting the contrast directly, the "beyond the information given" approach would then engage the learners in a number of thought-oriented activities that challenged them to apply and generalize their initial understandings, refining them along the way.

In contrast, a "without the information given" approach would hold back on direct instruction. The "official" characterization of heat versus temperature would never be offered, or only late in the game. Rather, the learners might be presented at the outset with phenomena involving thermometers and the heating of liquids (again, perhaps through computer simulations). They would be encouraged to try to explain such phenomena with their intuitive notions of temperature. Anomalies would emerge. To make sense of the anomalies, the learners would be encouraged to devise better models of what was occurring. The teacher would scaffold this process, heavily if necessary, but without directly providing answers.

Of course, to call this latter approach "without the information given" exaggerates somewhat. Certainly a great deal of information is available from the phenomena and the scaffolding provided by the teacher. However, direct information is withheld. On just this point, a considerable debate rages. Advocates of WIG constructivism urge that concepts are not truly and meaningfully learned in ways that empower learners unless those concepts are in good part rediscovered by the learners. Advocates of BIG constructivism urge that one can generally quite straightforwardly teach concepts, providing the overall instructional experience includes ample occasion for students to function generatively in testing and extending their evolving conceptions.

This is not a debate that has to be resolved in these pages. To confess my own viewpoint, let me say that education without any WIG episodes would rarely let students engage in and learn about processes of discovery and idea construction. However, education given over entirely to WIG constructivism would prove grossly inefficient and ineffective, failing to pass on in straightforward ways the achievements of the past. At any rate, the agenda of the moment is not to fine tune an appropriate balance of these perspectives, but to see how they illuminate the character of learning environments involving technology.

TECHNOLOGY MEETS CONSTRUCTIVISM

Information-processing technologies and constructivism, separately and often together, have remade substantially our conception of the challenges of learning. Apart from their practical applications to education, information-processing technologies have spawned the computer metaphor of the mind as an information processor. Constructivism has added that this information processor must be seen not as just shuffling data, but wielding it flexibly during learning—making hypotheses, testing tentative interpretations, and so on. The two have occasionally coalesced in detailed information-processing models that attempt to spell out the constructive processing of information in the human mind, according to traditional computer architectures (e.g., Anderson, 1983) or parallel-distributed processing architectures (e.g., Rumelhart, 1989).

But what does all this mean concretely for the practice of instructional design, where constructivism informs not only theory but the moment-to-moment choreography of the teaching-learning process and information-processing technology provides a practical tool as well as a useful metaphor? The implications become clearer with three facets of educational design in mind—the front-end analysis of tasks, instructional strategies, and assessment.

Morals for Front-End Analysis

A traditional task analysis of an area of performance—say algebra—might lay great stress on the retention of pieces of algebra knowledge and smoothly executed algebra skills. To be sure, understanding and active use of knowledge and skills would be seen as relevant goals, but not as problematic ones. Sufficient knowledge and agile skills would bring understanding and active use along with them.

The computer metaphor and the constructivist perspective offer quite another view of the matter. Understanding is not something that comes free with full databanks and thorough practice; it is something won by the struggles of the organism to learn—to conjecture, probe, puzzle out, forecast, and so on. Likewise, ready recall of information and smooth execution of procedures do not guarantee active use of knowledge and skills, as the learner later in life strives to cope creatively with new situations. On the contrary, there is considerable risk that a drill-and-practice regimen may yield knowledge and skills more "contextually welded" to very particular circumstances, less labile, less easily transferred (Salomon & Perkins, 1989). In summary, understanding and active use, become central goals of instruction to be pursued with particular care rather than taken for granted.

One immediate implication concerns the kind of task analysis that might be conducted for an area of performance such as writing paragraphs or solving algebra equations. The "subtasks" in question should include tasks that display understandings, not just knowledge and smooth executions. The subtasks should involve, for example, explanation, extrapolation, evidence giving, and the like. Writing elsewhere, my colleagues and I have called such tasks "understanding performances" (Perkins, 1989; Perkins, Crismond, Simmons, & Unger, in press).

Another implication is that caution should be observed in partitioning off overly narrow kinds of performances. For example, from a constructivist perspective, "writing paragraphs" might be viewed as a topic at risk of dissociation from the larger contexts of authentic communication that make paragraph writing meaningful. It is not that focused attention on topics like paragraphs is disallowed, but rather that whatever focused attention they get should be part of some larger enterprise transparent not just to the teacher but the learner. After all, the learner is not just learning information and routines, but engaged in sense making. And how much sense is the learner likely to be able to make of performances stripped of the contexts that give them meaning?

Morals for Instructional Strategy

Constructivist perspective brings with it quite a different conception of the kinds of tasks that learners should be tackling as they learn. This different conception touches every facet of the five mentioned earlier. Information banks become less central; symbol pads, places not just for recording but working through ideas. A construction kit or a phenomenarium is the center ring in many constructivist-oriented innovations, because it places the learner directly and emphatically in position of having something to make sense *with* or *of*, respectively. Also, task management is given over much more to the learner him or herself, albeit with appropriate scaffolding from a teacher.

Thus, for example, the *Geometric Supposer* environment developed by Schwartz and Yerushalmy (1987) provides a software support environment in which learners can easily make geometric constructions and formulate conjectures about possible theorems. The Supposer is at once a construction kit and a phenomenarium, facilitating construction of geometric configurations out of modules and making easy the detection and testing of geometric phenomena—parallels, symmetries, and so on.

Of course, how far this swing toward phenomenaria and construction kits goes depends somewhat on the brand of constructivism. WIG constructivism—"without the information given"—discourages information banks fed to the learner and encourages learner task management, construction kits, and phenomenaria. Not told very much at all, but supported in numerous ways, the learner works his or her way into and through the meanings to be learned.

BIG constructivism—merely "beyond the information given"—may preserve information banks and feed some of their contents directly to the learner. But then the tasks the learner engages in to make this information meaningful characteristically involve "understanding performances" as defined earlier, and often occur in the settings of construction kits or phenomenaria.

Morals for Assessment

Constructivism's largest impact on the assessment component of an educational treatment concerns the sorts of performances that need to be assessed. With a constructivist perspective comes an increased awareness of understanding and the active use of knowledge as crucial facets of learning not to be taken for granted. Now it is "understanding performances"—in their variety and, often, open-endedness—that requires assessment. Also, evaluating the active use of knowledge calls for measures of transfer of learning.

In contrast with classic CAI, one of the principal effects is to throw assessment "off line," because it requires nuance and understanding not readily encoded into the technology. To be sure, the technology can offer both support for and some limited kinds of on-line assessment. However, instruction in a constructivist idiom is likely to involve open-ended student projects, conjectures or interpretations expressed in natural language, and other such "outcomes" not readily gauged by the most adroitly programmed artificial intelligence at the present state of the art. The press to place assessment "off line" becomes particularly acute in WIG constructivism, with its emphasis on the learner bootstrapping himself or herself into understandings with minimal direct input of information and maximal room to strive to make sense of things along personally chosen paths.

More Than the Sum of the Parts

It is clear that, independently of one another, constructivism and information-processing technologies have much to offer to contemporary approaches to instruction. This can be seen in how each separately impacts upon the five facets of a learning environment identified earlier, expanding the opportunities afforded by each facet and encouraging new patterns of emphasis among the five.

Beyond the point that each contributes, it is fair to ask whether there is anything especially synergistic about their respective offerings, anything that makes a partnership between the two particularly advantageous in the enterprise of instructional design. And here the answer is assuredly yes. The constructivist perspective, whether of BIG or WIG style, places demands on the educational setting that are not so readily met: Phenomenaria and construction kits are at a premium, including ones that deal with rather abstract concepts and domains. Coaching-like interactions with learners suit the constructivist agenda better than more conventionally didactic patterns of interaction, with the inevitable question being where these coaches are to come from given present and foreseeable teacher-student ratios.

In these, and no doubt other, respects, information-processing technologies offer special help, because they allow building the kinds of more intimate, supportive, learning environments called for by the constructivist perspective. Accordingly, together, information-processing technologies and the constructivist point of view fashion an image of education much more attentive to understanding and the active use of knowledge and skills.

REFERENCES

Anderson, J. R. (1983). *The architecture of cognition.* Cambridge, MA: Harvard University Press.

Anderson, J. R., Farrell, R., & Sauers, R. (1984). Learning to program in LISP. *Cognitive Science, 8,* 87-129.

Anderson, J. R., & Thompson, R. (1989). Use of analogy in a production system architecture. In S. Vosniadou & A. Ortony (Eds.), *Similarity and analogical reasoning* (pp. 267-297). New York: Cambridge University Press.

Boyer, E. (1983). *High school: A report on secondary education in America.* New York: Harper & Row.

Bransford, J. D., Franks, J. J., Vye, N. J., & Sherwood, R. D. (1989). New approaches to instruction: Because wisdom can't be told. In S. Vosniadou & A. Ortony (Eds.), *Similarity and analogical reasoning.* New York: Cambridge University Press.

Brown, J. S., Collins, A., & Duguid, P. (1989). Situated cognition and the culture of learning. *Educational Researcher, 18*(4), 32-42.

Bruner, J. (1973). *Beyond the information given: Studies in the psychology of knowing.* New York: Norton.

Clement, J. (1982). Students' preconceptions in introductory mechanics. *American Journal of Physics, 50,* 66-71.

Clement, J. (1983). A conceptual model discussed by Galileo and used intuitively by physics students. In D. Gentner & A. L. Stevens (Eds.), *Mental models.* Hillsdale, NJ: Lawrence Erlbaum Associates.

Goodlad, J. (1984). *A place called school: Prospects for the future.* New York: McGraw-Hill.

McCloskey, M. (1983). Naive theories of motion. In D. Gentner & A. L. Stevens (Eds.), *Mental models* (pp. 299-324). Hillsdale, NJ: Lawrence Erlbaum Associates.

Papert, S. (1980). *Mindstorms: Children, computers, and powerful ideas.* New York: Basic Books.

Perkins, D., Crismond, D., Simmons, R., & Unger, C. (In press). Inside understanding. In D. Perkins, M. West, J. Schwartz, & M. Wiske (Eds.), *Making sense of the future: Teaching for understanding in the age of technology.*

Perkins, D. N. (1989). Art as understanding. In H. Gardner & D. Perkins (Eds.), *Art, mind and education: Research from project zero.* Urbana, IL: University of Illinois Press.

Perkins, D. N., & Simmons, R. (1988). Patterns of misunderstanding: An integrative model of misconceptions in science, mathematics, and programming. *Review of Educational Research, 58*(3), 303-326.

Ravitch, D., & Finn, C. (1987). *What do our 17-year-olds know?: A report on the first national assessment of history and literature.* New York: Harper & Row.

Rumelhart, D. E. (1989). Toward a microstructural account of human reasoning. In S. Vosniadou & A. Ortony (Eds.), *Similarity and analogical reasoning* (pp. 298-312). New York: Cambridge University Press.

Salomon, G., & Perkins, D. N. (1989). Rocky roads to transfer: Rethinking mechanisms of a neglected phenomenon. *Educational Psychologist, 24*(2), 113-142.

Schwartz, J. L., & Yerushalmy, M. (1987). The geometric supposer: Using microcomputers to restore invention to the learning of mathematics. In D. N. Perkins, J. Lochhead, & J. Bishop (Eds.), *Thinking: Proceedings of the second international conference* (pp. 525-536). Hillsdale, NJ: Lawrence Erlbaum Associates.

White, B. (1984). Designing computer games to help physics students understand Newton's laws of motion. *Cognition and Instruction, 1*, 69-108.

White, B., & Horwitz, P. (1987). *ThinkerTools: Enabling children to understand physical laws* (BBN Inc. Report No. 6470). Cambridge, MA: BBN Laboratories Inc.

5

Cognitive Flexibility, Constructivism, and Hypertext: Random Access Instruction for Advanced Knowledge Acquisition in Ill-Structured Domains

Rand J. Spiro
Center for the Study of Reading
University of Illinois

Paul J. Feltovich
Southern Illinois University
School of Medicine

Michael J. Jacobson
Center for the Study of Reading
University of Illinois

Richard L. Coulson
Southern Illinois University
School of Medicine

INTRODUCTION: THE COMPLEX CONTEXT OF LEARNING AND THE DESIGN OF INSTRUCTION

A central argument of this chapter is that there is a common basis for the failure of many instructional systems. The claim is that these deficiencies in the outcomes of learning are strongly influenced by underlying biases and assumptions in the design of instruction which represent the instructional domain and its associated performance demands in an unrealistically simplified and well-structured manner. We offer a constructivist theory of learning and instruction that emphasizes the real-world complexity and ill-structuredness of many knowledge domains. Any effective approach to instruction must simultaneously consider several highly intertwined topics, such as:

- the constructive nature of understanding;

- the complex and ill-structured features of many, if not most, knowledge domains;
- patterns of learning failure; and
- a theory of learning that addresses known patterns of learning failure.

Based on a consideration of the interrelationships between these topics, we have developed a set of principled recommendations for the development of instructional hypertext systems to promote successful learning of difficult subject matter (see Spiro, Coulson, Feltovich, & Anderson, 1988; Spiro & Jehng, 1990). This systematic, theory-based approach avoids the ad hoc character of many recent hypertext-based instructional programs, which have too often been driven by intuition and the power of the technology.

In particular, we argue that:

- Various forms of conceptual complexity and case-to-case irregularity in knowledge domains (referred to collectively as ill-structuredness) pose serious problems for traditional theories of learning and instruction.
- Cognitive and instructional neglect of problems related to content complexity and irregularity in patterns of knowledge use leads to learning failures that take common, predictable forms. These forms are characterized by conceptual oversimplification and the inability to apply knowledge to new cases (failures of transfer).
- The remedy for learning deficiencies related to domain complexity and irregularity requires the inculcation of learning processes that afford greater cognitive flexibility: This includes the ability to represent knowledge from different conceptual and case perspectives and then, when the knowledge must later be used, the ability to construct from those different conceptual and case representations a knowledge ensemble tailored to the needs of the understanding or problem-solving situation at hand.
- For learners to develop cognitively flexible processing skills and to acquire contentive knowledge structures which can support flexible cognitive processing, flexible learning environments are required which permit the same items of knowledge to be presented and learned in a variety of different ways and for a variety of different purposes (commensurate with their complex and irregular nature).
- The computer is ideally suited, by virtue of the flexibility it can provide, for fostering cognitive flexibility. In particular, multidimensional and nonlinear hypertext systems, if appropriately designed to take into account all of the considerations discussed above, have the power to convey ill-structured aspects of knowledge domains and to promote features of cognitive flexibility in ways that traditional learning environments (textbooks, lectures, computer-based drill) could not (although such traditional media can be very successful in other contexts or for other purposes). We refer to the principled use of flexible features inherent in computers to produce nonlinear

learning environments as Random Access Instruction (Spiro & Jehng, 1990).

Following our injunction to consider all crucial issues in the learning and instruction environment jointly, we will develop the following compound argument, which integrates the claims just presented:

- Characteristics of ill-structuredness found in most knowledge domains (especially when knowledge application is considered) lead to serious obstacles to the attainment of advanced learning goals (such as the mastery of conceptual complexity and the ability to independently use instructed knowledge in new situations that differ from the conditions of initial instruction). These obstacles can be overcome by shifting from a constructive orientation that emphasizes the retrieval from memory of intact preexisting knowledge to an alternative constructivist stance which stresses the flexible reassembly of preexisting knowledge to adaptively fit the needs of a new situation. Instruction based on this new constructivist orientation can promote the development of cognitive flexibility using theory-based hypertext systems that themselves possess characteristics of flexibility that mirror those desired for the learner.

In summary, ill-structured aspects of knowledge pose problems for advanced knowledge acquisition that are remedied by the principles of Cognitive Flexibility Theory. This cognitive theory of learning is systematically applied to an instructional theory, Random Access Instruction, which in turn guides the design of nonlinear computer learning environments we refer to as Cognitive Flexibility Hypertexts.

SELECTIVE FOCUS ON ADVANCED KNOWLEDGE ACQUISITION IN ILL-STRUCTURED DOMAINS

The argument developed in this chapter is not intended to cover all aspects of constructive mental processing. Similarly, instructional technology is a broad topic that will not be exhaustively addressed in this chapter. Rather, we will focus on a set of issues implicated by consideration of some special instructional objectives (Merrill, 1983) and the factors contributing to their attainment. In particular, we will be concerned only with learning objectives important to advanced (post-introductory) knowledge acquisition: to attain an understanding of important elements of conceptual complexity, to be able to use acquired concepts for reasoning and inference, and to be able to flexibly apply conceptual knowledge to novel situations. Furthermore, we will consider only complex and ill-structured domains (defined later). This combination of ambitious learning goals and the unobliging nature of characteristics associated with certain knowledge domains will be seen to present special problems for learning and instruction that call for special responses at the level of cognitive theory and related instructional interventions.

We will argue that one kind of hypertext approach is particularly appropriate for this constellation of features associated with the instructional context. The omission of other varieties of computer-based instruction from our discussion does not imply any negative evaluation of their merits. Indeed, in other instructional contexts the kinds of hypertexts we will discuss would be inappropriate (e.g., computer-based drill would be better suited to the instructional objective of memorizing the multiplication tables; see Jacobson & Spiro, 1991b, for the presentation of a framework for analyzing instructional contexts to determine the choice of educational technologies).

In what follows, we illustrate how a particular set of factors in the instructional context (including learning goals and the nature of the knowledge domain) and a set of observed learning deficiencies jointly lead to a recommended cognitive theory-based instructional approach.

THE NATURE OF ILL-STRUCTURED KNOWLEDGE DOMAINS AND PATTERNS OF DEFICIENCY IN ADVANCED KNOWLEDGE ACQUISITION

Ill-Structured Knowledge Domains: Conceptual Complexity and Across-Case Irregularity

An ill-structured knowledge domain is one in which the following two properties hold: (a) each case or example of knowledge application typically involves the simultaneous interactive involvement of multiple, wide-application conceptual structures (multiple schemas, perspectives, organizational principles, and so on), each of which is individually complex (i.e., the domain involves concept- and case-complexity); and (b) the pattern of conceptual incidence and interaction varies substantially across cases nominally of the same type (i.e., the domain involves across-case irregularity). For example, understanding a clinical case of cardiovascular pathology will require appreciating a complex interaction among several central concepts of basic biomedical science; and that case is likely to involve differences in clinical features and conceptual involvements from other cases assigned the same name (e.g., other cases of "congestive heart failure"). Examples of ill-structured domains include medicine, history, and literary interpretation. However, it could be argued that even those knowledge domains that are, in the main, more well-structured, have aspects of ill-structuredness as well, especially at more advanced levels of study (e.g., mathematics). Furthermore, we would argue that all domains which involve the application of knowledge to unconstrained, naturally occurring situations (cases) are substantially ill-structured. For example, engineering employs basic physical science principles that are orderly and regular in the abstract and for textbook applications (Chi, Feltovich, & Glaser, 1981). However, the application of these more well-structured concepts from physics to "messy" real-world cases is another matter. The nature of each engineering case (e.g., features of terrain, climate, available materials, cost, etc.) is so complex and differs so much from other cases that it is difficult to categorize it under any single principle, and any kind of case (e.g., building a bridge) is likely to involve different patterns of principles from instance to instance. Similarly, basic arithmetic is well-structured, while the process of applying arithmetic in solving "word problems" drawn from real situations is more ill-structured. For example, consider the myriad ways that arithmetic principles may be signaled for access by different problem situations and problem wordings.

Advanced Knowledge Acquisition: Mastery of Complexity and Preparation for Transfer

The objectives of learning tend to differ for introductory and more advanced learning. When first introducing a subject, teachers are often satisfied if students can demonstrate a superficial awareness of key concepts and facts, as indicated by memory tests that require the student only to reproduce what was taught in roughly the way that it was taught. Thus, in introductory learning, ill-structuredness is not a serious problem. Learners are not expected to master complexity or independently transfer their acquired knowledge to new situations. These latter two goals (mastery of complexity and transfer) become prominent only later, when students reach increasingly more advanced treatments of the same subject matter. It is then, when conceptual mastery and flexible knowledge application become paramount goals, that the complexity and across-case diversity characteristic of ill-structured domains becomes a serious problem for learning and instruction.

Patterns of Advanced Learning Deficiency in Ill-Structured Domains and Remedies in "Cognitive Flexibility Theory"

In this section we briefly review two related bodies of research: the nature of learning failures in advanced knowledge acquisition and new theoretical approaches to more successful advanced learning and instruction.

Forms of a "Reductive Bias" in Deficient Advanced Knowledge Acquisition. Advanced knowledge acquisition, that very lengthy stage between introductory treatments of subject matter and the attainment of expertise for the subject, has been very little studied (certainly in comparison to the large number of studies of novices and experts—e.g., Chase & Simon, 1973; Chi et al., 1981; Feltovich, Johnson, Moller, & Swanson, 1984). However, in our own recent investigations of advanced learning in ill-structured domains, we have found a number of notable results, some of which were somewhat surprising (Coulson, Feltovich, & Spiro, 1989; Feltovich, Spiro, & Coulson, 1989; Myers, Feltovich, Coulson, Adami, & Spiro, 1990; Spiro, Feltovich, Coulson, & Anderson, 1989). These results may be summarized as follows:

- Failure to attain the goals of advanced knowledge acquisition is common. For example, when students are tested on concepts that are consensually judged by teachers to be of central importance and that have been taught, conceptual misunderstanding is prevalent.
- A common thread running through the deficiencies in learning is oversimplification. We call this tendency the reductive bias, and we have observed its occurrence in many forms. Examples include the additivity bias, in which parts of complex entities that have been studied in isolation are assumed to retain their characteristics when the parts are reintegrated into the whole from which they were drawn; the discreteness bias, in which continuously dimensioned attributes (like length) are bifurcated to their poles and continuous processes are instead segmented into discrete steps; and the compartmentalization bias, in which conceptual elements that are in reality highly interdependent are instead treated in isolation, missing important aspects of their interaction (see Coulson et al., 1989; Feltovich et al., 1989; Myers et al., 1990; Spiro et al., 1989, for presentations and discussion of the many reductive biases that have been identified). Of course, the employment of strategies of this kind is not a problem if the material is simple in ways consistent with the reductive bias. However, if real complexities exist and their mastery is important, such reduction is an inappropriate oversimplification.
- Errors of oversimplification can compound each other, building larger scale networks of durable and consequential misconception.
- The tendency toward oversimplification applies to all elements of the learning process, including cognitive strategies of learning and mental representation, and instructional approaches (from textbooks to teaching styles to testing). These various sources of simplification bias reinforce each other (e.g., one is more likely to oversimplify if an inappropriately easier learning strategy is also employed in textbooks or teaching because it is simple).

As we will see in the next section, more appropriate strategies for advanced learning and instruction in ill-structured domains are in many ways the opposite of what works best for introductory learning and in more well-structured domains. For example, compartmentalization of knowledge components is an effective strategy in well-structured domains, but blocks effective learning in more intertwined, ill-structured domains that require high degrees of knowledge interconnectedness. Instructional focus on general principles with wide scope of application across cases or examples works well in well-structured domains (this is one thing that makes these domains well-structured), but leads to seductive misunderstandings in ill-structured domains, where across-case variability and case-sensitive interaction of principles vitiates their force. Well-structured domains can be integrated within a single unifying representational basis, but ill-structured domains require multiple representations for full coverage. For example, consider one kind of single unifying representation, an analogy to a familiar concept or experience. We have found that a single analogy may help at early stages of learning, but actually interfere with more advanced treatments of the same concept later on (Spiro et al., 1989; see also Burstein & Adelson, 1990). Any single analogy for a complex concept will always be limited in its aptness, and misconceptions that will develop when the concept is treated more fully can be predicted by knowing the ways in which the introductory analogy is misleading about or under represents the material to be learned. To summarize, we have found that the very things that produce initial success for the more modest goals of introductory learning may later impede the attainment of more ambitious learning objectives.

There is much that appears to be going wrong in advanced learning and instruction (see also GPEP, 1984; Perkins & Simmons, 1989). The cognitive theories and instructional practices that work well for introductory learning and in well-structured domains not only prove inadequate for later, more advanced treatments of the same topics, but adherence to those theories and practices may produce impediments to further progress. Our conclusion is that a reconceptualization of learning and instruction is required for advanced knowledge acquisition in ill-structured domains (see also Feltovich, Spiro, & Coulson, in press; Spiro & Jehng, 1990; Spiro et al., 1987, 1988, 1989). Such a reconceptualization, taking into account the problems posed by domain ill-structuredness and the patterns of advanced learning deficiency observed in our studies, is presented next, in our discussion of constructivism and a new constructive orientation, Cognitive Flexibility Theory. After a brief survey of the tenets of that theory, we show its implications for the design of computer hypertext learning environments that are targeted to the features of difficulty faced by advanced learners in ill-structured domains.

CONSTRUCTIVISM, OLD AND NEW: COGNITIVE FLEXIBILITY THEORY AND THE PROMOTION OF ADVANCED KNOWLEDGE ACQUISITION

Our interpretation of constructivism, as it is applied to learning and instruction, is complex. We argue that there are different points in cognitive acts where constructive mental processes occur. First, we take it as an accepted cognitive principle that understanding involves going beyond the presented information. For example, what is needed to comprehend a text is not solely contained in the linguistic and logical information coded in that text. Rather, comprehension involves the construction of meaning: The text is a preliminary blueprint for constructing an understanding. The information contained in the text must be combined with information outside of the text, including most prominently the prior knowledge of the learner, to form a complete and adequate representation of the text's meaning (see Spiro, 1980, for a review; also see Ausubel, 1968; Bartlett, 1932; Bransford & Johnson, 1972; Bruner, 1963).

However, our approach to constructivist cognition goes beyond many of the key features of this generally accepted view (see Spiro et al., 1987). The interpretation of constructivism that has dominated much of cognitive and educational psychology for the last 20 years or so has frequently stressed the retrieval of organized packets of knowledge, or schemas, from memory to augment any presented information that is to be understood or any statement of a problem that is to be solved. We argue that conceptual complexities and across-case inconsistencies in ill-structured knowledge domains often render the employment of prepackaged ("precompiled") schemas inadequate and inappropriate. Rather, because knowledge will have to be used in too many different ways for them all to be anticipated in advance, emphasis must be shifted from the retrieval of intact knowledge structures to support the construction of new understandings, to the novel and situation-specific assembly of prior knowledge drawn from diverse organizational loci in preexisting mental representations. That is, instead of retrieving from memory a previously packaged "prescription" for how to think and act, one must bring together, from various knowledge sources, an appropriate ensemble of information suited to the particular understanding or problem-solving needs of the situation at hand. Again, this is because many areas of knowledge have too diverse a pattern of use for single prescriptions, stored in advance, to cover enough of the cases that will need to be addressed. (For other discussions of issues related to cognitive flexibility and "inert knowledge," see Bereiter & Scardamalia, 1985; Bransford, Franks, Vye, & Sherwood, 1989; Brown, 1989; Whitehead, 1929.)

Thus, in Cognitive Flexibility Theory, a new element of (necessarily) constructive processing is added to those already in general acceptance, an element concerned primarily with the flexible use of preexisting knowledge (and, obviously, with the acquisition and representation of knowledge in a form amenable to flexible use). (However, also see Bartlett's, 1932, notion of "turning round upon one's schema.") This "new constructivism" is doubly constructive: (a) understandings are constructed by using prior knowledge to go beyond the information given; and (b) the prior knowledge that is brought to bear is itself constructed, rather than retrieved intact from memory, on a case-by-case basis (as required by the across-case variability of ill-structured domains). (Also see Bereiter, 1985.) Cognitive Flexibility Theory is a "new constructivist" response to the difficulties of advanced knowledge acquisition in ill-structured domains. It is an integrated theory of learning, mental representation, and instruction. We now turn our attention to that theory. (Having discussed the relationship of Cognitive Flexibility Theory to constructivism, the latter term will not be used explicitly very often in the remainder of the chapter—but it should be understood that when we talk about Cognitive Flexibility Theory, we are referring to a particular constructivist theory.)

Cognitive Flexibility Theory: A Constructivist Approach to Promoting Complex Conceptual Understanding and Adaptive Knowledge Use for Transfer

Limitations of space will not permit a detailed treatment of the key features of Cognitive Flexibility Theory in this section. Let it suffice to say that the tenets of the theory are direct responses to the special requirements for attaining advanced learning goals, given the impediments associated with ill-structured features of knowledge domains and our findings regarding specific deficiencies in advanced learning—knowing what is going wrong provides a strong clue for how to fix it. In lieu of any comprehensive treatment, we will discuss here one central aspect of the theory. Then, we will show how that aspect creates implications for the design and use of hypertext learning environments. For more detailed treatments of Cognitive Flexibility Theory, see Spiro et al. (1987, 1988), Spiro and Jehng (1990), and Feltovich et al. (in press).

The aspect of Cognitive Flexibility Theory that we will briefly discuss here and use for illustrative purposes involves the importance of multiple juxtapositions of instructional content. Some other aspects of the theory will be referred to in passing in the context of that discussion. (Many key tenets of Cognitive Flexibility Theory will not be mentioned at all; e.g., the vital importance of students' active participation in learning.) A central claim of Cognitive Flexibility Theory is that revisiting the same material, at different times, in rearranged contexts, for different purposes, and from different conceptual perspectives is essential for attaining the goals of advanced knowledge acquisition (mastery of complexity in understanding and preparation for transfer). Content must be covered more than once for full understanding because of psychological demands resulting from the complexity of case and concept entities in ill-structured domains, combined with the importance of contextually induced variability and the need for multiple knowledge representations and multiple interconnectedness of knowledge components (see Spiro et al., 1988, for justifications of all these requirements). Any single explanation of a complex concept or case will miss important knowledge facets that would be more salient in a different context or from a different intentional point of view. Some of the representational perspectives necessary for understanding will be grasped on a first or second exploration, while others will be missed until further explorations are undertaken. Some useful connections to other instructed material will be noticed and others missed on a single pass (with connections to nonadjacently presented information particularly likely to be missed). And so on. Revisiting material in an ill-structured domain is not a simple repetitive process useful only for forming more durable memories for what one already knows. For example, re-examining a case in the context of comparison with a case different from the comparison context (i.e., the first time the case was investigated) will lead to new insights (especially if the new "reading" is appropriately guided); this is because partially nonoverlapping aspects of the case are highlighted in the two different contexts. The more complex and ill-structured the domain, the more there is to be understood for any instructional topic; and therefore, the more that is unfortunately hidden in any single pass, in any single context, for any restricted set of purposes, or from the perspective of any single conceptual model.

For example, consider the importance of multiple knowledge representations, which is one thing made possible by multiple passes through the same material. A key feature of ill-structured domains is that they embody knowledge that will have to be used in many different ways, ways that cannot all be anticipated in advance. Knowledge that is complex and ill-structured has many aspects that must be mastered and many varieties of uses that it must be put to. The common denominator in the majority of advanced learning failures that we have observed is oversimplification, and one serious kind of oversimplification is looking at a concept or phenomenon or case from just one perspective. In an ill-structured domain, that single perspective will miss important aspects of conceptual understanding, may actually mislead with regard to some of the fuller aspects of understanding, and will account for *too* little of the variability in the way knowledge must be applied to new cases (Spiro et al., 1989). Instead, one must approach all elements of advanced learning and instruction with the tenet of multiple representations at the center of consideration.

Cognitive Flexibility Theory makes specific recommendations about multiple approaches that range from multiple organizational schemes for presenting subject matter in instruction to multiple representations of knowledge (e.g., multiple classification schemes for knowledge representation). Knowledge that will have to be used in a large number of ways has to be organized, taught, and mentally represented in many different ways. The alternative is knowledge that is usable only for situations like those of initial learning; and in an ill-structured domain that will constitute just a small portion of the situations to which the knowledge may have to be applied.

Given all of this, it should not be surprising that the main metaphor we employ in the instructional model derived from Cognitive Flexibility Theory (and in our related hypertext instructional systems) is that of the criss-crossed landscape (Spiro et al., 1987; Wittgenstein, 1953), with its suggestion of a nonlinear and multidimensional traversal of complex subject matter, returning to the same place in the conceptual landscape on different occasions, coming from different directions. Instruction prepares students for the diversity of uses of ill-structured knowledge, while also demonstrating patterns of multiple interconnectedness and context dependency of knowledge, by criss-crossing the knowledge domain in many ways (thereby also teaching students the importance of considering complex knowledge from many different intellectual perspectives, tailored to the context of its occurrence). This should instill an epistemological belief structure appropriate for ill-structured domains and provide a repertoire of flexible knowledge representations that can be used in constructing assemblages of knowledge, taken from here and from there, to fit the diverse future cases of knowledge application in that domain.

CONSTRAINTS ON THE DESIGN OF HYPERTEXT LEARNING ENVIRONMENTS DRAWN FROM IMPLICATIONS OF COGNITIVE FLEXIBILITY THEORY

Thus far, we have discussed the relationship between the nature of ill-structured knowledge domains and difficulties in the attainment of advanced learning goals (mastery of complexity and transfer to new situations). A principle of Cognitive Flexibility Theory was then introduced as one antidote to the problems of advanced knowledge acquisition in ill-structured domains. Now, we will briefly point to some of the ways that these cumulative considerations impinge on the design and use of hypertext learning environments.

First, the preceding discussion should make it reasonably clear that hypertext environments are good candidates for promoting cognitive flexibility in ill-structured domains. We have referred to the need for rearranged instructional sequences, for multiple dimensions of knowledge representation, for multiple interconnections across knowledge components, and so on. Features like these correspond nicely to well known properties of hypertext systems, which facilitate flexible restructuring of instructional presentation sequences, multiple data codings, and multiple linkages among content elements. It appears straightforward that a nonlinear medium like hypertext would be very well suited for the kinds of "landscape criss-crossings" recommended by Cognitive Flexibility Theory (and needed in ill-structured knowledge domains; see also Bednar, Cunningham, Duffy, & Perry, chapter 2).

However, it is not that easy. Implementing Cognitive Flexibility Theory is not a simple matter of just using the power of the computer to "connect everything with everything else." There are many ways that hypertext systems can be designed, and there is good reason to believe that a large number of those do not produce successful learning outcomes (e.g., because they lead the learner to become lost in a confusing labyrinth of incidental or ad hoc connections). What is needed is the discipline of grounding hypertext design in a suitable theory of learning and instruction. That is what we have done in several prototype hypertext systems derived from Cognitive Flexibility Theory and tailored to the known obstacles to advanced learning in difficult and ill-structured domains (Spiro et al., 1988; Spiro & Jehng, 1990). To provide some idea of how theory informs design, consider just one very simple example of a hypertext design decision that responds to an aspect of Cognitive Flexibility Theory-based logic discussed in the last section: rearrangement of the presentation sequence of content (that has been investigated previously), in order to produce different understandings when that content is "re-read."

Illustrating the Theory- and Context-Based Logic of Hypertext Design

Because of the feature of conceptual instability in ill-structured domains (i.e., the same conceptual structure takes on many more meanings across instances of its use than in well-structured domains), Cognitive Flexibility Theory dictates, as discussed in the last section, that one kind of instructional revisiting should produce an appreciation in the learner of the varieties of meaning "shades" associated with the diversity of uses. As Wittgenstein argued (1953), the meaning of ill-structured concepts is in their range of *uses*, rather than in generally applicable definitions—there is no simple "core meaning." We extend Wittgenstein's claim to larger units than the individual concept (e.g., complex conceptual structures such as a theme of a literary work). So, a feature built into our hypertexts is conceptual structure search: Content is automatically re-edited to produce a particular kind of "criss-crossing" of the conceptual landscape that visits a large set of case examples of a given conceptual structure in use. The learner then has the option of viewing different example cases in the application of a concept he or she chooses to explore. That is, the instructional content is re-edited upon demand to present just those cases and parts of cases that illustrate a focal conceptual structure (or set of conceptual structures). Rather than having to rely on sporadic encounters with real cases that instantiate different uses of the concept, the learner sees a range of conceptual applications close together, so conceptual variability can easily be examined. Learning a complex concept from erratic exposures to complex instances, with long periods of time separating each encounter, as in natural learning from experience, is not very efficient. When ill-structuredness prevents telling in the abstract how a concept should be used in general, it becomes much more important to show together the many concrete examples of uses. In sum, a hypertext design feature is incorporated as a response to a learning difficulty caused by a characteristic of ill-structured knowledge domains. (Of course, the issue of example selection and sequencing in concept instruction has been dealt with before, e.g., Tennyson & Park, 1980. What is novel about the present approach is the particular way that this issue is addressed and the kinds of higher-order conceptual structures that are studied. Even more important is the fact that that single issue is addressed within a larger, integrative framework. That is, the treatment of conceptual variability is just one aspect of a complete approach in which the diverse aspects are theoretically united.)

Following this same kind of logic, we will sketch briefly some of the other ways that hypertext design features can be made to match the goals of advanced learning—under the constraints of domain ill-structuredness and according to the tenets of Cognitive Flexibility Theory. For this purpose we will use one of our Cognitive Flexibility Hypertext prototypes, "Exploring Thematic Structure in *Citizen Kane* " ("KANE," for short—Knowledge Acquisition in Nonlinear Environments; see Spiro and Jehng, 1990, for details), which teaches processes of literary interpretation in a post-structuralist mode (e.g., Barthes, 1967).

KANE is a learning environment that goes beyond typical instructional approaches to literary interpretation that too often settle on a single, integrative understanding ("The theme of Citizen Kane is X"). Instead, students are shown that literary texts (in this case a videodisc of a literary film) support multiple interpretations, the interpretations combine and interact, they take on varying senses in different contexts, and so on. For example, the issue of conceptual variability that was discussed earlier is addressed by providing an option that causes the film to be re-edited to show just those scenes that illustrate any selected conceptual theme of the film (e.g., "Wealth Corrupts," " Hollow, Soulless Man," etc.). Using this option, the learner could, for example, see five scenes in a row, taken from various places in the film, that illustrate different varieties or "flavors" of the "Wealth Corrupts" theme. Each scene essentially forms a miniature case of the Kane character's behavior that illustrates the targeted theme. (Although the student is assumed to have already seen the film one or more times—this is advanced knowledge acquisition for Citizen Kane—the nonlinear presentation may still occasionally confuse. Therefore, to deal with this and other kinds of out-of-sequence criss-crossings, a design feature of Cognitive Flexibility Hypertexts is the provision of optional background information on the contexts immediately preceding the one being explored.) Because of the inability of abstract definitions (as might be construed for a theme such as "Soulless Man") to cover conceptual meanings-in-use in ill-structured domains, supplementary guidance about the way meaning is used in a particular situation (Brown, Collins, & Duguid, 1989) is required. This is provided for in KANE by giving the learner the option of reading an expert commentary on the special shade of meaning associated with the conceptual theme, as applied to a scene, immediately after the scene is viewed. These functional and context-sensitive (particularized) definitions explain why the scene is considered to be a case of a theme, such as "Wealth Corrupts." Note that a particularized representation of meaning is not the same as a dictionary sense of a word: The latter refers to different subtypes of a word's meaning, but with an implied similarity or overlap across instances of the same type—so there is less need to tailor to the individual case; in contrast, particularizing, as we mean it, implies a representation of a concept that is necessarily expressed in terms of an instance of usage (case, example, scene, occasion of use), as required in an ill-structured domain. Commentaries also include information about knowledge *access*: what cues in the case context should provide a "tip-off" that a particular concept might be relevant for analyzing a case—if one cannot access relevant conceptual information in memory, this knowledge will not be useful on subsequent occasions.

The commentaries also provide cross-references to other instantiations of the conceptual structure that constitute an instructionally efficacious set of comparisons (e.g., other cases/scenes in which either a roughly similar or saliently different particularized sense of that conceptual theme occurs). The guiding commentaries also include another important kind of cross-reference, namely to other conceptual themes that have interpretive relevance in accounting for the same case of Kane's behavior, concepts that interact with and influence the meaning of each other in that scene. (Note that these different kinds of cross-references counter the reductive tendencies toward compartmentalization of concepts and their cases of application that we have found to be harmful in advanced learning.) Thus there is a double particularization in Cognitive Flexibility Hypertexts: The generic conceptual structure is particularized not only to the context of a specific case, but also to the other concepts simultaneously applicable for analyzing that case. That is, each case or example is shown to be a complex entity requiring for its understanding multiple conceptual representations, with the role of non-additive conceptual interdependencies highlighted.

Each of the conceptual themes used in KANE is itself a wide-scope interpretive schema that has been argued for in the secondary literature on the film as being the most important theme for understanding the character of Kane. In reality, however, an ill-structured domain has no single schema that is likely to cover everything of interest for an individual case, nor is any schema/theme/concept likely to dominate across a wide range of cases. Therefore, the greater the number of such broad-gauge schemata that are available (and KANE provides ten), the greater the utility for understanding in two senses. First, there will be adequate coverage of the complexity of an individual case by an appropriately diverse set of schemata (something which is also modeled in KANE by the simultaneous display of all the relevant conceptual themes in each scene). Second, the likelihood is increased that the most apt set of conceptual schemata will be cognitively available for understanding any one of the highly diverse new cases that will be encountered in an ill-structured domain—the more conceptual structures there are to choose from, each a powerful schema itself and each taught in its complex diversity of patterns of use, the greater the chance that you will find a good fit to a given case. A related virtue is that configurations of combinations of conceptual structures are thereby demonstrated; since multiple conceptual representations will be required for each instance of knowledge application, the ability to combine conceptual entities and to recognize common patterns of their combination is crucial. The process of situation-specific knowledge construction, so important for transfer in ill-structured domains, is thus supported in at least two important ways: The processes of adaptive knowledge assembly are demonstrated, and the flexible knowledge structures required for this assembly are acquired. Furthermore, as users of the program shift over time into more of a "free exploration" mode, where they independently traverse the themes of the film in trying to answer questions of interpretation (posed by teachers or themselves), their active participation in learning the processes of knowledge assembly increases.

Flexible tools for covering content diversity and for teaching knowledge assembly combine to increase the resources available for future transfer/application of knowledge (e.g., interpreting a scene that has not yet been viewed or assembling prior knowledge to facilitate comprehension of a critique written about the film). By making many potential combinations of knowledge cognitively available—either by retrieval from memory or by context-sensitive generation—the learner develops a rich palette to paint a knowledge structure well fit to helping understand and act upon a particular case at hand. This is especially important in an ill-structured domain because there will be great variety in the demands on background knowledge from case to case (and with each case individually rich in the knowledge blend required).

This discussion could continue for many other features of hypertext learning environments that are specifically derived from Cognitive Flexibility Theory. What would be in common across any such discussion is that each feature could be shown to have the following purpose: to counter an advanced learning difficulty endemic to ill-structured domains.

CONCLUDING REMARKS

We have just discussed a few of the many kinds of revisitings of instructional content in rearranged contexts that are implied by Cognitive Flexibility Theory and embodied in our hypertext systems. However, our goals in this chapter were necessarily limited. Our purpose was merely to begin to illustrate the way design features of a particular kind of computer learning environment are related to cognitive and instructional theories that are themselves based on the problems posed by the interaction of learning objectives and characteristics of ill-structured knowledge domains. That is, our intention was to illustrate a way of thinking about the design of hypertext learning environments that is sensitive to and dependent upon the cognitive characteristics necessary for advanced knowledge acquisition in ill-structured domains. In particular, these are the characteristics of the "new constructivism" that we discussed earlier and that are properties of Cognitive Flexibility Theory. The realm of constructive processes must be taken beyond the retrieval of knowledge structures from memory (for the purpose of "going beyond the information given" in some learning situation), to also include the independent, flexible, situation-specific assembly of the background knowledge structures themselves.

In sum, we consider our work to be moving toward a systematic theory of hypertext design to provide flexible instruction appropriate for developing cognitive flexibility. We have called the instructional theory that is derived from Cognitive Flexibility Theory and applied in flexible computer learning environments Random Access Instruction. It, and the developing hypertext theory, is laid out in considerable detail in Spiro and Jehng (1990). We are encouraged so far about the robustness, systematicity, and generality of our hypertext design principles, in that they have been applied in very similar ways to develop hypertext prototypes in domains as diverse as cardiovascular medicine, literary interpretation, and military strategy. Preliminary data on the effectiveness of these Cognitive Flexibility Hypertexts is also encouraging. For example, Jacobson and Spiro (1991a) investigated two different design approaches for structuring a hypertext learning environment to provide instruction in a complex and ill-structured domain (the social impact of technology). The results of this experiment revealed that while the design which emphasized the mastery of declarative knowledge led to higher performance on measures of memory for presented facts, the design based on Cognitive Flexibility Theory (which highlighted different facets of the material by explicitly demonstrating critical interrelationships between abstract and case-centered knowledge components, in multiple contexts on different passes through the same content) promoted superior transfer to a new problem-solving situation. More empirical testing is clearly required, and numerous other issues of hypertext design remain to be discussed. However, those are stories for another time.

ACKNOWLEDGMENTS

The research reported in this chapter was supported in part by the Basic Research Office of the Army Research Institute (MDA903-86-K-0443) and the Office of Educational Research and Improvement (OEG0087-C1001). Some of the background research on the learning and understanding of complex conceptual material was supported in part by the Office of Naval Research, Cognitive Science Division (N00014-87-G 0165, N00014-88-K-0077). The chapter does not necessarily reflect the views of these agencies.

We would like to express our gratitude to Susan Ravlin for her first-rate programming work on the Cognitive Flexibility Hypertexts, and to Tom Duffy and Jane Adami for several very helpful comments on an earlier draft of the chapter.

REFERENCES

Ausubel, D. P. 1968). *Educational psychology: A cognitive view.* New York: Holt, Rinehart & Winston.

Barthes, R. (1967). *S/Z.* New York: Hill, Wang.

Bartlett, F. C. (1932). *Remembering.* Cambridge, England: Cambridge University Press.

Bereiter, C. (1985). Toward a solution of the learning paradox. *Review of Educational Research, 55,* 201-226.

Bereiter, C., & Scardamalia, M. (1985). Cognitive coping strategies and the problem of "inert knowledge." In S. F. Chipman, J. W. Segal, & R. Glaser (Eds.), *Thinking and learning skills: Current research and open questions* (Vol. 2, pp. 65-80). Hillsdale, NJ: Lawrence Erlbaum Associates.

Bransford, J. D., Franks, J. J., Vye, N. J., & Sherwood, R. D. (1989). New approaches to instruction: Because wisdom can't be told. In S. Vosniadou & A. Ortony (Eds.), *Similarity and analogical reasoning* (pp. 470-497). Cambridge, England: Cambridge University Press.

Bransford, J. D., & Johnson, M. K. (1972). Contextual prerequisites for understanding: Some investigations of comprehension and recall. *Journal of Verbal Learning and Verbal Behavior, 11,* 717-726.

Brown, A. (1989). Analogical learning and transfer: What develops? In S. Vosniadou & A. Ortony (Eds.), *Similarity and analogical reasoning* (pp. 369-412). Cambridge, England: Cambridge University Press.

Brown, J. S., Collins, A., & Duguid, P. (1989). Situated cognition and the culture of learning. *Educational Researcher, 18,* 32-42.

Bruner, J. S. (1963). *The process of education.* Cambridge, MA: Harvard University Press.

Burstein, M. H., & Adelson, B. (1990). Issues for a theory of analogical learning. In R. Freedle (Ed.), *Artificial intelligence and the future of testing.* Hillsdale, NJ: Lawrence Erlbaum Associates.

Chase, W. C., & Simon H. (1973). Perception in chess. *Cognitive Psychology, 4,* 55-81.

Chi, M. T. H., Feltovich, P. J., & Glaser, R. (1981). Categorization and representation of physics problems by experts and novices. *Cognitive Science, 5,* 121-152.

Coulson, R. L., Feltovich, P. J., & Spiro, R. J. (1989). Foundations of a misunderstanding of the ultrastructural basis of myocardial failure: A reciprocation network of oversimplifications. *The Journal of Medicine and Philosophy* (special issue on "The Structure of Clinical Knowledge"), *14*, 109-146.

Feltovich, P., Johnson, P. E., Moller, J. H., & Swanson, D. B. (1984). LCS: The role and development of medical knowledge in diagnostic expertise. In W. J. Clancey & E. H. Shortliffe (Eds.), *Readings in medical artificial intelligence: The first decade.* Reading, MA: Addison Wesley.

Feltovich, P. J., Spiro, R. J., & Coulson, R. L. (1989). The nature of conceptual understanding in biomedicine: The deep structure of complex ideas and the development of misconceptions. In D. Evans & V. Patel (Eds.), *Cognitive science in medicine: Biomedical modeling.* Cambridge, MA: MIT (Bradford) Press.

Feltovich, P. J., Spiro, R. J., & Coulson, R. L. (in press). Learning, teaching, and testing for complex conceptual understanding. In N. Frederiksen, R. Mislevy, & I. Bejar (Eds.), *Test theory for a new generation of tests.* Hillsdale, NJ: Lawrence Erlbaum Associates.

[GPEP] Panel on the General Professional Education of the Physician. (1984). *Physicians for the twenty-first century: The GPEP report.* Washington, DC: American Association of Medical Colleges.

Jacobson, M. J., & Spiro, R. J. (1991a). *Cognitive flexibility, hypertext learning environments, and the acquisition of complex knowledge: An empirical investigation.* Manuscript submitted for publication.

Jacobson, M. J., & Spiro, R. J. (1991b). *A framework for the contextual analysis of computer-enhanced learning environments.* Manuscript submitted for publication.

Merrill, M. D. (1983). Component display theory. In C. M. Reigeluth (Ed.), *Instructional-design theories and models: An overview of their current status* (pp. 282-333). Hillsdale, NJ: Lawrence Erlbaum Associates.

Myers, A. C., Feltovich, P. J., Coulson, R. L., Adami, J. F., & Spiro, R. J. (1990). Reductive biases in the reasoning of medical students: An investigation in the domain of acid-base balance. In B. Bender, R. J. Hiemstra, A. J. J. A. Scherbier, & R. P. Zwierstra (Eds.), *Teaching and assessing clinical competence.* Groningen, the Netherlands: BoekWerk Publications.

Perkins, D. N., & Simmons, R. (1989). Patterns of misunderstanding: An integrative model for science, math, and programming. *Review of Educational Research, 58*, 303-326.

Spiro. R. J. (1980). Constructive processes in prose comprehension and recall. In R. J. Spiro, B. C. Bruce, & W. F. Brewer (Eds.), *Theoretical issues in reading comprehension* (pp. 245-278). Hillsdale, NJ: Lawrence Erlbaum Associates.

Spiro, R. J., Coulson, R. L., Feltovich, P. J., & Anderson, D. K. (1988). Cognitive flexibility theory: Advanced knowledge acquisition in ill-structured domains. In *The tenth annual conference of the cognitive science society*. Hillsdale, NJ: Lawrence Erlbaum Associates.

Spiro, R. J, Feltovich, P. J., Coulson, R. L., & Anderson, D. K. (1989). Multiple analogies for complex concepts: Antidotes for analogy-induced misconception in advanced knowledge acquisition. In S. Vosniadou & A. Ortony (Eds.), *Similarity and analogical reasoning* (pp. 498-531). Cambridge, England: Cambridge University Press.

Spiro, R. J., & Jehng, J. C. (1990). Cognitive flexibility and hypertext: Theory and technology for the nonlinear and multidimensional traversal of complex subject matter. In D. Nix & R. J. Spiro (Eds.), *Cognition, education, and multimedia: Exploring ideas in high technology* (pp. 163-205). Hillsdale, NJ: Lawrence Erlbaum Associates.

Spiro, R. J., Vispoel, W., Schmitz, J., Samarapungavan, A., & Boerger, A. (1987). Knowledge acquisition for application: Cognitive flexibility and transfer in complex content domains. In B. C. Britton (Ed.), *Executive control processes* (pp. 177-200). Hillsdale, NJ: Lawrence Erlbaum Associates.

Tennyson, R. D., & Park, O. (1980). The teaching of concepts: A review of instructional design research literature. *Review of Educational Research, 50,* 55-70.

Whitehead, A. N. (1929). *The aims of education.* New York: Macmillan.

Wittgenstein, L. (1953). *Philosophical investigations.* New York: Macmillan.

6

Technology and the Design of Generative Learning Environments

Cognition and Technology Group
Learning Technology Center
Peabody College of Vanderbilt University

INTRODUCTION

The rationale for recent work at the Vanderbilt University Learning Technology Center derives from widespread concern about the failures of our schools and our society to help students learn to think more effectively, and to help them develop effective problem solving, reasoning and learning skills (e.g., Bransford, Goldman, & Vye, 1991; Carey, Flower, Hayes, Schriver, & Hass, 1989; Jones & Idol, 1990; Nickerson, 1988; Resnick, 1987; Resnick & Klopfer, 1989; Voss, Perkins, & Segal, 1990). One source of concern about the need to teach thinking stems from poor national test scores, especially on tasks involving problem solving and reasoning (e.g., Carpenter, 1980; Kouba, Brown, Carpenter, Lindquist, Silver, & Swafford, 1988; Jones & Idol, 1990; NAEP, 1981, 1983; National Commission on Excellence in Education, 1983). Nickerson (1988) summarizes the results of national tests by noting that "In the aggregate, the findings from these studies force the conclusion that it is possible to finish 12 or 13 years of public education in the United States without developing much competence as a thinker" (Nickerson, 1988, p. 5).

The thinking activities that are of concern include the ability to write persuasive essays, engage in informal reasoning, explain how data relate to theory in scientific investigations, and formulate and solve moderately complex problems that require mathematical reasoning. These are generative tasks that are important in a variety of everyday contexts. As an illustration, consider the task of planning to go on a trip. Successful planning requires that one generate the sub-problems to be solved (e.g., the need to find shelter and food, to estimate time of arrival, etc.); this is different from being asked to solve simple word problems that already define the problems to be solved (e.g., If you will travel 120 miles at 60 mph, how long will the trip take?). In our previous research, we found that sixth grade students who scored in the 8th and 9th stanine on math tests did well on simple word problems yet were almost totally unable to perform planning tasks that asked them to formulate and solve sets of analogous problems (e.g., Van Haneghan et al., in press). Of course, many other students also have trouble even with the simple word problems. Similarly, many of the students with whom we worked could easily memorize facts from their science texts yet had great difficulty explaining how various sets of data were linked to possible scientific explanations (e.g., Cognition & Technology Group at Vanderbilt, 1990).

Many argue that a major cause of poor performance on tasks that require the generation of relevant subproblems, arguments, and explanations is that most curricula emphasize the memorization of facts and the acquisition of relatively isolated subskills that are learned out-of-context and hence result in knowledge representations that tend to remain inert (e.g., see Brown, Collins, & Duguid, 1989; Cognition & Technology Group at Vanderbilt, 1990; Resnick & Klopfer, 1989). Alternatives to fact memorization and out-of-context practice include an emphasis on in-context learning that is constructive or generative in nature and is organized around authentic tasks that often involve group discussions (e.g., Brown, et al., 1989; Cognition & Technology Group at Vanderbilt, 1990; Gragg, 1940).

THEORETICAL FRAMEWORK OF GENERATIVE LEARNING ENVIRONMENTS

The generative learning environments that we have developed over the past five years are based on a theoretical framework that emphasizes the importance of anchoring or situating instruction in meaningful, problem-solving contexts that allow one to simulate in the classroom some of the advantages of apprenticeship learning (e.g., Brown, Collins, & Duguid, 1989; Cognition & Technology Group at Vanderbilt, 1990, in press). A major goal of this approach is to create shared environments that permit sustained exploration by students and teachers and enable them to understand the kinds of problems and opportunities that experts in various areas encounter and the knowledge that these experts use as tools. Theorists such as Dewey (1933), Schwab (1960) and Hanson (1970) emphasize that experts in an area have been immersed in phenomena and are familiar with how they have been thinking about them. When introduced to new theories, concepts, and principles that are relevant to their areas of interest, the experts can experience the changes in their own thinking that these ideas afford. For novices, however, the introduction of concepts and theories often seems like the mere introduction of new facts or mechanical procedures to be memorized. Because the novices have not been immersed in the phenomena being investigated, they are unable to experience the effects of the new information on their own noticing and understanding. Novices especially need help in moving from a general goal to the generation and definition of distinct subgoals necessary to achieve the overall goal.

Clearly, generative learning environments can be constructed in a variety of domains. Much of our work has focused in the area of mathematics. For our mathematics environments, the cognitive theory on which our approach is based interfaces with the instructional recommendations issued by the National Council of Teachers of Mathematics (NCTM) Curriculum Standards Group (1989). The NCTM's suggestions for changes in classroom activities include more emphasis on complex, open-ended problem solving, communication, and reasoning; more connections from mathematics to other subjects and to the world outside the classroom; more uses of calculators and powerful computer-based tools such as spreadsheet and graphing programs for exploring relationships (as opposed to having students spend an inordinate amount of time calculating by hand). In proposing a more generative approach to mathematics learning, the NTCM states:

> ...[T]he mathematics curriculum should engage students in some problems that demand extended effort to solve. Some might be group projects that require students to use available technology and to engage in cooperative problem solving and discussion. For grades 5-8 an important criterion of problems is that they be interesting to students. (NCTM, 1989, p.75)

In the following section we describe seven design principles that we believe will enhance teachers' abilities to encourage the kinds of generative problem-solving activities that we and others (e.g., the NCTM) emphasize.

DESIGN PRINCIPLES FOR GENERATIVE LEARNING ENVIRONMENTS

The generative learning environments that we have developed in mathematics involve a series of video-based adventures about a person named Jasper Woodbury. The adventures have been designed for fifth- and sixth-grade students, although we have used the series with students as young as first grade and as old as college freshmen. The series currently has four episodes completed and two more are in the planning stage. The following set of design principles have served as a framework for developing the series.

1. Video-based presentation format. Although some excellent work on applied problem solving has been conducted with materials that are supplied orally or in writing (e.g., Lesh, 1981), we decided to use the video medium for several reasons. One is that it is easier to make the information more motivating because characters, settings, and actions can be much more interesting. A second reason for using the video medium is that the problems to be communicated can be much more complex and interconnected than they can be in the written medium—this is especially important for students who have difficulty with reading. Modern theories of reading comprehension focus on the construction of mental models of situations; students can more directly form a rich image or mental model of the problem situation when the information is displayed in the form of dynamic images rather than text (McNamara, Miller, & Bransford, 1991). Teachers who have worked with our pilot videos have consistently remarked that our video-based adventures are especially good for students whose reading skills are subaverage. In addition, since there is a great deal of rich background information on the video, there is much more of an opportunity to notice scenes and events that can lead to the construction of additional, interesting problems in other content areas as well as in mathematics.

2. Narrative format. A second design principle is the use of a narrative format to present information. One purpose of using a well-formed story is to create a meaningful context for problem solving (for examples of other programs that use a narrative format, see Lipman, 1985; Bank Street College of Education, 1984). Stories involve a text structure that is relatively well understood by middle-school students (Stein & Trabasso, 1982). Using a familiar text structure as the context for presentation of mathematical concepts helps students generate an overall mental model of the situation and lets them understand authentic uses of mathematical concepts (e.g., Brown, Collins, & Duguid, 1989).

3. Generative learning format. The stories in the Jasper series are complete stories with one exception. As with most stories, there is setting information, a slate of characters, an initiating event and consequent events. The way in which these stories differ is that the resolution of the story must be provided by students. (There is a resolution on each disc, but students see it only after attempting to resolve the story themselves.) In the process of reaching a resolution, students generate and solve a complex mathematical problem. One reason for having students generate the ending—instead, for example, of guiding them through a modeled solution—is that it is motivating; students like to determine for themselves what the outcome will be. A second reason is that it allows students to actively participate in the learning process. Research findings suggest that there are very important benefits from having students generate information (Belli, Soraci, & Purdon, 1989; Slamecka & Graf, 1978; Soraci, Bransford, Franks, & Chechile, 1987).

4. Embedded data design. An especially important design feature of the Jasper series—one that is unique to our series and is instrumental in making it possible for students to engage in generative problem solving—is what we have called "embedded data" design. All the data needed to solve the problems are embedded somewhere in the video story. The mathematics problems are not explicitly formulated at the beginning of the video and the numerical information that is needed for the solutions is incidentally presented in the story. Students are then able to look back on the video and find all the data they need (this is very motivating). This design feature makes our problem-solving series analogous to good mystery stories. At the end of a good mystery, one can see that all the clues were provided, but they had to be noticed as being relevant and put together in just the right way.

5. Problem complexity. The Jasper videos pose very complex mathematical problems. For example, the first episode in the series contains a problem comprised of more than 15 interrelated steps. In the second episode, multiple solutions need to be considered by students in order to decide the optimum one. The complexity of the problems is intentional and is based on a very simple premise: Students cannot be expected to learn to deal with complexity unless they have the opportunity to do so (e.g., Schoenfeld, 1985). Students are not routinely provided with the opportunity to engage in the kind of sustained mathematical thinking necessary to solve the complex problem posed in each episode. The video makes the complexity manageable. We believe that a major reason for the lack of emphasis on complex problem solving (especially for lower achieving students) is the difficulties teachers face in communicating problem contexts that are motivating and complex yet ultimately solvable by students.

6. Pairs of related adventures. All Jasper videos have been designed in pairs. One reason for pairs of videos stems from the cognitive science literature on learning and transfer. Concepts that are acquired in only one context tend to be welded to that context and hence are not likely to be spontaneously accessed and used in new settings (e.g., Bransford & Nitsch, 1978; Bransford, Franks, Vye, & Sherwood, 1989; Bransford, Sherwood, Vye, & Rieser, 1986; Brown, Bransford, Ferrara, & Campione, 1983; Brown, Collins, & Duguid, 1989; Gick & Holyoak, 1980; Salomon & Perkins, 1989; Simon, 1980). Pairs of videos can help students analyze exactly what they are able to carry over from one context to another and what is specific to each context but not generalizable. For example, the first two episodes of "The Adventures of Jasper Woodbury" focus on the general issue of "trip planning." This pair of "trip planning" adventures allows students to learn to deal with the complexity in the first episode and then attempt to apply what they have learned in the second episode (plus learn some important, additional information). Pairs of adventures provide students with the opportunity to use mathematical concepts in a variety of contexts; thus enhancing considerably their abilities to transfer these skills to new situations spontaneously.

7. **Links across the curriculum.** Each narrative episode contains the data necessary to solve the specific complex problem posed at the end of the video story. As well, the narration provides many opportunities to introduce topics from other subject matters. For example, in the trip-planning episodes, maps are used to help figure out the solutions. These provide a natural link to geography, navigation, and other famous trips in which route planning was involved (e.g., Charles Lindbergh's flight across the Atlantic).

In sum, the videodisc-based problem solving "Jasper" adventures have been specially designed to recreate some of the advantages of apprenticeship training and to support the kinds of teaching activities that invite thinking and that have been recommended by groups such as the NCTM curriculum standards group (1989). Taken together, the seven design principles described above lead to the creation of video-based environments that are very different from the typical approach to educational videos (most simply involve lectures on tape). We believe that these design principles have implications for encouraging problem solving and reasoning in many areas of instruction.

DESCRIPTION OF EPISODES FROM "THE ADVENTURES OF JASPER WOODBURY"

The best way to understand the instructional design principles, as well as the intended intervention outcomes, is to "walk" through one of the episodes of the initial pair on trip planning. Each video in the Jasper series has a main story that is 17 to 20 minutes in length. The "end" of each video narration features one of the characters (Jasper in the first episode; Emily in the second) stating the problem that has to be solved; it is posed as a challenge and the students have to generate the relevant sub-problems in order to figure out the solution. All the data needed to solve the problems are provided in the video, and the problem to be solved is very complex. Each pair of videos in the series involves similar types of problems (e.g., trip planning for the first pair, developing a business plan in the second pair). There are many links in each video that allow students and teachers to extend their explorations across the curricula. (Please note that the verbal descriptions of these adventures fail to capture the excitement in them. In this case, a video is truly worth a thousand words.).

The first episode of the pair of trip planning videos is entitled *Journey to Cedar Creek.* This episode opens with Jasper Woodbury practicing his golf swing. The newspaper is delivered and Jasper turns to the classified ads for boats. Jasper sees an ad for a 1956 Chris Craft cruiser and decides to take a trip to Cedar Creek where it is docked. He rides his bicycle to the dock where his small "row" boat, complete with outboard motor, is docked. We see Jasper as he prepares for the trip from his dock to Cedar Creek: He is shown consulting a map of the river route from his home dock to the dock at Cedar Creek, listening to reports of weather conditions on his marine radio, and checking the gas for his outboard. As the story continues, Jasper stops for gas at Larry's dock. Larry is a comical-looking character who knows lots of interesting information. For example, as he hands Jasper the hose on the gas pump, he just happens to mention all the major locations where oil is found. When Jasper pays for the gas, we discover the only cash he has is a $20 bill. As Jasper makes his way up river, he passes a paddle-wheeler, a barge, and a tug boat and some information is provided about each of these. Next, Jasper runs into a bit of trouble when he hits something in the river and breaks his shear pin. He has to row to a repair shop, where he pays to have the pin fixed. Later, Jasper reaches the dock where the cruiser is located and meets Sal, the cruiser's owner. She tells him about the cruiser and they take the boat out for a spin. Along the way, Jasper learns about its cruising speed, fuel consumption, and fuel capacity, including the fact that the cruiser's temporary fuel tank only holds 12-gallons. He also learns that the boat's running lights don't work, so the boat can't be out on the river after sunset. Jasper eventually decides to buy the old cruiser, and pays with a check. He then thinks about whether he can get to his home dock by sunset. The episode ends by turning the problem over to the students to solve.

It is at this point that students move from the passive, television-like viewing to the active generation mode discussed earlier. They must solve Jasper's problem. Students have to generate the kinds of problems that Jasper must consider in order to decide whether he can get the boat home before dark without running out of fuel. The problem looks deceivingly simple; in reality it involves many sub-problems. But all the data needed to solve the problem were presented in the video. For example, to determine whether Jasper can reach home before sunset, students must calculate the total time the trip will take. To determine total time, they need to know the distance between the cruiser's and Jasper's home dock and the boat's cruising speed. The distance information can be obtained by referring to the mile markers on the map Jasper consulted when he first began his trip. The time needed for the trip must be compared to the time available for the trip by considering current time and the time of sunset, information given over the marine radio. The problems associated with Jasper's decision about whether he has enough fuel to make it home are even more complex. As it turns out, he does not have enough gas and he must plan where to purchase some—at this point money becomes a relevant issue. In this manner, students identify and work out the various interconnected sub-problems that must be faced to solve Jasper's problem.

THE ADDED VALUE OF VIDEODISC & HYPERMEDIA

Although videotape can be used as the medium for generative learning environments, the value of the environments can be enhanced by placing the environments on videodisc. The ability to instantaneously and randomly access any of the 54,000 frames that make up the 30 minutes of video on one side of the disc provides considerable advantage over the slow and cumbersome search-and-find method of linear videotape. With videodisc, segments can be played in slow motion or frozen clearly for detailed study so that students can take advantage of this rich source of information, or the video can be scanned rapidly looking for important events (these features were previously available on only the most expensive videotape players). This ease of access to any part of the video changes its function, from a linear element used to introduce or enhance instruction to an integral resource that can be explored and analyzed in detail. Using a hand controller for the videodisc player, teachers can rapidly locate and replay scenes in order to illustrate particular points or to invite class discussion. Segments of video that are not contiguous can be juxtaposed easily and contrasted to develop pattern recognition skills. This type of access can be accomplished using only a videodisc player and a simple hand-held remote control device, an inexpensive system comparable in price to an ordinary videotape player.

In addition to videodisc, we have taken advantage of the recent advances in "hypermedia," in which computing and communication technology are combined to make flexible connections between formerly distinct media such as writing, photographs, television, video, sound, graphics and computing. Thus, in addition to the mathematical problem-solving encouraged by the videodisc environments, we have developed several sets of ancillary hypermedia materials that extend the use of the video-based environment on a wide range of skills.

The ancillary hypermedia materials that we have developed are linked to the video but may be presented either via computer or print. There are several possible extensions to the problem-solving video. One form of extension involves practice in a basic skill or concept area such as decimals, fractions, money, time, etc. Within each area, different skill levels are represented in the form of exercises. In general, each area has a basic-concepts level (differentiating the basic units of that subject), a conversions (between the different units) or rounding level (for decimals and money), and a computation level using simple word problems. For example, to develop fluency with units of measurement, students are shown various objects and people who were seen in the episode and they are asked to estimate some dimension (e.g., the size). The task involves discriminating among common units of measurement (e.g., pounds, ounces, tons, inches, feet, weight).

Another form of extension involves an analog solution problem for the entire adventure. To develop proficiency at applying the problem solution for a given episode, the parameters of the original problem setting are changed. For example, by changing the fuel capacity of the temporary fuel tank, Jasper may be able to make it home without refueling. In these analogs we can also change the scenario by adding new locations or goals, thereby maintaining student interest in the problem-solving activity. These exercises allow students to explore the problem space by testing the changes in goals, obstacles and subgoals as a result of reasonable changes in situational elements. To develop proficiency with trip planning, there are available a number of "perturbed" mini-adventures that utilize the trip-planning schema as well.

The Jasper episodes were also designed to provide natural contexts for exploring scientific, geographical, and historical information related to the Jasper adventures and to use this information to solve real-world problems that people such as explorers and others throughout history have had to solve. To capitalize on these linkages across other content areas, we have developed hypermedia software called the *Database Publisher* that can be used by students and teachers.

The databases constructed by students using the *Publisher* provide them with an opportunity to explore scientific, geographical, and historical information related to the Jasper adventures and to use this information to solve real-world problems that people such as explorers and others throughout history have had to solve. As a simple illustration, the database for the *Journey to Cedar Creek* includes historical information relevant to life during the times of Mark Twain. When studying Mark Twain's world, it is very instructive for students to see how plans to go certain distances by water in *Journey to Cedar Creek* would be different if the mode of travel were steamboat or raft. A three-hour trip for Jasper by motorboat would have taken the better part of a day on Huckleberry Finn's raft. This means that drinking water, food, and other necessities would need to be included in one's plans.

SUMMARY

As a nation, we face the problem that the mathematical and scientific problem-solving ability of our students is falling short of what is needed for today's technological world. Results from national studies reinforce the need to increase achievement in mathematics and science (e.g., Kouba et al., 1988).

In this paper we have discussed a generative approach for teaching problem solving. The generative learning environments we have described are based on a theoretically motivated set of design principles that derive from a number of years of research. Several of these design principles are unique to our proposed series and appear to be extremely important for enhancing motivation among students and developing powerful skills of complex problem formulation and problem solving.

We also discussed the role of technology as a delivery medium for generative learning environments, as well as the use of hypermedia for extending the use of the video to a variety of contexts. The learning environments are designed so that they can be implemented at three levels of technological sophistication. The simplest level is videotape. A second level involves the use of videodisc with a hand-held remote control. The third level involves computer-based control of the videodisc plus video-related hypermedia software. Each level of sophistication adds value for teachers and students, so there is a motivation to move from videotape to videodisc to videodisc plus computer. In this way, we hope to help schools become technologically more sophisticated without making it impossible for them to use the materials if they cannot yet afford the extra equipment necessary to go beyond the use of videotape. In addition, this arrangement allows teachers to develop new skills in a gradual manner rather than be expected to learn a vast amount of new information (e.g., about new teaching strategies and about computers) all at once.

ACKNOWLEDGMENTS

Preparation of this chapter was supported in part by a grants from the James S. McDonnell Foundation and the National Science Foundation.

Members of the Cognition and Technology Group who contributed to this chapter include: Linda Barron, John Bransford, Bill Corbin, David Edyburn, Ben Ferron, Laura Goin, Elizabeth Goldman, Susan Goldman, Ted Hasselbring, Allison Heath, Jim Pellegrino, Kris Rewey, Robert Sherwood, Nancy Vye, Susan Warren, and Susan Williams.

REFERENCES

Bank Street College of Education (1984). *Voyage of the Mimi*, Scotts Valley, CA: Wings for Learning, Inc., Sunburst Co.

Belli, R., Soraci, S., & Purdon, S. (1989). *The generation effect in learning and memory: Implications for theory and practice.* Unpublished manuscript, Vanderbilt University, Learning Technology Center, TN.

Bransford, J. D., Franks, J. J., & Vye, N. J. & Sherwood, R. D. (1989). New approaches to instruction: Because wisdom can't be told. In S. Vosniadou & A. Ortony (Eds.), *Similarity and analogical reasoning* (pp. 470-497). NY: Cambridge University Press.

Bransford, J. D., Goldman, S. R., & Vye, N. J. (1991). Making a difference in people's abilities to think: Reflections on a decade of work and some hopes for the future. In L. Okagaki & R. J. Sternberg (Eds.), *Directors of development: Influences on the development of children's thinking* (pp. 147-180). Englewood Cliffs, NJ: Lawrence Erlbaum Associates.

Bransford, J. D., & Nitsch, K. E. (1978). Coming to understand things we could not previously understand. In J. F. Kavanaugh & W. Strange (Eds.), *Speech and language in the laboratory, school, and clinic.* Cambridge, MA: MIT Press. (Reprinted in H. Singer & R. Ruddell (Eds.), *Theoretical models and processes of reading.* Newark, DE: International Reading Association.)

Bransford, J. D., Sherwood, R., Vye, N., & Rieser, J. (1986). Teaching thinking and problem solving: Research foundations. *American Psychologist, 41,*1078-1089.

Brown, A. L., Bransford, J. D., Ferrara, R., & Campione, J. (1983). Learning, understanding and remembering. In J. Flavell & E. Markman (Eds.), *Mussen handbook of child psychology* (Vol. 1, 2nd ed.). Somerset, NJ: John Wiley & Sons.

Brown, J. S., Collins, A., & Duguid, P. (1989). Situated cognition and the culture of learning. *Educational Researcher, 17,* 32-41.

Carey, I., Flower, L., Hayes, J. R., Schriver, K. A., & Hass, C. (1989). Establishing an epistemological base for science teaching in the light of contemporary notions of the nature of science and how children learn science. *Journal of Research in Science Teaching, 27,* 429 - 447.

Carpenter, E. T., (1980). Piagetian interviews of college students. In R. G. Fuller et al., (Eds.), *Piagetian programs in higher education.* Lincoln: ADAPT, University of Nebraska-Lincoln.

Cognition and Technology Group at Vanderbilt. (1990). Anchored instruction and its relationship to situated cognition, *Educational Researcher, 19*(3), 2-10.

Cognition and Technology Group at Vanderbilt (in press). Anchored instruction and science education. In R. Duschl & R. Hamilton (Eds.), *Philosophy of science, cognitive psychology and educational theory and practice.* NY: SUNY Press.

Dewey, S. (1933). *How we think: Restatement of the relation of reflective thinking to the educative process.* Boston: Heath.

Gick, M. L., & Holyoak, K. J. (1980). Analogical problem solving. *Cognitive Psychology, 15,* 1-38.

Gragg, C. I. (1940). *Because wisdom can't be told. Harvard Alumni Bulletin,* 78-84.

Hanson, N. R. (1970). A picture theory of theory meaning. In R. G. Colodny (Ed.), *The nature and function of scientific theories* (pp. 233-274). Pittsburgh: University of Pittsburgh Press.

Jones, B. F., & Idol, L. (1990). Conclusions. In B. F. Jones & L. Idol (Eds.), *Dimensions of thinking and cognitive instruction* (pp. 511-532). Hillsdale, NJ: Lawrence Erlbaum Associates.

Kouba, V. L., Brown, C. A., Carpenter, T. P., Lindquist, M. M., Silver, E. A., & Swafford, J. O. (1988). Results of the fourth NAEP assessment of mathematics: Number, operations, and word problems. *Arithmetic Teacher, 35*(8), 14-19.

Lesh, R. (1981). Applied mathematical problem solving. *Educational Studies in Mathematics, 12*, 235-264.

Lipman, M. (1985). Thinking skills fostered by philosophy for children. In J. Segal, S. Chipman, & R. Glaser (Eds.), *Thinking and learning skills: Relating instruction to basic research* (Vol. 1, pp. 83-108). Hillsdale, NJ: Lawrence Erlbaum Associates.

McNamara, T. P., Miller, D. L., & Bransford, J. D. (1991). Mental models and reading comprehension. In R. Barr, M. Kamil, P. Mosenthal, & T. D. Pearson, (Eds.), *Handbook of reading research.* (Vol. 2, pp. 490-511). NY: Longman.

National Assessment of Educational Progress (NAEP). (1981). *Reading, thinking, and writing: Results from the 1979-1980 national assessment of reading and literature.* Report No. 11-L-01. Denver, CO: Education Commission of the States.

National Assessment of Educational Progress (NAEP). (1983). *The third national mathematics assessment: Results, trends and issues.* (Report No. 13-MA-01). Denver, CO: Educational Commission of the States.

National Commission on Excellence in Education. (1983). *A nation at risk: The imperative for educational reform.* Washington, DC: US Government Printing Office.

National Council of Teachers of Mathematics. (1989). *Curriculum and evaluation standards for school mathematics.* Reston, VA: Author.

Nickerson, R. S. (1988). On improving thinking through instruction. *Review of Research in Education, 15*, 3-57.

Resnick, L. (1987). *Education and learning to think.* Washington, DC: National Academy Press.

Resnick, L. B., & Klopfer, L. E. (Eds.) (1989). *Toward the thinking curriculum: Current cognitive research.* Alexandria, VA: American Society for Curriculum Development.

Salomon, G., & Perkins, D. N. (1989). Rocky road to transfer: Rethinking mechanisms of a neglected phenomenon. *Educational Psychologist,* 24(2), 113-142.

Schoenfeld, A. (1985). *Mathematical problem solving.* Orlando, FL: Academic Press.

Schwab, J. J. (1960). What do scientists do? *Behavioral Science, 5*, 1-27.

Simon, H. A. (1980). Problem solving and education. In D. T. Tuma & R. Reif (Eds.), *Problem solving and education: Issues in teaching and research* (pp. 81-96). Hillsdale, NJ: Lawrence Erlbaum Associates.

Slamecka, N. J., & Graf, P. (1978). The generation effect: Delineation of a phenomenon. *Journal of Experimental Psychology: Human Learning and Memory, 4,* 592-604.

Soraci, S. A., Jr., Bransford, J. D., Franks, J. J., & Chechile, R. (1987). A multiple-cue model of generation activity. *Proceedings of the 1987 Psychonomics Society.* New Orleans.

Stein, N. L., & Trabasso, T. (1982). What's in a story: An approach to comprehension and instruction. In R. Glaser (Ed.), *Advances in instructional psychology,* (Vol. 2, pp. 213-267). Hillsdale, NJ: Lawrence Erlbaum Associates.

Van Haneghan, J., Barron, L., Young, M., Williams, S., Vye, N., & Bransford, J. (in press). The Jasper Series: An experiment with new ways to enhance mathematical thinking. In D. Halpern (Ed.), *Concerning the development of thinking skills in science and mathematics.* Hillsdale, NJ: Lawrence Erlbaum Associates.

Voss, J. F., Perkins, D., & Segal, J. (1990). *Informal reasoning and education.* Hillsdale, NJ: Lawrence Erlbaum Associates.

III INSTRUCTIONAL TECHNOLOGY PERSPECTIVES

7

An Instructional Designer's View of Constructivism

Walter Dick
Florida State University

INTRODUCTION

There is no question that the major principles of instructional design have been derived from Skinnerian psychology and Gagné's conditions of learning. These theories have been integrated, along with other principles, into systematic models for designing instruction. Instructional designers are now being challenged by constructivists to reconsider the theories they use in their design work. That challenge is well represented in the chapters by Perkins, Bransford et al., Cunningham and Spiro et al. (see Chapters 4, 6, 3, and 5, respectively). The purpose of this chapter is to review the work of each of these authors from the point of view of an instructional designer and to explore several general reactions that emerge from a review of Parts I and II of this book.

REACTIONS TO PERKINS' "TECHNOLOGY MEETS CONSTRUCTIVISM"

Perkins presents an interesting contrast between the classroom of the past and present, and the electronic classroom of the future. He indicates that computer-based classrooms will support the use of databases, microworlds, word processors, intelligent tutors, and laboratory simulations. The roles of teacher and student will change dramatically as learning becomes more of an interactive process.

The classroom of the future will support the constructivist belief that learning must be at least BIG, if not WIG. Students must construct concepts and apply them by going "beyond the information given." Some would prefer that they operate more "without the information given," that is, by discovering concepts without being directly given the information they need. The more the problem-solving learning situation represents the real world, the more likely it is that the student will transfer the skills to other problem-solving situations.

Designers will recognize this strategy as an alternative form of discovery learning which has been present in the literature for many years. There may be a tendency to reject this approach as inefficient and questionable in its effectiveness. This would be unfortunate because the constructivists have presented some important criticisms and alternative approaches that deserve the consideration of designers.

Perkins clarifies for designers the constructivist view by discussing front-end analysis, instructional strategies, and assessment. He makes the important point that the *context* in which skills will be used must be identified in the needs assessment, and subsequently incorporated, to the extent possible, in the instruction that is provided to the student. With the BlG/WlG approach to teaching, there is an emphasis on learner control and the capability to manipulate information. No more linear chains of core instruction for the constructivists! And, when the student is done, assessment must focus on the transfer of the skills that have been learned to other contexts. (Cunningham has much more to say on this.)

Perkins, along with the other three authors, stresses two major points: American education is failing to prepare our students to be successful in today's world and, in order to remedy this situation, instruction must focus on retention, understanding, and active use of what is learned. Designers would not disagree with either of these points.

REACTIONS TO BRANSFORD'S "GENERATIVE LEARNING ENVIRONMENTS"

Bransford echoes the theme that we must teach students to think effectively, reason, problem solve, and develop learning skills. This can be done by anchoring learning in meaningful contexts which simulate apprenticeship learning. He presents seven major design principles and a description of their application.

Designers would have little problem with Bransford's principles when the desired learning outcomes are taken into consideration. His use of video stories with embedded data (BlG) provide for motivating scenarios such as that of Jasper Woodbury. Particularly appealing are the presentations of *pairs* of scenarios so that the student must apply newly acquired skills in at least two contexts. It is also possible to change the parameters within a scenario so that the student does not simply memorize a single solution to a problem.

One of Bransford's principles is problematic. He advocates the use of very complex problem situations, some of which require up to 15 steps to solve. Some students probably are capable of dealing with this level of complexity, but certainly some must be overwhelmed. What provision is made for the less capable learner? Bransford makes reference to some basic-skills ancillary materials but does not make clear exactly how they are used. This raises a major issue about entry behaviors which will be discussed at a later point.

REACTIONS TO CUNNINGHAM'S "DIALOGUE"

Cunningham has presented a delightful dialogue in which we find ourselves swayed first one way and then another. He contrasts the objectivist's view of design with that of the constructivist, who takes the position that learning consists of the building up of structures and that what is learned depends on what is already known and how the new information is interpreted by the learner. Finally, knowledge emerges in contexts in which it is relevant, that is, in a setting that is meaningful to the learner.

According to Cunningham, the constructivist designer begins by selecting tasks that are relevant to a child's experiences, gives him tools to work on a problem, has the child work with other children to solve the problem, and the test of success is "is the task successfully completed?" This description highlights the approach often favored by constructivists of having children work in groups on problem-solving tasks. The cooperative learning approach is apparent in a number of constructivist applications.

The area of greatest challenge in Cunningham's dialogue is that of assessment. He argues for the assessment to be embedded in the context of the learning in order to be valid. He clearly objects to assessments that occur in what he calls the decontextualized school situation. Designers would agree that whatever "conditions" are included in the statement of a terminal objective (e.g., given a role-play situation, the learner will...) should be the conditions that apply when the objective is assessed. No quarrel here!

The designer's problem comes with *what* is assessed. For the constructivist, the focus of the assessment should be on what has been constructed by the learner as a result of the learning situation. What has been constructed will likely differ from student to student. In "assessing the construction" it appears that we would be measuring learning *gain* rather than whether the student has mastered a specific set of predetermined skills. There is also a problem of assessing group work. How are individuals evaluated and with what degree of confidence?

The designer's questions about assessment have relevance not only for grading the learners but also for the whole process of formative evaluation. How do constructivists conduct formative evaluations without objective performance data? It might also be noted that many of Cunningham's points seem to be directed more at psychometricians and people who believe in teaching context-free problem-solving skills. Designers have problems with these same people!

REACTIONS TO SPIRO'S "COGNITIVE FLEXIBILITY, CONSTRUCTIVISM, HYPERTEXT, RANDOM ACCESS INSTRUCTION," ETC.

Spiro describes his theory as "new constructivism" and he provides a persuasive argument that links learning problems in ill-defined knowledge domains to the need for cognitive flexibility which results from learning knowledge in a variety of ways and contexts. Hypertext systems are ideally suited to the presentation of what he describes as random access instruction.

Spiro provides us with examples of ill-defined domains: history, medicine, and literary interpretation. This highlights a major difference between many designers and constructivists, namely the emphasis of the former on skills to be learned versus the latter's focus on learning a "domain" of knowledge. Designers don't think of teaching knowledge, they identify skills that must be acquired and then apply hierarchical analysis to identify the subskills that are required in order to learn the terminal skills. This difference does not detract from the other points that Spiro makes regarding the need for cognitive flexibility.

It is interesting to note that Spiro is examining those skills that fall between novice and expert. Cognitive psychologists have studied the two extremes in expertise, but little is known about the mid-ground.

Spiro points out that the approaches used to teach novices are countereffective when developing higher level transfer skills. This is another way of saying that we first learn to discriminate and categorize concepts by placing each example in its appropriate slot. Later, as we learn principles and problem solving, we must learn to generalize our knowledge rather than categorize it. If we have effectively learned the lower level skills, it is difficult to transfer to other situations. We can speculate that this may be wired in as a means of preserving the species by preventing us from overgeneralizing our behaviors to inappropriate, and possibly life-threatening, situations. In other words, appropriate and effective transfer in one situation can be inappropriate and ineffective generalization in another. It is sometimes a thin line, and therefore is not surprising that transfer of training has been a difficult process that has been studied throughout the history of psychology.

Spiro's approach to instruction focuses on multiple presentations of information. Content must be covered a number of times with different purposes; therefore there are many concrete examples of the uses of a concept. A hypertext system provides the ideal vehicle for presenting this type of instruction. A designer would probably respond to this approach by asking "How many different examples?" Designers have always used examples and nonexamples as the basic approach to concept learning. Spiro would appear to broaden this emphasis. The question remains of how many of these examples does an individual student actually see? Is learner control again an issue? Is the learner "guided" through an entire range of examples or is this decision left to the student?

At the end of Spiro's chapter he refers to a study in which his approach was contrasted with one which stressed the acquisition of declarative knowledge. Clearly this type of study is critically important to the advancement of the constructivist position and a better understanding of the constructivist view through its representation in concrete experimental treatments.

As an aside to the reader it may be noted that one of the learning strategies presented by the constructivists is rereading a passage with a different purpose in mind. I suggest that Spiro's chapter deserves just such a rereading. It is so compact in ideas, as well as new terminology, that a single reading only provides the initial scaffolding for later, more purposeful readings.

GENERAL OBSERVATIONS ABOUT THE CHAPTERS

It has been observed that the constructivist movement is a natural reaction to the major emphasis in recent years on statewide skills-based testing and the poor performance of American students in international comparisons. Several of the chapters refer to inadequate problem-solving skills of students as the rationale for advancing the constructivist position. It should be noted that instructional designers cannot be blamed for poor student performance because designers have had almost no part in shaping the American public school curriculum. Nearly all advances made by designers, aside from those carrying computers, have been rejected by the schools over the last 2O years. So designers share the same concern as the constructivists for student performance and how it can be improved.

A problem that is being faced by designers is the application of appropriate strategies for the new technologies. The front end of the instructional design model is constantly changing to accommodate new approaches to analysis. However, theory-based instructional strategies for multi-media systems have not kept pace. In essence, the technology has driven the applications, with theory nowhere to be found. Constructivism provides one theoretical approach to the use of computer-based systems such as hypertext, and, as such, deserves careful consideration.

Of particular importance is the fact that these theorists are developing instructional sequences that typify their theory and they have begun conducting research and evaluations. We can only hope that they will continue to do so. It is of particular significance that they are focusing on the context in which skills must be used and trying to replicate that context in the learning situation. This is an important lesson for all designers, regardless of their organizational affiliation.

Problems and Concerns

A review of the constructivist chapters reveals a number of areas in which there are either unanswered questions or direct differences with a typical instructional design approach. Some of these points were indicated in the reviews of the specific chapters while others emerge from a consideration of the chapters as a whole.

1. While the authors make it clear that they are focusing on problem-solving skills other spokespeople for constructivism would make it appear that the theory applies to all domains of human learning. What are the boundaries of the theory? And, is it really a theory, or is it an instructional strategy for a particular type of learning outcome?

2. Domains of knowledge and domains of learning are very different. Designers are not concerned with students learning everything in a domain, they are concerned with their learning everything that is required in order to be effective. How inefficient and ineffective is constructivist instruction because it tries to cover too much?

3. Why does there appear to be almost no concern for the entry behaviors of students? Designers use analytic techniques to determine what a student *must know or be able to do* before beginning instruction, because without these skills research shows they will likely not be able to learn new skills. Why are constructivists not concerned that the gap will be too great between the schema of some students and the tools and information that they are provided? Do we have so many failing students and dropouts today because the schools don't show enough concern for entry behaviors?

4. There is a major difference in approaches to assessment. Designers use objectives to describe the setting in which behaviors must occur. Constructivists also are concerned about context—but more for instruction than individual assessment. Designers are concerned that a reasonable percent of the learners achieved a reasonable percent of the objectives, and that they do so efficiently. Constructivists, perhaps because all of their examples are from public education, show no concern for efficiency, and little apparent concern for certifying the competency level of individual students.

5. An unspoken issue throughout the chapters is that of learner control. Designers typically provide learners with only those choices that will insure mastery performance. Constructivists seem to offer the learner almost unlimited discretion to select what is studied, from among available resources, and how it is studied. What accountability is there that students will learn? This leads into the last, and perhaps most interesting, issue.

6. Although few formal definitions of "Instruction" are available (according to a colleague who has been searching for them), it is fair to say that an instructional designer would say that a minimalist definition of instruction is an educational intervention that is driven by specific outcome objectives, materials or procedures that are targeted on these objec-

tives, and assessments that determine if the desired changes in behavior (learning) have occurred.

What about the constructivist interventions. Do they have specific learning objectives for each student? Apparently not. Is the organization of content, as well as practice and feedback activities, focused on specific outcomes? Apparently not. Are criterion-referenced assessments provided for each learner to determine if they have mastered the desired skills? Apparently not. Therefore, if instructional designers design instruction, then constructivists are constructing something else. This "something else" may be a desirable educational intervention, but it does not appear to be instruction.

SUGGESTIONS FOR CONSTRUCTIVISTS

The interventions that you are developing have three significant characteristics: They are costly to develop, they require technology to implement, and they are very difficult to evaluate. Based on what we know about the dissemination of innovations, it is unlikely that your efforts will find rapid acceptance in the public schools. The "bells and whistles" associated with your interventions are attractive and fun. Your basic approach will be appealing to the humanistic orientation of the public schools. But, it is hoped, that you will continue the research and evaluations, to identify the real strengths and weaknesses of your approach, and to continue to interact with instructional designers about your findings.

SUGGESTIONS FOR INSTRUCTIONAL DESIGNERS

In the closing scene of Cunningham's chapter, his character Simplicio says, "And l have become convinced more than ever that constructivism is simply a label for fuzzy, unscientific thinking. The logic underlying what we have here been calling objectivism is simply so compelling in my mind, despite your wonderful arguments, that I cannot seriously consider constructivism as a viable alternative." As a trained objectivist instructional designer, it may be difficult not to find yourself in almost knee-jerk agreement with Simplicio. But don't fall into this trap.

Constructivists are responding, in part, to limitations in present instructional design theory and practice. Their ideas regarding learning contexts and multiple learning exposures are extremely important if designers are to be concerned with the transfer of skills from the learning site to the site at which they will be used. Stay in touch with this area of the literature; there may be some exciting developments in the future.

ACKNOWLEDGMENTS

The author expresses his appreciation to his colleagues, Marcy Driscoll and Mike Hannafin, as well as several graduate students who read the constructivist chapters and shared their interpretations and reactions. Any errors of fact or judgment in this chapter remain the responsibility of the author.

8

Constructivism and Instructional Design

M. David Merrill
Utah State University

INTRODUCTION

After careful review of chapters 1 through 6, we have concluded that extreme constructivism[1] does indeed represent an alternative view to Instructional Systems Technology (IST), but that some of the assumptions and prescriptions of a more moderate constructivism are consistent with our views of instructional design. Constructivism advocates are fond of characterizing the instructional view in order to make their points stand out in bold relief against what they believe are inappropriate assumptions and practices. It is unfortunate that in making these characterizations they have not cited the work of instructional design theorists, but rather supporters of the constructivist movement. Too often such characterizations become straw men which are also not supported by members of the IST community.[2] For example, Bednar, Cunningham, Duffy, and Perry (chapter 2) and Cunningham (chapter 3) cite the extreme views of Lakoff (1987), which he labels "objectivism," as the theoretical foundation of IST. We do not accept these extreme views as foundational to our own work, and would surmise that other instructional design theorists would be equally hesitant to acknowledge this view as representative of their work.

At Utah State University we are attempting to extend instructional design theory or IST. Our work may not reflect the views of the IST community at large. Nevertheless, we have been careful to identify our own assumptions and their implications for second generation instructional design theory (ID_2).[3] In this chapter, I will review these assumptions and contrast them with corresponding assumptions of constructivism as reflected by the authors of chapters 1 through 6. In this effort I shall identify those constructivistic assumptions that are consistent with our assumptions and those which are clearly in opposition to our view.

In addition, I will identify the instructional design implications of our ID_2 assumptions and will contrast these with the instructional design implications of constructivism as represented by the authors of chapters 1 through 6.

Finally, I will take a very pragmatic stance and argue that the assumptions of both ID_2 and constructivism may be equally valid or invalid. I will suggest a set of pragmatic criteria which has led us to accept the assumptions of ID_2 and to reject the opposing assumptions of extreme constructivism. Ultimately the instructional design prescriptions of either position must be established by empirical verification. I will also suggest some of the difficulties in obtaining such verification, including the possibility that the instructional products resulting from either position may have far more in common than they have in opposition, making an adequate empirical test extremely difficult.

ASSUMPTIONS OF ID_2

ID_2 is based on the following assumptions. The first three are quoted from Merrill, Li, and Jones (1990b).

Mental Models

> Our concept of ID_2 is cognitive rather than behavioral. We start from the basic assumption that learning results in the organizing of memory into structures, which we may term *mental models*. To this we adopt two propositions about the learning process from cognitive psychology:
> - organization during learning aids in later retrieval of information, and
> - elaborations generated at the time of learning new information can facilitate retrieval.
>
> Organization refers to the structuring of knowledge, while elaboration refers to the explicit specification of relations among knowledge units.

Categories of Knowledge

> From ID_1 [first generation instructional design[4]] we retain Gagné's fundamental assumption:
> - there are different learning outcomes and different conditions are required to promote each of these different outcomes (Gagné, 1965, 1985).
>
> We propose to extend these fundamental ideas as follows:
> - a given learned performance results from a given organized and elaborated cognitive structure, which we will call a mental model. Different learning outcomes require different types of mental models;

- the construction[5] of a mental model by a learner is facilitated by instruction that explicitly organizes and elaborates the knowledge being taught, during the instruction;
- there are different organizations and elaborations of knowledge required to promote different learning outcomes.

Knowledge Representation

We assume that knowledge can be represented in a knowledge base external to the learner.

We make no claims about how cognitive structure is organized and elaborated, as this is not well understood. We stand on the weaker, and more defensible assumption, that we can analyze the organization and elaborations of knowledge outside the mind, and presume that there is some correspondence between these and the representations in the mind.

Enterprises

A complex mental model enables the learner to engage in some complex human enterprise or integrated activity. We assume that ID_2 should teach the organized and elaborated knowledge needed to facilitate the development of mental models, thus enabling students to engage in complex enterprises.

Knowledge Strategy Separation

We assume that instructional strategy is somewhat independent of the knowledge to be taught. We assume that the same strategy can be used to teach different topics and even different subject matters.

Strategy Categories

In the previous paragraphs we assumed that different organizations and elaborations of knowledge are required to promote different learning outcomes; we further assume that there are different kinds of instructional strategies necessary to promote these different kinds of learning outcomes. Different instructional strategies are required to promote the acquisition of different kinds of knowledge and skill. We assume that these strategy categories are not domain specific. Using the appropriate instructional strategy will facilitate the student's acquisition of that knowledge or skill, while using an inappropriate instructional strategy will decrement the student's acquisition of the knowledge or skill.

Strategy Universality

We assume that these instructional strategies are somewhat universal; that is, to learn a particular type of knowledge or skill, a particular learner must engage in a set of instructional transactions similar to those required by any other learner.

ASSUMPTIONS OF CONSTRUCTIVISM

The authors of chapters 1 through 6 seem to subscribe to the following (the quotations are from Bednar et al., chapter 2):

Learning Constructed

Knowledge is constructed from experience. "...[L]earning is a constructive process in which the learner is building an internal representation of knowledge...."

Interpretation Personal

There is no shared reality, learning is a personal interpretation of the world. "...[L]earning results in...a personal interpretation of experience."

Learning Active

Learning is active. "Learning is an active process in which meaning is developed on the basis of experience."

Learning Collaborative

Meaning is negotiated from multiple perspectives. "Conceptual growth comes from the sharing of multiple perspectives and the simultaneous changing of our internal representations in response to those perspectives...." Sagredo (Cunningham, chapter 3) agrees: "The role of education...is...to promote collaboration with others to show the multiple perspectives that can be brought to bear on a particular problem and to arrive at self-chosen positions to which they can commit themselves...."

Learning Situated

Learning should occur in realistic settings (situated or anchored). "...[L]earning must be situated in a rich context, reflective of real-world contexts...."

Testing Integrated

Testing should be integrated with the task, not a separate activity. "...[T]he measure of learning...is how instrumental the learner's knowledge structure is in facilitating thinking in the content field...."

COMPARISON OF CONSTRUCTIVISM AND ID_2

On the surface these premises seem to be consistent with our ID_2 perspective. However, the implications of these assumptions, as stressed by some of the authors of chapters 1 through 6, make most of them inconsistent with the assumptions of ID_2.

Mental Models Versus Constructed Learning

"Knowledge [a mental model] is constructed from experience." We agree. We do not subscribe to the *tabula rasa* straw man of extreme objectivism. I don't know anyone who seriously assumes that knowledge is merely "transferred" to the memory of the student. Mental models are constructed by the learner as a result of experience. The student needs a variety of experiences to construct an adequate mental model. A mental model is modified as a result of every new experience. On this point ID_2 has no disagreement with constructivism.

Categories of Knowledge and Personal Interpretation

"There is no shared reality, learning is a personal interpretation of the world." This is a point of major disagreement. While ID_2 subscribes to learning as constructed, we do not assume that the resulting cognitive structure is completely idiosyncratic, unique to each individual. We assume that the semantics or content of cognitive structure are unique to each individual, but that the syntax or structure is not. By analogy, there are an infinite number of declarative sentences in the English language, but, while their semantics can differ significantly, they all have the same syntax. In a like way, the content of each individuals mental models may be different, but ID_2 assumes that the structure is the same. Whatever the mechanisms of mind—electrical, chemical—and the functioning of mind—encoding, memory, retrieval—ID_2 assumes that in this respect all people are created equal. Further, we assume that such functions can be known and used to guide instruction.

Knowledge Representation and Constructed Learning

Some of the authors of chapters 1 through 6 have taken a strong stand for constructivism with regard to knowledge analysis and representation (e.g., chapter 2). Their corollaries of these assumptions include the following:

Content cannot be prespecified. There are no different types of learning, especially separate from content. There can be "no meaningful construction (nor authentic activity) if relevant information is prespecified." Furthermore, they have suggested that there can be no categories of objectives independent of subject matter or domain, that all objectives are unique to different subject matters. The only allowable content is "authentic tasks," which if "decontextualized" (i.e., taken from the milieu in which they occur) are no longer "authentic" and hence have lost their value for enabling the student to construct knowledge, except for the "artificial context of the classroom."

ID_2 stands in direct opposition to these extreme constructivist views. We have proposed a syntax for knowledge representation (Jones, Li, & Merrill, 1990) that assumes that knowledge, across subject matter areas, can be represented in knowledge frames of three types—entities, activities, and processes. We have further assumed that these frames can be elaborated in four ways—via properties, components, abstractions, and associations. This knowledge structure enables us to represent knowledge in a knowledge base. This representation is independent of any particular individual. The same knowledge structure can be used for a wide variety of knowledge domains. Furthermore, we assume that in order for adequate instruction to occur that knowledge must be prespecified. Technology-based delivery systems such as CBI or interactive video require that knowledge be prespecified and represented in some form of knowledge base. ID_2 proposes that this representation has a syntax that will allow the representation of diverse domains, using the same knowledge structure.

Some of the advocates of constructivism have equated prespecified with linear, nonflexible, or nonexecutable. These are unwarranted extrapolations. An intelligent tutoring system that can carry on a dialogue with a student must have prespecified knowledge. In fact, specifying enough knowledge to make such systems viable is one of the challenges ITS has encountered. Prespecification does not mean that the knowledge is static or linear, or that all student responses have been anticipated. An appropriate syntax for representation makes such intelligent systems possible. Hence, it should not be assumed that because ID_2 advocates a particular syntax that this syntax enables only static, linear, or noninteractive presentation of the knowledge.

Two of the authors (Spiro et al., and Bransford et al.) have described technology-delivered instruction in the constructivist tradition. Spiro et al. (chapter 5) describe technology-based hypermedia delivery based on Cognitive Flexibility Theory. This requires that the knowledge be represented in some knowledge base. The Cognitive Technology Group (chapter 6) describe video scenarios of complex problem-solving situated in real-world like settings. This requires some form of knowledge base implemented by the technology. If knowledge is represented, then there must be some form of representation. In our opinion, the knowledge representation system of ID_2 could be used to represent the information described by both of these research groups. It is not clear from the information available whether Spiro, Bransford, and their colleagues subscribe to the view that each of these representations must be unique, or whether they would accept a common syntax for knowledge representation. However, they must disagree with Bednar, Cunningham, Duffy, and Perry (chapter 2) concerning the prespecification of knowledge. In both cases the knowledge has been prespecified.

Enterprises

We have indicated that some of the limitations of first-generation instructional design, including our own work, are that "ID_1 content analysis does not use integrated wholes which are essential for understanding complex and dynamic phenomena," and "ID_1 teaches pieces but not integrated wholes." Some of the authors (chapter 2) have also expressed this limitation of Objectivism in the following way:

> Knowledge can be completely characterized using the techniques of semantic analysis (or its second cousin, task analysis)....[T]hought is atomistic in that in can be completely broken down into simple building blocks, which form the basis for instruction. Thus, this transfer of knowledge is most efficient if the excess baggage of irrelevant content and context can be eliminated.

In order to contrast constructivist views these authors have stated the most extreme view of objectivism.

Constructivism assumes that, "Learning should occur in realistic settings (situated or anchored)." These authors (chapter 2) go to the opposite extreme, however, and suggest that an "authentic task" must contain no isolated tasks, must be a real-world task, must be in context, and must involve no simplification of that context. Furthermore they argue that context cannot be separated from use. While advocating the teaching of more integrated enterprises (see Gagné & Merrill, 1990), ID_2 still holds that these enterprises are constructed of components of known syntax and that analyzing a task into these components enables the use of transaction shells to efficiently and effectively enable student interaction as described later in this chapter. ID_2 feels that teaching authentic tasks in context is a desirable part of the instruction. But to deny simplification, to deny isolating a generality from context, to insist on all instruction occurring only in the context of use, is to deny some of the great advantages of learning from instruction versus learning only from experience.

To insist on context never being separated from use is to deny the teaching of abstractions. An abstraction is one of the powerful capabilities of the human mind, the ability to decontextualize ideas from context and apply them in a new context. We agree that the initial instruction must be contextualized, that the learner must experience the abstraction in a variety of contexts and applications; but we emphatically insist that at some point in the instruction these abstractions not only can, but must, be decontextualized if the student is to gain the maximum benefit and ability to transfer generalities and tools to new situations.

Knowledge Strategy Separation

While the basic assumptions identified for constructivism don't seem to demand such a narrow view, some of the authors (chapter 2) insist that there can be no content independent instructional strategies. As indicated, a fundamental assumption of ID_2 is that strategy and subject matter content are somewhat independent.

Strategy Categories

While the basic assumptions identified for constructivism don't seem to demand such a narrow view, some of the authors (chapter 2) insist that there are no categories of objectives and hence there can be no categories of strategies. They further insist that all objectives are unique to the context in which they are embedded. As indicated, a fundamental assumption of ID_2 is that there are classes of instructional transactions which are appropriate for promoting acquisition of particular types of mental models, that these fundamental instructional transactions can be adapted to a wide variety of situations and used with different subject matter contents.

Strategy Universality

While the basic assumptions identified for constructivism don't seem to demand such a narrow view, some of the authors (chapter 2) insist that there is no "average learner," that each learner is unique. Furthermore, they insist on no external control of instructional events, implying that all instruction must be under learner control. This extreme view would insist that all learners must have instruction that is unique to them—that all learners must control their own instruction. This makes instructional design prescriptions via any universal set of instructional strategies impossible. As indicated a fundamental assumption of ID_2 is that there are classes of instructional strategies which are appropriate for all learners to enable them to construct appropriate mental models of particular kinds of learning tasks.

Active Learning

Yes! Yes! ID_2 insists on an active learner and that this activity be meaningful, not just response for the sake of response (see Merrill, 1988). The name *Instructional Transaction* was deliberately chosen to represent an active learner. An instructional transaction is defined as "a mutual, dynamic, real-time, give-and-take between an instructional system and a student in which there is an exchange of information" (Li & Merrill, 1990; Merrill, Li, & Jones, 1990b, 1991).

Collaborative Learning and Meaning Negotiated from Multiple Perspectives

This assumption is not inconsistent with ID_2 except that we would insist that not all learning need be collaborative. There are occasions when individual learning is more effective and more efficient.

We agree that a divergent set of examples and contexts is necessary for promoting adequate transfer to new situations. However, some of the authors (chapter 2) have argued that the use of examples to "highlight critical attributes and systematically manipulate the complex of irrelevant attributes" is not appropriate since life seldom consists of nicely organized examples; hence, they advocate "slices of life" as more authentic. They are right of course, life is not regular; that is why learning form instruction is more efficient than learning only from experience. We agree that multiple perspectives are necessary, but we also advocate that these multiple perspectives should be carefully chosen (preselected) to enable the learner to abstract from these situations that which is relevant and that which is not. It is a straw man to insist, as these authors do, that the selection of cases which highlight attributes necessarily means that these cases are "clear-cut examples with only one correct solution" or that "...there is little that is authentic about the examples."

Salviati (Cunningham, chapter 3) argues that "...the role of education...is to promote collaboration with others to show the multiple perspectives that can be brought to bear on a particular problem and to arrive at self-chosen positions to which they can commit themselves, while realizing the basis of other views with which they may disagree." "...[L]earning is infinite and not subject to the sorts of analyses favored by objectivists except in the most trivial cases."

These constructivists argue that specific learning objectives are not possible—that meaning is always constructed by, and unique to, the individual; that all understanding is negotiated. In our opinion this is a very extreme position. Let me speak up for the vast amount of "trivial cases," those situations where shared meaning is not only possible but necessary.

Do we want students to have a "self-chosen position" with regard to the sound of letters in learning to read? Do we want students to have a "self-chosen position" about the meaning of the integers. Will a machine allow us to have a "self-chosen position" about how it works? Can students have a "self-chosen position" about which keys on a keyboard correspond to certain letters on the screen? Do we want students to have a "self-chosen position" about how to do the arithmetic operations of add and subtract? About how to solve a linear equation? Do we want drivers to have a "self-chosen position" about the meaning of a red light? Of a stop sign? Will a natural law allow us to have a "self-chosen position" about its relationships? Can a student have a "self-chosen position" about Ohm's law?

If I hire a surgeon to do heart surgery, PLEASE let me have one who has learned the trivial case and knows that my heart looks like every other human heart. Please don't let him negotiate new meanings and hook up my veins in some "self-chosen position to which [she/he] can commit [herself/himself]." I want her/him committed to the standard objective view. The trivial case is not so trivial. To dismiss so casually the objective case is perhaps the greatest danger of radical constructivism.

Integrated Testing

On the surface there is nothing inconsistent about this assumption and ID_2. We have also advocated that testing be more integrated and that it should be consistent with the learning objectives of the task. However, we would not insist that all testing must be integrated. It is possible to have a separate assessment of learning achievement.

Constructivists, however, insist on integrated testing for another reason, and with this argument, we do have disagreement. They insist that learning cannot be decontextualized; hence, testing cannot be decontextualized. Thus, the only possible measure is to observe the learner's performance in the context of the authentic task. We would insist that generalities (abstraction models) can be abstracted (decontextualized) and then applied in another context. We would argue that the most adequate assessment is not performance on the learning task, but performance on another, previously unencountered, task where the abstracted (decontextualized) learning can be applied. To deny this transfer of knowledge is to deny one of the mind's most remarkable capabilities and to limit the transfer of learning which, ironically, is one of the concerns of constructivism in the first place.

ID_2 AND INSTRUCTIONAL DESIGN

Using the previously identified assumptions, ID_2 is a technology-enabled approach to instructional design that has as primary goals: to enable subject matter experts with minimal training or experience in instructional technology to develop effective technology-delivered instructional materials; to ensure that these instructional materials provide learning experiences that use the advanced capabilities of the computer to provide meaningful experiential learning activities; and to decrease the cost of instructional development by an order of magnitude with no loss in instructional effectiveness.

We are designing an instructional design and delivery system (see Merrill, Li, & Jones, 1990a, 1990b, 1990c, 1991) composed of two primary subsystems: a knowledge base and a family of instructional transaction shells. The knowledge base is a representation of all of the knowledge and skill to be taught. Transaction shells enable the learners to interact with this knowledge in ways that best enable them to build appropriate mental models.

Instructional transactions[6] are instructional algorithms, patterns of learner interactions (far more complex than a single display and a single response) which have been designed to enable the learner to acquire a certain kind of knowledge or skill. Different kinds of knowledge and skill require different kinds of transactions. The necessary set of these instructional transactions is designed and programmed once, like other applications such as spread sheets and word processors. These instructional programs are called *instructional transaction shells.* These transaction shells can then be used with different content topics as long as these topics are of a similar kind of knowledge or skill.

Authoring by way of *instructional transaction shells* consists of selecting those patterns of interactions which are appropriate for a given topic and merely supplying the subject matter content to the knowledge base in a form that can be used by the transaction shell. There is no need to determine every display, to determine a branching structure, to select what kind of questions to use, to specify answer processing. Once the transaction shells have been developed, they can be used over and over again with no need for extensive instructional design or programming.

CONSTRUCTIVISM AND INSTRUCTIONAL DESIGN

Sagredo (in chapter 3) suggests that instructional design for a constructivist consists of the following:

> ...[S]electing tasks which are relevant to the child's lived experience....The teacher or instructional developer then provides access to tools which can be used to better understand or construct solutions to the problem....[O]ften approached with a collaborative group. No separate test is required. The 'proof'...is the successful completion of the task.

While IST has a well-documented methodology, it is not clear how a constructivist would go about carrying out these steps. How does one select relevant problems? By job analysis? By deciding what students should know? By looking at learner capabilities? By task analysis? But these are the techniques of IST. If we set an objective, if we assess learner capabilities, if we do a task analysis, are we going to choose irrelevant tasks? On the surface, I see little difference between the task analysis of IST and selecting a relevant task for constructivism, except that a constructivist may be less systematic about the procedures for choosing relevant tasks.

Is selecting a process, discovery orientation (provide tools and encourage students to construct solutions to problems) selecting an instructional strategy? Is guiding a student in the discovery (problem-solving) process using these tools an instructional strategy? Is using a collaborative (cooperative) problem-solving approach a strategy? Are there occasions when individual effort is more appropriate? Constructivism advocates a discovery process—collaborative instructional strategy—whereas instructional design does not exclude this strategy, but may also choose alternative strategies when they are appropriate. On the surface the constructivism instructional strategy seems to merely have a narrower point of view and be limited to certain types of instructional outcomes.

Can data be gathered during the execution of an activity? Combined with other data from observation can this constitute a test? Instructional design would say yes. Constructivism seems to be merely a limiting position excluding more objective measures, whereas instructional design would advocate using that assessment technique most appropriate to the situation.

On the surface the instructional design procedures recommended for constructivism do not seem contrary to IST or ID_2. ID_2 certainly would not select an irrelevant task (although the straw man arguments of Sagredo (in chapter 3) seem to imply that this is the case for typical instructional design). A transaction is, among other things, providing access to the student of the tools necessary to understand and solve the problem. ID_2 certainly supports successful completion of the task but would not object to an external assessment of achievement. It is the extreme interpretation of the authors (chapters 2 and 3) which is troublesome.

They argue that to be relevant a task must be imbedded in a real-world context. It cannot be simplified. It cannot be equated to any other task and must therefore be unique. It cannot be prespecified. It cannot be classified as to type of knowledge or skill required. The learning must be completely unique; no two learners will necessarily come to understand the task in the same way. The teacher must model the process rather than provide any conclusions, but the teacher must not be scripted. The generalities cannot be decontextualized or they will lose meaning. Are these restrictions necessary limitations of constructivism?

The examples of experiential instruction described by Spiro et al. (chapter 5) and Bransford et al. (chapter 6) do not adhere to this strict interpretation of constructivism. They meet the fundamental assumptions of active learning and situated problems but necessarily involve prespecification and identification of intended outcomes. In fact, the technology-based instruction described by these authors is very consistent with that which would be developed using ID_2. It is our hope that the experiential environments resulting from the application of Instructional Transaction Theory would result in learning interactions very similar to those described by Spiro, Bransford, and their associates.

CONSTRUCTIVISM AND INSTRUCTIONAL TRANSACTION THEORY

As indicated earlier, Instructional Transaction Theory (ID_2) is consistent with a moderate interpretation of some of the assumptions of constructivism. However, ID_2 is inconsistent with the extreme views put forth by some of the authors in this book.

Who is right? In the eternal scheme of things, none of us understands very much about how humans learn, how the mind functions. What is mind? What is knowledge? Both sets of assumptions may be wrong together. They are undoubtedly both incomplete. So, how does one choose?

We take the pragmatic stand that there may be competing systems of instruction based on different assumptions about learners and learning. It is difficult to establish the truth of our assumptions, but the propositions that follow from these assumptions can be submitted for empirical verification. Support for a given proposition still does not establish the truth of the assumption on which it is based, since the same proposition may be derived from a different set of assumptions. Such is the case with the more moderate views of constructivism. The instructional prescriptions that follow from ID_2 are very similar to those that follow from a moderate constructivism: relevant tasks, active learning, and experiential learning. As compelling as the arguments of the constructivists may be, there is no empirical evidence in support of their assumptions, and little empirical evidence in support of the instructional design propositions derived from these assumptions. On the other hand there is little empirical support for ID_2 either.

However, an extreme constructivist position, while it may be appropriate for some types of learning in a general education environment, is contrary to the solution of some of our most pressing educational problems.

As argued earlier, much of what needs to be learned must be shared. There are, in fact, agreed upon concepts, principles, facts, processes, procedures, and activities that learners must learn. The extreme constructivist position that learners can "arrive at self-chosen positions" is nonsense. A significant amount of what every child must learn—and certainly what any adult must learn to earn a living and function in society—is objective, must be shared, can be very similar, must be very similar from one individual to the next. The world is composed of Cunningham's "trivial cases."

Second, instructional development is too cost intensive. We cannot afford well-designed effective instruction because of the tremendous cost of developing it. Hence, most of our instruction is stand-up presentation that everyone acknowledges as inadequate, irrelevant, incomplete. Those existing cases of dynamic, effective, appealing, experiential environments (such as the environment described by Bransford et al. in chapter 6), which everyone recognizes as significant improvements over our usual instructional experiences, are extremely expensive to develop and are thus out of reach for most learners.

The real challenge is how to make such effective learning environments available to all learners most of the time. To assume that these environments do not exist because instructional designers have a theoretical bias which prescribes less effective instruction (as suggested by Bednar et al., chapter 2) is an insult to those who have dedicated their life to trying to build better instruction. It is not the theoretical bias, but rather the existence of practical tools available for building such systems that is the real limitation. Constructivism provides a rationale for such learning systems. We subscribe with enthusiasm to the work of Spiro and his associates in delineating Cognitive Flexibility Theory. It provides a theoretical rationale for what we are trying to do. But we resent the implications of Bednar et al., which suggest that IST has deliberately developed instruction which is ineffective because instructional designers believe that this inadequate instruction is better.

ID_2 is an attempt to build a technology that enables a significantly more cost effective approach to instructional development. The output of this technology would be effective, situated (in the moderate sense), experiential learning environments enhanced by more directed instructional strategies. This technology is made possible by the assumptions of ID_2: that knowledge has a syntax that is universal across domains; that knowledge can be represented using this syntax in a knowledge base external to the learner; that learners can interact with this knowledge in a variety of ways, but that certain types of interactions are necessary if a learner is to acquire a particular type of knowledge or skill; that prespecified computer programs (transaction shells) can enable these interactions and thus enable a learner to construct appropriate mental models of this knowledge.

Extreme constructivism, represented by some of the authors of this book, make such a technology difficult, if not impossible. Rather than contributing to a more efficient and effective instructional technology, extreme constructivism may in fact inhibit technological solutions to our pressing instructional needs. A technology built on the assumptions of extreme constructivism—that content cannot be prespecified because every learning task is unique; that learners learn in idiosyncratic ways; that objectives or learning outcomes are content specific; that there are no categories of objectives; that there is no domain-independent instructional strategy; that there can be no external control of the instructional events except that which the learner chooses; that there are no isolated tasks, only real-world tasks; that there can be no simplification of content; that content cannot be separated from use; that the teacher must model the process but must not be scripted; and that there must always be alternative views—is extremely hard to conceive. In an attempt to solve what they perceive as inadequacies in our current instruction approaches, extreme constructivists propose a methodology that is even more labor intensive, thus insuring that even less effective instruction will be available in the future than is now the case.

CONCLUSION

IST as represented by our own work, ID_2, applauds the creative work of Spiro et al. and Bransford et al. Much of our own work is an attempt to provide tools that enable the development of the type of experiential environments that they describe. We would advocate that moderate constructivism has much that should be considered by instructional designers. On the other hand, extreme constructivism, as represented by the other authors in this book, goes to the other extreme. The assumptions that they make about the learning process are unnecessarily restrictive and may actually prevent the more effective instruction that they seek.

NOTES

1. I have tried to reflect Constructivism as represented by the authors of the chapters in Parts of I and II.
2. IST, Instructional Systems Technology, is the term used in chapter 2 to refer to those of us who advocate a systems approach to instructional design and technology. I will adopt their acronym for use in this chapter.
3. I will not try to represent the IST community at large in this chapter, but will concentrate on our own view of instructional design and the assumptions underlying our approach. I will refer to our approach throughout this chapter as ID_2 or second generation instructional design.
4. First generation instructional design includes the theories represented in Reigeluth (1983, 1987) and similar positions, such as that of Englemann and Carnine (1982).
5. Our use of the word *construction* in this context is not an accident. We do not subscribe to the notion that mental models are merely

"transferred" into the head of the student, but that students must be actively involved in constructing meaning, building an appropriate knowledge structure. However, we do believe that the structure necessary to engage in certain types of tasks must have similar syntax across different students. The syntax of the structure thus constructed is not therefore idiosyncratic to a particular student.

6. We first introduced the idea of an instructional transaction in Merrill 1983, 1987. Subsequently Li and Merrill (1990) described instructional transactions in more detail.

REFERENCES

Englemann, S., & Carnine, D. (1982). *Theory of instruction: Principles and applications.* NewYork: Irvington Publishers.

Gagné, R. M. (1965). *The conditions of learning* (1st ed.). New York: Holt, Rinehart & Winston.

Gagné, R. M. (1985). *The conditions of learning* (4th ed.). New York: Holt, Rinehart & Winston.

Gagné, R. M., & Merrill, M. D. (1990). Integrative goals for instructional design. *Educational Technology Research & Development, 38*(1), 23-30.

Jones, M. K., Li, Z., & Merrill, M. D. (1990). Domain knowledge representation for instructional analysis. *Educational Technology, 30*(10), 7-32.

Lakoff, G. (1987). *Women, fire and dangerous things.* Chicago: University of Chicago Press.

Li, Z., & Merrill, M. D. (1990). Transaction shells: A new approach to courseware authoring. *Journal of Research on Computing in Education, 23*(1), 72-86.

Merrill, M. D. (1987). Prescriptions for an authoring system. *Journal of Computer-Based Instruction, 14*(1), 1-8.

Merrill, M. D. (1988). Applying component display theory to the design of courseware. In D. H. Jonassen (Ed.), *Instructional designs for microcomputer courseware.* Hillsdale, NJ: Lawrence Erlbaum Associates.

Merrill, M. D., Li, Z., & Jones, M. K. (1990a). Limitations of first generation instructional design (ID_1). *Educational Technology, 30*(1), 7-11.

Merrill, M. D., Li, Z., & Jones, M. K. (1990b). Second generation instructional design (ID_2). *Educational Technology, 30*(2), 7-14.

Merrill, M. D., Li, Z., & Jones, M. K. (1990c). The second generation instructional design research program. *Educational Technology, 30*(3), 26-30.

Merrill, M. D., Li, Z., & Jones, M. K. (1991). Instructional transaction theory: An introduction. *Educational Technology, 31*(6), 7-12.

Reigeluth, C. M. (Ed.). (1983). *Instructional-design theories and models: An overview of their current status.* Hillsdale, NJ: Lawrence Erlbaum Associates.

Reigeluth, C. M. (Ed.). (1987). *Instructional theories in action.* Hillsdale, NJ: Lawrence Erlbaum Associates.

IV CLARIFYING THE RELATIONSHIP

9

Some Thoughts About Constructivism and Instructional Design

Cognition and Technology Group (CTGV)
Learning Technology Center
Peabody College of Vanderbilt University

Our goal in this chapter is to focus on two issues that were raised by Dick (chapter 7) and Merrill (chapter 8). The first involves the general concept of constructivism and our way of thinking about it. The second involves concerns raised by Dick (chapter 7) regarding the complexity of our Jasper problems. At the heart of our response on both issues is (perhaps) a fundamental departure from more traditional instructional design conceptions of the nature of knowledge, the teaching-learning process, and the implications of these for the design of instruction.

ON CONSTRUCTIVISM

We contrast our view with one that holds that knowledge is an identifiable entity with some absolute truth value. The goal of instruction is met if students acquire this knowledge, usually as transmitted by whatever teaching mechanisms are in place (e.g., a teacher, a tutoring machine, etc.). Under this view of knowledge, the transmittal process is optimized if the knowledge can be specified and an ideal acquisition sequence identified. All that remains is for this sequence to be delivered in as "teacher-proof" a fashion as possible. In many cases systematic instructional design seems to have been a response to the pragmatic reality of instructors with little or no teaching knowledge or expertise.

An alternative conception, one that our group and many other constructivists adhere to, represents a blend of ecological psychology (e.g., Gibson, 1977; Shaw & Bransford, 1977) and constructivism (e.g., Bransford, Barclay, & Franks, 1972). On the ecological side, we believe that there is structure in the world, both the physical world and the epistemological world, that places constraints on knowing (e.g., Gibson & Gibson, 1955). On the constructivist side, we believe that there are sufficient degrees of freedom in the structure of physical and epistemological worlds to allow people to construct their own personal theories of their environments, of what is "known" or believed by others about those environments, and of themselves.

So how do people come to agree on events or find ways to settle differences? Here we join others (e.g., Kuhn, 1962; Vygotsky, 1978) in emphasizing the social nature of cognition. The constraints on constructed knowledge come largely from the community of which one is a member. In the absence of any community, we suppose that it would be possible for an individual to have an idiosyncratic view of the world—but then, because there is no community, the idiosyncrasy is irrelevant. As soon as there are two views, one of two things must occur: The idiosyncratic views must be brought into harmony or the individuals involved must "agree to disagree." In other words, the individual is free to build his or her own interpretation of the world, so long as that interpretation is coherent with the general zeitgeist. Knowledge is a dialect process the essence of which is that individuals have opportunities to test their constructed ideas on others, persuade others of the virtue of their thinking, and be persuaded. By continually negotiating the meaning of observations, data, hypotheses, and so forth, groups of individuals construct systems that are largely consistent with one another. One of our major goals in instruction is to encourage students to develop socially acceptable systems for exploring their ideas and their differences in opinion. For example, we want to help them appreciate rules of "good argumentation" and to continually look for appropriate ways to test their ideas. But we also want them to realize that these ideas of "goodness" (good theory, good science, good debate, etc.) are subject to change over time (e.g., Cleminson, 1990).

ON COMPLEXITY

In his recent discussion article, Dick (chapter 7) questions one of the design principles underlying our Jasper series; namely, the principle of complexity. We noted that our Jasper problems were purposely complex (averaging approximately 15 steps) and were designed to mimic the levels of complexity found in many problems that occur in everyday life. Dick (chapter 7) was worried about the effects of this complexity, especially on low-achieving students. Dick (chapter 7) has helped us realize that we did not devote nearly enough time to explaining why we felt that complexity was both manageable and useful.

Thanks in part to Dick's (chapter 7) concerns, we recently wrote an article that explores the issue of complexity in more detail (CTGV, in press). In the article, we note that our Jasper materials are not assumed to produce learning on their own; they require effective teaching. More specifically, we note that our Jasper materials afford (in the sense of Gibson, 1977) specific types of teaching and learning activities but do not guarantee them. The degree to which complexity is or is not problematic depends on the teacher's approach, since this will impact the learner's approach. For example, we discuss the work of an experienced teacher who, by re-defining the goals of a Jasper adventure and using manipulables, was able to successfully use it with first and second graders.

At a broader level, we believe that the realistic nature of our Jasper problems (including their complexity) helps students construct important sets of ideas and beliefs and refrain from constructing misconceptions. For example, theorists such as Schoenfeld (1985) and Spiro and colleagues (chapter 5) discuss frequently held misconceptions that result from over-simplifications of the curricula. Many of today's students believe that (a) problems are something that are presented by teachers rather than discovered by good learners, (b) that good learners almost instantly know the answer to all problems (e.g., Whimbey & Lockhead, 1982), and (c) that if they can't solve a problem in 5 minutes, then they can never solve it. We are interested in discovering the combinations of materials and teaching activities that can help students realize the value of discovering the need for future learning. When our Jasper adventures are taught in this way, we think that they provide excellent contexts for helping students learn to value their own abilities and learn to learn on their own.

We recently had the opportunity to meet with a group of 20 individuals who had used four Jasper adventures in fifth- and sixth-grade classrooms during the past year. Without prompting from us, every one of them stated how pleasantly surprised they were by the thinking abilities of low-achieving students in their classroom. They felt that the challenging nature of the Jasper adventures had made it possible for everyone to contribute. One benefit of the complexity in Jasper is that no individual student can immediately come up with "the" answer and hence make it impossible for others to contribute. Another benefit is that the students knew that they were working on "real" problems rather than on "baby stuff." The teachers also noted that the students gained a great deal of confidence in their abilities to deal with complexity, even if solution of parts of the problem was still beyond their current ability level (similar techniques are used in medical education; see Williams, 1991).

The teachers' impressions are confirmed by students' responses on attitude scales—the students agree that with the Jasper adventures they are forced to think and work "harder" than is the case for typical math class but they also agree that this makes math more fun and more meaningful. The result is that they much prefer solving Jasper problems when compared with "simpler" word problems.

We should also mention that the Jasper materials are not simply meant to benefit low-achieving students. Indeed, another reason for using complex problems is that even high achieving math students are ill-prepared to deal with this level of complexity. Data we have collected from uninstructed high-achieving fifth- and sixth-grade math students indicate extremely limited solution success with Jasper problems (Goldman et al., 1991). However, following instruction that scaffolds generative problem solving, we have found dramatic improvements in the solution of a similarly complex problem (e.g., Van Haneghan et al., in press). If we expect students to be able to deal with complex problems in the real world, we must provide them with opportunities to learn how to solve them.

As we noted earlier, positive ideas and attitudes about learning and about what remains to be learned are not an automatic consequence of working with Jasper. They depend on effective teaching. Nevertheless, we believe that the potential advantages of working with complex problems that allow students to "see the need" for further learning are very important and worthy of further analysis and research.

ACKNOWLEDGMENTS

Preparation of this chapter was supported in part by grants from James S. McDonnell Foundation #91-6 and the National Science Foundation #MDR9050191. The views expressed are ours and not necessarily theirs.

Members of the CTGV who contributed to this chapter are John Bransford, Susan Goldman, and Jim Pellegrino.

REFERENCES

Bransford, J. D., Barclay, J. R., & Franks, J. J. (1972). Sentence memory: A constructive vs. interpretive approach. *Cognitive Psychology, 3,* 193-209.

Cleminson, A. (1990). Establishing an epistemological base for science teaching in the light of contemporary notions of the nature of science and how children learn science. *Journal of Research in Science Teaching, 27,* 429-447.

Cognition and Technology Group at Vanderbilt. (in press). The Jasper experiment: An exploration of issues in learning and instructional design. *Educational Technology Research and Development.*

Gibson, J. J. (1977). The theory of affordance. In R. Shaw & J. Bransford (Eds.), *Perceiving, acting, and knowing.* Hillsdale, NJ: Lawrence Erlbaum Associates.

Gibson, J., & Gibson, E. (1955). Perceptual learning: Differentiation or enrichment. *Psychological Review, 62,* 32-51.

Goldman, S. R., Vye, N. J., Williams, S. M., Rewey, K., Pellegrino, J. W., & the Cognition and Technology Group at Vanderbilt. (1991, April). *Solution space analyses of the Jasper problems and students' attempts to solve them*. Paper presented at the American Educational Research Association, Chicago, IL.

Kuhn, T. S. (1962). *The structure of scientific revolutions*. Chicago: University of Chicago Press.

Schoenfeld, A. (1985). *Mathematical problem solving*. Orlando, FL: Academic Press.

Shaw, R. E., & Bransford, J. D. (1977). Psychological approaches to the problem of knowledge. In R. E. Shaw & J. D. Bransford (Eds.), *Perceiving, acting and knowing: Toward an ecological psychology*. Hillsdale, NJ: Lawrence Erlbaum Associates.

Van Haneghan, J., Barron, L., Young, M., Williams, S., Vye, N., & Bransford, J. (in press). The Jasper series: An experiment with new ways to enhance mathematical thinking. In D. Halpern (Ed.), *Concerning the development of thinking skills in science and mathematics*. Hillsdale, NJ: Lawrence Erlbaum Associates.

Vygotsky, L. L. (1978). *Mind in society*. Cambridge, MA: Harvard University Press.

Whimbey, A., & Lockhead, J. (1982). *Problem solving and comprehension*. Philadelphia: The Franklin Institute Press.

Williams, S. M. (1991). *Case-based approaches to instruction in medicine and law*. Unpublished manuscript, Vanderbilt University, Nashville, TN.

10

Knowledge Representation, Content Specification, and the Development of Skill in Situation-Specific Knowledge Assembly: Some Constructivist Issues as They Relate to Cognitive Flexibility Theory and Hypertext

Rand J. Spiro
Center for the Study of Reading
University of Illinois

Paul J. Feltovich
Southern Illinois University
School of Medicine

Michael J. Jacobson
Center for the Study of Reading
University of Illinois

Richard L. Coulson
Southern Illinois University
School of Medicine

The following brief set of remarks is a response to the thoughtful discussions by Merrill (chapter 8) and Dick (chapter 7) of chapter 5, which first appeared in the special issue of *Educational Technology* on the topic of constructivism. Given the generally positive tenor of their comments about our chapter, we will obviously not find much to disagree with. Instead, we will clarify and amplify a few issues raised in and by our chapter about the nature of our theory and the instructional approach derived from it. (All we will be able to do here is state general positions; readers seeking detailed explication should see our papers, especially: Spiro, Coulson, Feltovich, & Anderson, 1988; Spiro, Feltovich, Coulson, & Anderson, 1989; Spiro & Jehng, 1990; Spiro, Vispoel, Schmitz, Samarapungavan, & Boerger, 1987.)

COGNITIVE FLEXIBILITY THEORY AND OBJECTIVIST VERSUS CONSTRUCTIVIST CONCEPTIONS OF KNOWLEDGE: MULTIPLE KNOWLEDGE REPRESENTATIONS FOR ADEQUACY OF COVERAGE AND PREPARATION FOR TRANSFER

Spiro et al. (chapter 5) offered a constructivist rationale derived from Cognitive Flexibility Theory (Spiro et al., 1987, 1988) for the systematic development of nonlinear and multidimensional computer learning environments called Cognitive Flexibility Hypertexts (CFHs). We will not recapitulate that argument here. However, since it was clear from the articles in the special issue that there are many variations on what is meant by "constructivist," it may be useful to situate our position along the continuum of potential viewpoints. Our constructivist position, as it applies to complex and ill-structured domains, rejects any view that says either that there is *no* objective reality, or that there is a an objective reality that can be "captured" in any *single and absolute* way. Rather, one of our principal tenets is that the phenomena of ill-structured domains are best thought of as evincing *multiple truths*: Single perspectives are not *false*, they are *inadequate*. That is why *multiple knowledge representations* are so central to Cognitive Flexibility Theory. And it is why the multidimensional and nonlinear "criss-crossing" of conceptual and case landscapes, to demonstrate the context-dependent diversity of *warranted and valid* understandings (where there is more than one right answer, it is not a matter of "anything goes"—candidate understandings must be justified), is so important a feature of CFHs. In an ill-structured knowledge domain, individual cases can be reasonably interpreted from different conceptual perspectives, each adding something useful that the others miss. And the domain as a whole will be inadequately characterized by any fixed organization of superordinate and subordinate conceptual structures (given the variability across cases in the relative importance of concepts in the domain). To be ready to use knowledge flexibly, to be able to find the most useful of the valid representations to fit the needs of a particular case, one must have available a diverse repertoire of ways of *constructing* situation-sensitive understandings (again, with appropriate justification required). In an ill-structured domain, any overly limited version of what is "correct" will miss too much of the complexity that must be mastered for sufficiency of rich conceptual understanding and fullness of case coverage. This point is crucial and worth restating: Single, prespecifiable truths will not account for enough of the across-case variability and individual case complexity that is a hallmark of ill-structuredness. As we have said in other places, knowledge that will have to be used in many ways, as will be the case in ill-structured domains, must be taught and mentally represented in many ways.

PRESPECIFICATION OF KNOWLEDGE AND THE TEACHING OF CONTENT VERSUS SKILL: COGNITVE FLEXIBILITY HYPERTEXTS PROVIDE BUILDING BLOCKS FOR FLEXIBLE, SITUATION-SENSITIVE KNOWLEDGE ASSEMBLY, NOT FINAL PRODUCTS OF KNOWLEDGE

Related to the issue of multiple knowledge representations are the topics of *prespecification* of knowledge and the *teaching of content versus skill.* Merrill argues (chapter 8) that an important difference between our position and that of other constructivists is that we prespecify the knowledge that students should learn—that the knowledge is "represented in some knowledge base." This point is also related to Dick's assertion (chapter 7) that we teach domains of knowledge (i.e., content), *not* skills of thinking. These characterizations are not entirely accurate. CFHs do not *fully* prespecify the knowledge that will be presented to learners, and the instructional philosophy of Cognitive Flexibility Theory is very much oriented towards the development of the special cognitive processing skills needed in ill-structured domains (as well as providing an exploration environment which can foster the apprehension of content and structural relationships useful for the learner to represent).

There is *some* prespecification in our systems. However, we would not say that the representation of the knowledge that we want learners to acquire is fully and explicitly contained in the knowledge base of a CFH. What is prespecified is not some final product of knowledge that learners are supposed to passively assimilate. Rather, CFHs provide *exploration environments,* organized around *building blocks for knowledge assembly,* that are useful for a process of constructivist thinking that is inculcated. A corollary of our argument that complex and ill-structured knowledge domains require multiple representations is that any single case of the use of knowledge in such a domain will require a selective assembly of appropriate subsets of those representational perspectives that must be appropriately integrated to fit the needs of the particular situation at hand. Accordingly, the extent of knowledge prespecification found in CFHs is limited to rough *guideposts* or *starting points* for thinking about the domain, with an emphasis on their flexibility rather than rigidity of structuration and use. The more extended treatments of our approach make it clear that what is impressed upon the learner is that the knowledge guidelines that are provided do not have prespecified meanings, definable in the abstract and in advance of their application in diverse contexts (e.g., see Spiro et al., 1988; Spiro & Jehng, 1990). Instead, meaning is partially determined by rough patterns of family resemblance and then filled out by interactions of those patterns with details of their specific contexts of use (Wittgenstein, 1953).

For example, although CFHs provide widely applicable themes of conceptual understanding, the instructional programs emphasize the variability of their meanings across cases, demonstrations of how those conceptual structures receive specific tailorings in individual case contexts and interact with other concepts in the shaping of meaning, and so on. So, the theme search option in CFHs (discussed in chapter 5) causes cases to be successively displayed that instantiate a given conceptual theme; however, the commentaries for each case stress the specialized aspects of the concept's use in that context, as well as interrelations with other conceptual themes in each case's environment.[1]

Thus, we follow a "middle road" between *rigid prespecification* (with rigid prestructuration and rigid prescription of routines for knowledge use), and associated passive reception by the learner (with a memory emphasis), at one extreme, and immersion in a *totally unstructured* environment, neglectful of the role of conceptual aspects of understanding, at the other extreme. Furthermore, we definitely advocate active participation of the learner, faded control from the "teacher" (e.g., the computer program) to the student as learning proceeds (Collins, Brown, & Newman, 1989), and options that permit customization by the learner to go beyond even the loose prestructuration that we provide (e.g., options to add conceptual themes and case analyses).

Addressing Dick's assertion (chapter 7) that we do not focus on "skills to be learned," we argue that where there is so much richness of potential understanding and so much variability across individually complex cases of knowledge application, a central role must be accorded to situation-sensitive knowledge *assembly*. This is because in an ill-structured domain the manner of use of knowledge varies too much across situations to be specified in advance and then retrieved intact from memory. CFHs would be useless in preparing learners to apply their knowledge widely to new cases (the learning objective of transfer) if they did not teach both the *learning skills* of context-dependent, multidimensional, noncompartmentalized knowledge acquisition, and the *application skills* of flexible, situation-sensitive knowledge assembly (those skills that are characteristic of a particular domain and those that are of more general utility).

Returning to the issue of prespecification, we agree with Merrill (chapter 8) that the equation of "prespecified with linear, nonflexible, or nonexecutable" is unwarranted. However, we question the aptness of the term "prespecification" to describe the nature of the information presented to students in CFHs. When so many safeguards are built into CFHs to make it likely that learners will not look for an exact specification of the knowledge they should acquire (that they could then passively record in memory), we would prefer to say that the *opportunity to learn flexible foundations for building case-dependent specifications on their own* is provided to them. In sum, where *flexibility and openness of potential warranted interpretations* are avowed as *primary virtues* of both system design and the intended cognitive structures and processes of students using the system, as they are in CFHs, we do not believe "prespecification" is an apt descriptor. If one considers the kinds of things CFHs teach (again, see our cited papers), and how they are taught, it should be clear that the prespecification is minimal, and that the goal is for students to develop an epistemological stance which treats knowledge as substantially not prespecifiable in ill-structured domains. CFHs are like intellectual "erector sets" that, by permitting open-ended exploration in the context of some flexible background structures, aspire to the goals of making knowledge a manipulable, "three-dimensional" entity for the learner, and providing the tools for creating knowledge arrangements for different purposes.

OCCASIONS FOR COGNITIVE FLEXIBILITY HYPERTEXTS: INSTRUCTIONAL CONTEXTS FOR NONLINEAR AND MULTIDIMENSIONAL CASE-BASED LEARNING

Finally, we want to say again that we do not believe that CFHs are ideally suited for all instructional situations. As we have said in our papers (see the citations listed later), in well-structured knowledge domains, where the application of general principles and abstract concepts can proceed in a routinized manner (i.e., in roughly the same way across large numbers of cases), there is little need to prepare people for the kind of situation-specific knowledge assembly process that CFHs are intended to develop. Therefore, in well-structured knowledge domains it is not necessary to engage in so complicated an instructional process as the multidimensional and nonlinear "landscape criss-crossing" of CFHs.[2] We have been explicit about the *kinds of knowledge domains* for which CFHs should be used and the learning objectives they are intended to foster. CFHs are for case-based instruction in complex and ill-structured domains for the purposes of advanced knowledge acquisition, that is, mastery of complexity and development of the ability to flexibly apply or transfer knowledge to a wide range of new, real-world cases.

An instructional approach should be no more complicated than it needs to be. However, instruction must be as complicated as is necessary to achieve the established goals of learning, given the constraints imposed by the features of the knowledge domain that is the subject of learning. We have found in our studies of advanced knowledge acquisition that initial simplifications of complex subject areas can *impede* the later acquisition of more complex understandings (Feltovich, Spiro, & Coulson, 1989; Spiro et al., 1989). CFHs offer an approach to instruction in which learners can be presented relatively early on (following as brief an introductory segment as possible) with features of complexity necessary for advanced understanding in a domain, providing a foundation that *can* be built upon as still more advanced treatments of the material are presented. And this (necessary) early introduction of some complexity is accomplished in a tractable manner made possible by a new approach to incremental instructional sequencing designed to minimize the extent to which students become overwhelmed by difficult subject matter they need to master.

NOTES

1. This point is relevant to a potential misunderstanding: Inevitably, there are superficial similarities that disguise quite fundamental differences between the CFH approach and more traditional ones. The relationship between how CFHs and other instructional design approaches use "examples" is illustrative of this point. It might seem at first blush that our conceptual-theme-search option is intended to highlight *defining features* of a concept's application, in the way traditional instructional design makes use of examples. However, we do not provide *examples* of a concept's use. We teach from rich, real-world cases, demonstrating a process by which case features and the context of other relevant concepts in the case influence conceptual application. Although it may appear that we are teaching concepts and abstract principles, we are in fact doing something quite different. We are teaching *cases* most centrally (because of the considerable across-case irregularity that characterizes ill-structured domains), and the ways in which concepts get woven through and tailored to the case contexts of their occurrence. In this sense, it becomes less relevant to ask, for example, *how many examples* we recommend presenting to a student. Each "example" is actually a complete case "experience" in itself; the more cases you encounter, the greater the amount of experience and the richer the understanding. In other words, our answer to the question "How many?" is "The more the better" (but you learn an awful lot just from a case or two—see Spiro & Jehng, 1990, for an example of how much can be learned from just a brief scene from a larger case). Furthermore, in a CFH the student revisits the same case in different contexts, to teach different lessons; it is not clear how a revisiting should be "counted." Advanced knowledge acquisition is very often not a discrete process with a finite endpoint; rather, knowledge must be cultivated and continuously developed—the more you interact with sources of knowledge, the more you learn. In sum, this brief discussion should make it clear that the imputation of similarity across instructional philosophies should be made with great caution. (This is not to say that there are not important affinities between the CFH approach and, say, that of Merrill. We believe that there are, along with some important points of divergence.)
2. See Jacobson and Spiro (1991) for a discussion of a proposed framework for analyzing instructional contexts to determine the kind of educational technology approach (e.g., drill and practice, intelligent tutoring system, hypertext) best suited to the context. It should also be noted that we believe ill-structuredness to be far more prevalent than is typically believed, especially with increasingly more advanced treatments of subject matter

and in any domain of knowledge application in unconstrained real-world settings, such as the professions.

ACKNOWLEDGMENTS

Preparation of this chapter was supported in part by the Office of Educational Research and Improvement (OEG0087-C1001). Some of the background research on the learning and understanding of complex conceptual material was supported in part by the Basic Research Office of the Army Research Institute (MDA903-86-K-0443) and the Office of Naval Research, Cognitive Science Division (N00014-87-G 0165, N00014-88-K-0077). The chapter does not necessarily reflect the views of these agencies.

REFERENCES

Collins, A., Brown, J. S., & Newman, S. E. (1989). Cognitive apprenticeship: Teaching the craft of reading, writing, and mathematics. In L. B. Resnick (Ed.), *Cognition and instruction: Issues and agenda.* Hillsdale, NJ: Lawrence Erlbaum Associates.

Feltovich, P. J., Spiro, R. J., & Coulson, R. L. (1989). The nature of conceptual understanding in biomedicine: The deep structure of complex ideas and the development of misconceptions. In D. Evans & V. Patel (Eds.), *Cognitive science in medicine: Biomedical modeling.* Cambridge, MA: MIT (Bradford) Press.

Jacobson, M. J., & Spiro, R. J. (1991). *A framework for the contextual analysis of computer-enhanced learning environments.* Manuscript submitted for publication.

Spiro, R. J., Coulson, R. L., Feltovich, P. J., & Anderson, D. K. (1988). Cognitive flexibility theory: Advanced knowledge acquisition in ill-structured domains. In *The tenth annual conference of the cognitive science society.* Hillsdale, NJ: Lawrence Erlbaum Associates.

Spiro, R. J, Feltovich, P. J., Coulson, R. L., & Anderson, D. K. (1989). Multiple analogies for complex concepts: Antidotes for analogy-induced misconception in advanced knowledge acquisition. In S. Vosniadou & A. Ortony (Eds.), *Similarity and analogical reasoning* (pp. 498-531). Cambridge, England: Cambridge University Press.

Spiro, R. J., & Jehng, J. C. (1990). Cognitive flexibility and hypertext: Theory and technology for the nonlinear and multidimensional traversal of complex subject matter. In D. Nix & R. J. Spiro (Eds.), *Cognition, education, and multimedia: Exploring ideas in high technology* (pp. 163-205). Hillsdale, NJ: Lawrence Erlbaum Associates.

Spiro, R. J., Vispoel, W., Schmitz, J., Samarapungavan, A., & Boerger, A. (1987). Knowledge acquisition for application: Cognitive flexibility and transfer in complex content domains. In B. C. Britton (Ed.), *Executive control processes* (pp. 177-200). Hillsdale, NJ: Lawrence Erlbaum Associates.

Wittgenstein, L. (1953). *Philosophical investigations.* New York: Macmillan.

11

Attempting to Come to Grips with Alternative Perspectives

Thomas M. Duffy
Indiana University

Anne K. Bednar
Eastern Michigan University

Where to begin, where to begin? Merrill's (chapter 8) interpretation of Bednar, Cunningham, Duffy, and Perry (chapter 2) in comparison to the ideas we intended to communicate and the interpretations many others have made in reading the chapter, is a clear example of the multiple realities that result from constructivist activity. He has, in our opinion, identified some of the clear points of contrast between his own ID_2 and constructivism; for example the issue as to whether process can be separated from content and the issue of whether learning can he categorized into well defined types of outcomes which match to various universal instructional strategies exclusive of content domain. We see constructivism, in all of the theoretical representations we have read, offering a clear alternative on these issues. However, much of the remainder of Merrill's (chapter 8) assertions concerning our perspective on constructivism are simply not consistent with our views.

For example, Merrill interprets us as suggesting that all opinions or constructions are equally viable. We have never subscribed to this view, which is better known as deconstructivism. Rather, we emphasize the importance of testing one's own understandings via collaborative activities. Consistent with Vygotsky (1978), we emphasize the social negotiation of meaning or understandings. Indeed, collaboration as a means of testing ideas and evaluating alternative perspectives is central to our view. With that example in mind we will begin our social negotiation of understanding the constructivist view in general and Bednar et al. (chapter 2) in particular by responding to Merrill's points.

Using a divide and conquer approach, Merrill draws a sharp contrast between the Cognition and Technology Group (chapter 6) and Spiro, Feltovich, Jacobson, and Coulson (chapter 5) on one hand and Bednar et al. (chapter 2) on the other, referring to the former as a "more moderate constructivism" with which his views are consistent and the latter as "extreme constructivism." A primary basis for this "grouping" of perspectives is Merrill's interpretation of how each views the prespecification of knowledge in building instruction. Before addressing that issue in particular, let us note that it is totally appropriate that there be different interpretations of the implications of a constructivist epistemology for instructional design. However, we believe our perspectives on constructivism are more similar than distinct from these other researchers, even in relation to the prespecification of knowledge.

Merrill's view of the prespecification of knowledge is heavily associated with what information is provided in the learning context. At the base, he seems to view knowledge and information as identical. For example, Merrill states:

> ID_2 stands in direct opposition to these extreme constructivist views. We have proposed a syntax for knowledge representation...which assumes that knowledge, across subject matter areas, can be represented in knowledge frames of three types—entities, activities, and processes. (chapter 8)

Merrill seems to imply that any learning situation which is not totally devoid of content is the result of the prespecification of the knowledge base. That is, the prespecification of knowledge is judged by the mere provision of any content. However, we view instructional designers as providing information, not knowledge. From our view the prespecification of knowledge becomes apparent in how you measure learning—in what the learner can do. Any learning activity will contain content, but if learners are not held responsible to "learn" that content domain in "the" way which reflects the developer's view of the domain, then prespecification of knowledge has not occurred.

What the Cognition and Technology Group (chapter 6), Spiro et al. (chapter 5), Bednar et al. (chapter 2), Perkins (chapter 4), and Cunningham (chapter 3) suggest is that the process of learning in any domain emerges from the domain and that any learning activity should be in the context of a larger task goal (a macrocontext). That is, the reason for learning something—the criterion for understanding—is always an integral part of the task complex. Providing that context has a vastly different impact on the cognitive demands, and hence the learning, than does simply providing a verbal description of the context or telling the learner about the relevance. The segment must be realistic (in terms of cognitive demands), have a large number of components from which the students extract those elements which are appropriate to their solution of the problem, and be part of a larger issue or task—one that, in an educational system, will almost certainly extend beyond a single discipline. Knowledge is not absent, it is simply not predetermined as the outcome of the learning experience.

If Merrill chooses to claim consistency with Spiro et al. and the Cognition and Technology Group, though disagreeing with Bednar et al., he would also have to believe that learners do not develop schema or propositional networks during learning that are later retrieved to guide performance (Spiro et al., chapter 5). Merrill would have to believe that instead learners develop rich, context-based meanings of concepts so that in new situations they have the flexibility to construct schemas that will guide performance (Spiro et al., chapter 5; Cognition and Technology Group, chapter 6). Further, Merrill would have to agree with Spiro et al. that instruction should not be sequenced from simple to complex, if simple means stripping away the complexity of the context (the richness of the environments in which the concept is relevant). Each of these characteristics of constructivist learning environments emerges as implications from the epistemology.

Merrill, however, asserts that instructional technology should be an eclectic field, free to draw in practice from any theoretical base, no matter how inconsistent the assumptions of those various bases. In fact, while he claims a cognitive science base to his own theory, he retains the concept of categories of knowledge from behaviorism and then suggests that "some of the assumptions and prescriptions" of constructivism are consistent with his theory. In his knowledge representation system he states:

> The philosophical question of the nature of meaning can be safely ignored. Instruction, in large measure, communicates accepted meaning. The developer of instruction explicitly desires that the learner adopt the meaning intended by the developer, and not reach a separate and personal interpretation of that meaning. Although being able to reach such personal interpretations is an important part of being educated, *most instruction,* particularly most uses of automated instruction, *concerns transferring, as effectively and efficiently as possible, previously determined interpretations.* (Jones, Li, & Merrill, 1990; italics added)

Obviously our perspective is directly opposed to this view of learning. In Bednar et al. (chapter 2), and in Duffy and Knuth (1990), we have suggested that one of the dominant views of instruction is that it consists of the transfer of knowledge from the instructor (or instructional system) to the learner. Merrill has accused us of presenting a straw-man view. However, the quotation above seems to reflect just such a view. Perhaps our most basic disagreements are over what the goals of education should be and what the nature of instructional science should be.

Merrill also seems to mistake constructivism for discovery learning, when he calls attention to the need for cost-effective instructional design. He implies that providing each learner with a unique instructional experience would be far too expensive. What he fails to see is that we are already providing each learner with a unique experience simply because each learner brings a unique set of understandings, experiences, and personal goals to each learning experience. The problem from a constructivist point of view is that we are not making that individual experience relevant to each learner in a way which facilitates development of a personal perspective, one that will transfer from the school environment to real-world application. What do we suggest instructional designers do from a constructivist approach? We would turn from structuring instruction to designing environments in which learning can take place—environments which are characterized by rich contexts, authentic tasks, collaboration for the development and evaluation of multiple perspectives, an abundance of tools to enhance communication and access to real-world examples and problems, reflective thinking, modeling of problem solving by experts in the content domain, and apprenticeship mentoring relationships to guide learning. The phenomenaria described by Perkins (chapter 4) are precisely the kind of ideal learning environments we would seek. It is possible that development of these environments would be less expensive than the intense analysis required by traditional instructional design just for the prespecification of knowledge and the establishment of learning objectives.

Since our original expression of our ideas did not communicate these characteristics to Merrill, let us put that text to the side and offer a different approach to our thinking. Let us provide two examples contrasting objectivist and constructivist learning.

A first example: Qualifying exams in which the students are all given a reading list and then tested on the contents of that reading list is an objectivist[1] strategy toward "Qualifying." The assessment questions in that system have nothing to do with the individual student—they have only to do with the committee's view of the content domain. Note also that the task of the student qualifying—to master this material to answer whatever questions might be asked—is not representative of what the individual will do as a PhD in the field.

An alternative constructivist strategy might be to ask the student to write publishable review papers in several areas of the content domain. This might take place over perhaps 2 years of the graduate work. It would be up to the student to define the issue or focus within the specified topic area and to decide on the approach to the issues. Evaluation might be how well the student considered and evaluated the perspectives on the issue both in the text and in an oral discussion during which the student would be asked to reflect upon his or her approach to the issues. Note that the task is one the student will hopefully engage in as a PhD—it is authentic. Note also that the content cannot be defined a priori except in general terms. Certainly there is no prespecification of knowledge.

A second example using technology: The most typical way of teaching history is to present facts, dates, personalities, trends and theories, either through lecture or readings. The objective is too often to learn dates, describe sequences of events, etc. More creative approaches, many of which have emerged as a result of a design process, typically share these sorts of content-oriented objectives.

Students in the first author's seminar recently designed a course to teach 10th-grade American History from a constructivist perspective and using hypertext. Three excellent designs were generated, but we will describe only one here (Honebein, Fishman, Chong, & Kim, 1991).[2] Through front-end analysis, including initial and ongoing dialogue with a 10th-grade American History teacher, the editor of the *Journal of American History*, and the director of the Center for History Making in America, the developers learned that the central issue in history is detective work, and that students must learn that any reporting of history represents a particular perspective. The fun of being a historian is in gathering and trying to understand these different perspectives.

A database of original documents is the core of the curriculum for the history course we designed. The complete database (the students only developed a prototype) is far more extensive than any domain of knowledge the learners could master, and certainly we did would not devise a test of that subject matter. Instead, access to the database is managed through a series of problem-solving tasks. For example, in the study of the Truman Doctrine, the 10th graders take the position of advisors to president Truman. They are given the choice of a problem area relevant to the development of the Truman Doctrine (e.g., political problems in Turkey or Greece) where Truman needed help. Students receive a brief scenario of the "situation" and the alternative kinds of advice they might offer. It is then up to them to work in the database to develop a perspective on the situation. They can also go to the Secretaries of Defense, State and Commerce to get their points of view on the "best" strategy (each Secretary provides a perspective on how he approaches problems—what databases he tends to focus on and what cautions he exercises in using that database). In the plan for the use of this system, the 10th graders would work in groups, sharing the workload and points of view. The instructor would serve as a coach and model, working with the groups as they developed and evaluated perspectives. Evaluation could not be based on the mastery of any prespecified information (or knowledge). Instead, evaluation would be of students' developing the perspective and, most importantly, of providing a rationale for, and defense of, their point of view.

What is distinct in each of these examples is that there is no prespecification of content to learn nor any expectation that each learner will take the same thing away from the learning experience. As much as possible the activity that the student engages in is authentic. The role of the instructor is to model and guide. Additionally, learner control—the learner's judgments as to what should be done and why—is seen as an integral part of the learning process. In each of these learning environments, it would be strange indeed, to consider the nature of the task without learner control. The approach does not preclude guiding the student. Indeed, apprenticeship is central to the pedagogy. Finally, with specific reference to the history example, we might note that while the Truman Doctrine was the topic, the students' learning extended well beyond the simple principle and statements or reason for the Truman Doctrine. They learned about a variety of military, social, political, and economic facts about the countries involved, some key members of the U.S. cabinet, and a variety of process and problem-solving skills.

We hope that these comments and examples will help to clarify the conceptual framework we were trying to present in Bednar et al. (chapter 2) and will highlight the potential value of this framework in the design of instruction. Merrill (chapter 8) suggests an empirical test to determine whether constructivism or ID_2 best serves the field. We have our doubts about the effectiveness of the experimental approach providing a test as to which approach best serves the field—at least in any near-term sense. The two approaches seem to be about different things; constructivism is not aiming to produce the kinds of outcomes Merrill advocates (acquisition of previously determined interpretations). Hence we see extreme difficulty in creating learning environments that provide reasonable tests of the two views. While we think the research will help clarify details of the points of view, we prefer a developmental model where practice in the field is constantly evaluated in a formative sense and the results are applied to examine and adapt the model in a continuous cycle. We also prefer the emergence of a collaborative dialogue in which we and our colleagues across the world present our perspectives and our evidence, each using the dialogue to adapt our personal practice and theory of instructional design.

That important dialogue is underway already. At professional discussions others have described the move to a constructivist epistemology as a paradigm shift with tremendous implications for the field. We look at Bednar et al. (chapter 2) as an invitation to dialog within a community of which we consider ourselves a part, not one we stand in opposition to. Merrill (chapter 8) asserts that our views are an insult to instructional designers "who have dedicated their life to trying to build better instruction." He states that we "suggest that IST has deliberately developed instruction which is ineffective because instructional designers believe that this inadequate instruction is better." Were Merrill's assertions true, we would be criticizing ourselves. Within the group of authors are more than 38 years of designing instruction applying traditional instructional design models. That we are now considering constructivism is our way, in the best tradition of instructional technology, of trying to build better instruction.

NOTES

1. Two points of clarification may be required. First, by "objectivist" we are referring to the view of learning best captured in the quotation from Jones, Li, and Merrill (1990) presented earlier and the position described by

Bednar et al. (chapter 2) and Cunningham (chapter 3), and presented in Dick and Carey (1990). Second, we do not mean to imply that the approach is a necessary outcome of an objectivist design—many different outcomes are possible. Rather, it is an acceptable and not atypical approach from that perspective but clearly not one that would arise from a constructivist perspective.

2. The other designs are described in Brown, Choi, Goldstein, and McMahon (1991) and Brescia, Carr, Chen, and Garfinkle (1991).

REFERENCES

Brescia, W., Carr, A., Chen, P., & Garfinkle, R. (1991). *A human-scale approach to history instruction: Design document for an American history course.* Unpublished report, Instructional Systems Technology, Indiana University, Bloomington.

Brown, B. F., Choi, W., Goldstein, L., & McMahon, T. (1991). *Perspectives '48: An election simulation involving student role play supported by a hypermedia database.* Unpublished report, Instructional systems Technology, Indiana University, Bloomington.

Dick, W., & Carey, L. (1990). *The systematic design of instruction* (3rd ed.). Glenview, IL: Scott, Foresman.

Duffy, T. M., & Knuth, R. (1990). Hypermedia and instruction: Where is the match? In D. Jonassen & H. Mandl (Eds.), *Designing hypermedia for learning.* Heidelberg, FRG: Springer-Verlag.

Honebein, P. C., Fishman, B., Chong, S-M., & Kim, Y. H. (1991). *Trumedia: Hypermedia design implications of a constructivist learning environment.* Unpublished report, Instructional Systems Technology, Indiana University, Bloomington.

Jones, M. K., Li, Z., & Merrill, M. D. (1990). Domain knowledge representation for instructional analysis. *Educational Technology, 30* (10).

Vygotsky, L. (1978). *Mind and society.* Cambridge, MA: Harvard University.

12

Evaluating Constructivistic Learning

David H. Jonassen
University of Colorado

At the NATO conference on "Designing Constructivistic Learning Environments," held in Leuven, Belgium, following the writing of chapters 1 through 8, I tried frequently to direct the discussion toward the problems in evaluation that are raised by constructivism. The implications of constructivism for instruction seem so much clearer (as evidenced by the chapters in this book) than those for evaluation. Since evaluation of learning from constructivistic environments is perhaps the most difficult issue related to constructivism, the conference participants seemed all too willing to ignore my pleas for clarification. However, since I have raised the issue so consistently, it seems only appropriate that I suggest the following ideas that will provide a fitting target, as it were.

PREMISE

Considerable interest has been paid recently to applications of constructivism and the design of constructivistic learning environments (chapters 1 and 2; Duffy & Jonassen, in press; Jonassen, 1991). Constructivism makes a decidedly different set of assumptions about learning and the processes for supporting it than do traditional curriculum-based or instructional systems approaches to designing instruction. Constructivism proposes that learning environments should support multiple perspectives or interpretations of reality, knowledge construction, and context-rich, experience-based activities. Since so many fine examples of constructivistic environments have been described in Part II of this book, perhaps the thorniest issue yet to be resolved regarding the implications of constructivism for learning is how to evaluate the learning that emerges from those environments.

This chapter begins by reviewing the constructivist position, first by comparing it with objectivism and second by listing its assumptions. From that brief review, the chapter argues that if constructivism is a valid perspective for delivering instruction, then it should also provide a valid set of criteria for evaluating the outcomes of that instruction. That is, the assumptions of constructivism should be applied to the process of evaluation. The chapter argues that constructivistic evaluation means more than goal-free evaluation. It then reviews the implications of constructivistic criteria for developing evaluation methods and suggests evaluation criteria based upon constructivistic principles.

ALTERNATIVE CONCEPTIONS

Objectivism and constructivism are often described as polar extremes on a continuum in order to contrast their assumptions (Jonassen, 1991); however most designers and theorists assume positions that fall somewhere between the extreme views (see chapter 8). For instance, while programmed instruction (PI) and instructional design (ID) possess more objectivistic assumptions, Piagetian and discovery learning tasks tend to be more constructivistic. In order to clarify the dialectic, let me describe the extreme positions.

objectivism<--------PI-------ID-------ITS------Piagetian-------->constructivism
externally mediated reality internally mediated reality

Objectivism

Jonassen (1991) describes the assumptions of objectivism. Objectivists believe in the existence of reliable knowledge about the world. As learners, our goal is to gain this knowledge; as educators, to transmit it. Objectivism further assumes that learners gain the same understanding from what is transmitted. Knowledge is stable because the essential properties of objects are knowable and relatively unchanging. The important metaphysical assumption of objectivism is that the world is real, it is structured, and that structure can be modeled for the learner. Objectivism holds that the purpose of the mind is to "mirror" that reality and its structure through thought processes that are analyzable and decomposable. The meaning that is produced by these thought processes is external to the understander, and it is determined by the structure of the real world. Learning therefore consists of assimilating that objective reality. The role of education is to help students learn about the real world. The goal of designers or teachers is to interpret events for them. Learners are told about the world and are expected to replicate its content and structure in their thinking.

Constructivism

Constructivism, on the other hand, claims that reality is more in the mind of the knower, that the knower constructs a reality, or at least interprets it, based on his/her experiences. Constructivism is concerned with how we construct knowledge from our experiences, mental structures, and beliefs that are used to interpret objects and events. Our personal world is created by the mind, so in the constructivist's view, no one world is any more real than any other. There is no single reality or any objective entity. Constructivism holds that the mind is instrumental and essential in interpreting events, objects, and perspectives on the real world, and that those interpretations comprise a knowledge base that is personal and individualistic. The mind filters input from the world in making those interpretations. An important conclusion from constructivistic beliefs is that we all conceive of the external world somewhat differently, based on our unique set of experiences with that world and our beliefs about those experiences.

Again, the descriptions of objectivism and constructivism given here are summaries of the extremes of the positions. Each individual must determine his or her own point of view which will likely fall somewhere along the continuum just described.

CONSTRUCTIVISTIC CRITERIA

Constructivism claims that learners can only interpret information in the context of their own experiences, and what they interpret will, to some extent, be individualistic. As objectivistic designers, we may intend to map a particular reality onto learners, but they ultimately interpret our messages in the context of their own experiences and knowledge and construct their own meaning relative to their needs, backgrounds, and interests. Rather than attempting to map the structure of an external reality onto learners, constructivists recommend that we help them to construct meaningful and conceptually functional representations of the external world.

If learning outcomes are individually constructed, how do we evaluate them? What standards can be applied to assess the meaningfulness of the learning from these cognitively sophisticated environments. The following criteria are suggested as a starting point for conceiving of evaluation methods from a constructivistic perspective. These criteria represent integral components of most definitions of constructivistic learning.

Goal-Free Evaluation

An obvious implication of constructivism for evaluation of learning is that evaluation should be more goal free. Goal-free evaluation is a construct that Scriven (1973) promoted to overcome the biasing of evaluation by the specific project goals. He believed that an evaluation was more objective if the evaluator was not informed in advance of what the goals were. Scriven used the Consumer Union approach as his archetype. It is impossible, he suggested, for a consumer agency to evaluate the effectiveness of a product while being programmed in advance by the goals of the product. Rather than relating evaluation in terms of goals, he recommended using needs-assessment methods to determine what the goals of education should be. He argued that verified needs provide the most objective standards by which to evaluate outcomes of any process.

Clearly, constructivistic outcomes may be better judged by goal-free evaluation methodologies. If specific goals are known before the learning process begins, the learning process as well as the evaluation would be biased. Providing criteria for referencing evaluation results in criterion-referenced instruction. That is, the goals of the learning drive the instruction, which in turn controls the student's learning activities. Criterion-referenced instruction and evaluation are prototypic objectivistic constructs and therefore not appropriate evaluation methodologies for constructivistic environments.

It is clear that the methods used to evaluate the outcomes of constructivistic learning systems need to be goal free. However, if constructivism is to become an accepted principle of learning, valid methodologies for assessing its outcomes must also be conceived. That is, it is not enough to say that evaluation should be goal free. The evaluation methodologies we use to assess constructivistic outcomes need to possess the cognitive sophistication implied by the goals of constructivism.

Authentic Tasks

An important criterion that is being suggested for restructuring schools is to focus education on authentic tasks. Authentic tasks are those that have real-world relevance and utility, that integrate those tasks across the curriculum, that provide appropriate levels of complexity, and that allow students to select appropriate levels of difficulty or involvement. We cannot all become masters of every content area. According to this belief, task and content analysis should focus less on identifying and prescribing a single, best sequence for learning and more on selecting tasks that are both meaningful and able to accommodate constructivistic applications.

Knowledge Construction

Nearly every definition of constructivism refers to knowledge construction rather than reproduction. That is, learners should actively engage in building knowledge structures. But what does that mean? It means that, as evaluators, we need to focus on learning outcomes that will reflect the intellectual processes of knowledge construction. Clearly, knowledge construction entails higher order thinking. So, outcomes of constructivistic environments should assess higher order thinking, such as that at the "find" level of Merrill's (1983) taxonomy, the "cognitive strategy" level of Gagné's (1987), and the "synthesis" level of Bloom's taxonomy. We might expect learners, for instance, to create new goals and methods for learning. Obviously, solving relevant problems would be a reasonable outcome. I would also recommend argumentation as an appropriate learning outcome, that is, developing and defending a particular position. A major criterion for assessing each of these knowledge-construction outcomes must be originality. The point here is not to subordinate the principle of goal-free evaluation, but rather to suggest that evaluators need to use evaluation filters that will permit them to focus only on these higher order skills.

Experiential Constructions (Process Versus Product)

If we assume that reality is dependent on human mental activity, that meaning is determined by the mental processes of the individual, and that these processes are grounded in perception and grow out of experience, then those are the things that we should evaluate—not the extant behavior or the product of that behavior. That is, if possible, it is the process of knowledge acquisition that should be evaluated, along with the product. Evaluating how learners go about constructing knowledge is more important, from a constructivist perspective, than the resulting product. This suggests that effective assessment should be integrated into instruction, that is, become a part of the instructional process. So, as learners are acquiring knowledge, evaluation guidelines should be available, so that both the student and the teachers may know how the student is progressing. The metacognitive awareness of learning that would result from this process should improve learning and ultimately the product that it produces.

Objectivists typically employ a criterion to reference the process or—most often—the product of learning. Why should students have only one opportunity to demonstrate their knowledge acquisition? If we accept that transfer is an integral higher order learning skill, then students should be provided several opportunities to demonstrate their abilities.

Context-Driven Evaluation

Most constructivistic environments that are described in this book assume that instruction should be anchored in some meaningful, real-world context. Therefore, it is equally important that evaluation occur in contexts that are just as rich and complex as those used during instruction. One of the clearest recommendations from the conference in Belgium was that simplified, decontextualized problems are inappropriate outcomes for constructivistic environments. So are they for evaluation, as well.

The criteria for evaluating reasoning in these evaluation environments will be suggested by the environments themselves; that is, evaluation is also context-dependent. If the tasks are authentic, then the real-world environment that is being modeled in the constructivistic environment will recommend the most relevant variables. For instance, we have been developing constructivistic, case-based learning environments in transfusion medicine, to prepare residents and third-year medical students in how to assess transfusion risks. The criteria for success in a medical diagnostic environment are clear—a correct diagnosis and prescription of treatment that will save the patient within a time period limited by the severity of the problem and at a cost acceptable to the patient, the hospital, the insurance company, and so on. True enough, real-world criteria may be very objective. But they are real-world, and to the extent that they reflect real-world criteria, they are meaningful.

(Learning) Context-Dependent Evaluation

Just as constructivistic learning is supported by rich contexts, designers and evaluators must consider the context in which learning is taking place. I would argue that constructivistic learning environments are most effective for the stage of advanced knowledge acquisition.

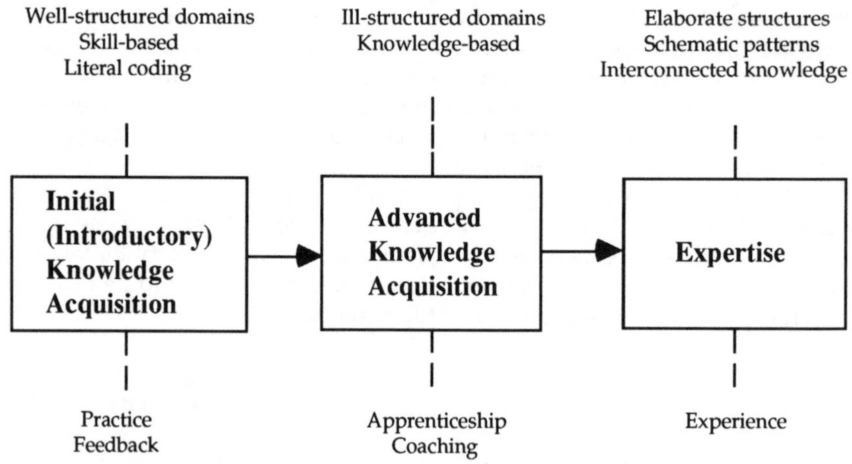

FIG. 12.1. Three stages of knowledge acquisition.

Let me explain. Jonassen (in press) has described three stages of knowledge acquisition; introductory, advanced, and expert (see Figure 12.1). Introductory learning occurs when learners have very little directly transferable prior knowledge about a skill or content area. It represents the initial stages of schema assembly and integration. The second phase of knowledge building is advanced knowledge acquisition, which is an intermediate stage in learning that follows introductory knowledge acquisition and precedes expertise (Spiro, Coulson, Feltovich, & Anderson, 1988). Learners must acquire advanced knowledge in order to solve complex, domain- or context-dependent problems. Expertise is the final stage of knowledge acquisition. We know that experts have more internally coherent yet more richly interconnected knowledge structures and that they represent problems differently.

Constructivistic learning environments are most appropriate for the second stage, advanced knowledge acquisition. (This claim is evaluated in the After Thoughts section at the end of this chapter.) It is at this stage that misconceptions, such as reductive bias are most likely to result from instruction that oversimplifies and prepackages knowledge (Spiro et al., 1988). Because learners have not assembled or integrated adequate knowledge structures during introductory knowledge acquisition, it likely that introductory knowledge acquisition is better supported by more objectivistic approaches, with a transition to constructivistic approaches that represent complexity and ill-structuredness as the learners acquire more knowledge. At the other end of the learning process, experts need very little instructional support and will likely be surfeited by the rich level of instructional support provided by most constructivistic environments. So, it is important to consider the context (and stage) in which the learning is occurring. Clearly, constructivistic environments can support advanced knowledge acquisition.

Multiple Perspectives

If it is appropriate to present multiple perspectives in learning environments with the expectation that learners will meaningfully accommodate these different perspectives, then it is equally important to reflect and accept those multiple perspectives in the evaluation process. Some obvious implications are that using a single set of criteria for assessing the quality of outcomes is unacceptable, and that using only a single type of outcome is also unacceptable. Rather than learning being referenced by a single behavior or set of behaviors, it should be referenced by a domain of possible outcomes, each of which would provide acceptable evidence of learning.

Another implication of this multiple perspective criteria of constructivism is that, since evaluation is necessarily subjective to some degree, the assumption that a single evaluator is capable of providing an objective or a complete appraisal from his or her single perspective is impossible. Constructivistic evaluation requires a panel of reviewers, each with a meaningful perspective from which to evaluate the outcomes and each with reasonable credentials for evaluating the learner. The panel may consist of novices as well as experts. It is likely that a novice could provide a much better evaluation than the expert, who frequently focuses on inappropriate criteria of learning.

As a result, evaluation of learning would necessarily become more goal free, because of the difficulty in corresponding the same set of goals to different evaluators. If you believe, as radical constructivists do, that no objective reality is uniformly interpretable by all learners, then assessing the acquisition of such a reality is not possible. A less radical view suggests that learners will interpret perspectives differently, so evaluation processes should accommodate a wider variety of response options.

Multimodal

If it is necessary to evaluate products of learning rather than the process, then a portfolio of products, rather than a single product of learning, should be evaluated. This portfolio should describe either different student interpretations of the assignment or different stages in its development. Few authentic tasks produce only a single product or outcome. Because constructivistic learning is multifaceted and multiperspectival, then it almost necessarily results in multiple outcomes. Each of those perspectives, modes, or dimensions of learning is best represented in different products. So each of those products may be created in different media or modes within media, and should therefore be evaluated in a somewhat different way. Of course, if a product is being evaluated, then it should be evaluated by more than one person, that is, multiple evaluators. Not all of these evaluators need be experts. A mixture of experts, novices, and journeymen may be the most useful mix of evaluators of learning products.

Socially Constructed (Negotiated) Meaning

Perhaps the greatest misinterpretation of constructivism is that it necessarily results in academic chaos. If all learners construct their own meaning from information, how can we share enough knowledge to even communicate? In fact, we do share the same meaning for objects, events, and ideas through a long process of negotiation. Individual differences will always still exist (if you don't believe me, try to get a group of people to agree on the critical attributes of a "chair"). However, we share enough meaning to communicate, to argue, to hypothesize, and so on.

If meaning is negotiated, why shouldn't we also negotiate the goals of learning or use the negotiation process, in the form of argumentation, as evidence of learning. Because learners interpret the world somewhat differently, the outcomes of learning will vary somewhat, and so objectives, if they are useful at all, can best be used as a negotiating tool for guiding learners during the learning process and for self-evaluation of learning outcomes. This prescription is especially problematic for training design, which is typically based on the solution of specific, perceived problems. Most training is almost, by definition, convergent and objectivistic, because it supports explicit, company performance goals.

Goals of Evaluation

Perhaps the most fundamental change in evaluation of constructivistic outcomes should be the putative goals of evaluation. Evaluation implies an appraisal or value judgment about a person or his/her performance relative to some criteria. If learning is a process involving knowledge construction, should not that provide the most appropriate goal. And who better can evaluate knowledge construction than the constructor? Evaluation from a constructivistic perspective should be less of a reinforcement and/or behavior control tool and more of a self-analysis and metacognitive tool. Constructivistic learning is not supposed to mirror reality, but rather to construct meaningful interpretations. Constructivistic evaluation is the mirror for viewing that construction process.

CONCLUSION

If constructivistic environments are created to engage learners in relevant and meaningful knowledge construction, then as designers we are obligated to implement alternative methods for evaluating learning form them. Objectivistic evaluation methods, like criterion-referencing, are not appropriate for evaluating learning and are likely too insensitive to perceive the types of learning that constructivistic environments are designed to support. The methods by which we evaluate learning from these environments should be more goal free; they should assess knowledge construction in relevant real-world contexts requiring authentic learning tasks that represent multiple perspectives and viewpoints.

AFTER THOUGHTS

Understanding, as averred by most of the authors in this book, is a dynamic, constructive-reconstructive process involving interpretation, negotiation, and reconceptualization. So it is with my understanding and beliefs about constructivism. Earlier, I stated that evaluation is context-dependent. I still believe that, but part of my argument contended that constructivistic approaches to learning are most appropriate for supporting advanced stages of knowledge acquisition. In chapter 16, Cathy Fosnot points out the weaknesses of this argument. I argued from an efficiency standpoint, that initial schema assembly occurs best (most efficiently) in the objectivistic mode. The temptations of objectivism are considerable for a generation of designers raised on a completely objectivist diet.

My statement ignored her work (Fosnot, 1989) with elementary school learning. McMahon and O'Neill (in press) on a Bubble Dialog, and the whole Piagetian and Vygotskian heritage argues that younger, novice learners are probably the most constructivistic learners. So in many (though not all) initial knowledge acquisition contexts, constructivistic environments are appropriate. And, in those contexts, the constructivistic principles of evaluation described earlier are even more important, providing teachers with tools for understanding how novice learners are building knowledge representations.

ADDENDUM: A SOCIETAL PERSPECTIVE ON BUILDING AND EVALUATING CONSTRUCTIVISTIC LEARNING ENVIRONMENTS

Evaluation in the U.S. is largely goal driven. The goals of learning are usually determined by the teacher, designer, or education agency. Most often, the teacher engages in acts of teaching and then attempts to assess what students should have learned from what he or she told them. The goals are implicit in what was "taught," but there are often tacit expectations about what should have been learned. The second most common scenario is the "criterion-referenced" approach to evaluation. The implicit assumptions of criterion-referenced evaluation are that it is possible to determine an objective reality, that reality is comprehensible and transferable in the same way by all learners, and (most insidiously) that other learning outcomes (incidental learning) are irrelevant to the process of education. In industrial training and in much of education, education agencies establish the criteria for the training or schooling process and select what they deem to be appropriate goals of learning for their students. Most often, the objectives of both teachers and trainers are convergent and reproductive. Nonetheless, they are the criteria by which learners' performances are evaluated. Evaluation is driven by these goals, implicit or explicit. This approach to evaluation is the most common in education at all levels.

Although goal-free evaluation has been a widely referenced approach to evaluation, it has not become a general evaluation methodology, in part because techniques for goal-free evaluation were either unspecified or they were very intricate and cumbersome. Also, they are dissonant with societal expectations about evaluation. Making judgments about the quality of work or thinking is a normal expectation of education. Society demands these judgments in order to select individuals for nearly every life endeavor.

The goals of education typically evolve from societal belief systems. These beliefs, which are so objectivistic yet so firmly entrenched, may preclude the proper use of constructivistic environments. I would argue that if it is impossible to extricate the process of evaluation of constructivistic learning outcomes from this convergent, criterion-referenced evaluation of largely reproductive expectations that drive most of education, then it may (unfortunately) be inappropriate to think about designing constructivistic environments. When the goals of the instruction are so dissonant with the goals that are expressed by the education agencies, then constructivistic learning, with its divergent outcomes, may well perform a disservice to students. If the students are rewarded only for outcomes that are not facilitated by constructivistic environments, are we not jeopardizing students by building them and engaging the students with them? Our experience has shown that learners using constructivistic environments for the first time experience difficulty because they misapply reproductive learning strategies. They do so because they expect that form of an evaluation. This very bleak conclusion is, in fact, a straw-man argument for suggesting that building and implementing constructivistic environments in education requires perhaps a larger revolution than any of us bargained for—that ultimately we must reconceptualize the outcomes of education from a societal perspective. Restructuring schools and training must start with the expectations that we have for them, but that is a more convoluted argument than space here permits. If we are to widely implement constructivistic learning environments, it will require that we reconceptualize the outcomes of education at a societal level so that divergent points of view, alternative conceptions of the world, and alternative means for reflecting those processes are more acceptable. And, if we are unable to alter those expectations, then as designers, our most important contribution may be to design more effective mnemonic systems for helping learners memorize more effectively. If our goal as designers is to facilitate learning, but if the only learning that is societally acceptable is reductive and reproductive, then do we have an obligation to facilitate that learning by building better objectivistic than constructivistic tools?

ACKNOWLEDGMENTS

My sincere thanks to Hans van der Meij for his very incisive review of a draft of this chapter (which was written in his second language) and for the colloquy that accompanied it. This chapter was written while I was a visiting faculty member in the Vakgroep Instructie Technologie, Toegepaste Onderwijskunde, Universiteit Twente, Netherlands. My thanks to them for their support.

REFERENCES

Duffy, T., & Jonassen, D. H. (in press). *Instructional principles for the design of constructivist learning environments*. Berlin: Springer-Verlag.

Fosnot, C. T. (1989). *Enquiring teachers, enquiring learners.* New York: Teachers College Press.

Gagné, R. M. (1987). *The conditions of learning* (4th ed.). New York: Holt, Rinehart & Winston.

Jonassen, D. H. (1991). Objectivism vs. constructivism: Do we need a new philosophical paradigm? *Educational Technology: Research & Development, 393*), 5-14.

Jonassen, D. H. (in press). Cognitive flexibility theory and its implications for designing CBI. In S. Dijkstra (Ed.), *Instructional models in computer based learning environments.* Heidelberg, FRG: Springer-Verlag.

McMahon, H., & O'Neill, W. (in press). Computer-mediated zones of engagement in learning. In T. M. Duffy, J. Lowyck, & D. H. Jonassen (Eds.), *Designing environments for constructivist learning.* Hillsdale, NJ: Lawrence Erlbaum Associates.

Merrill, M. D. (1983). Component display theory. In C. M. Reigeluth (Ed.), *Instructional-design theories and models* (pp. 282-333). Hillsdale, NJ: Lawrence Erlbaum Associates.

Scriven, M. (1973). Goal free evaluation. In E. R. House (Ed.), *School evaluation.* Berkeley, CA: McCutchan.

Spiro, R. J., Coulson, R. L., Feltovich, P. J., & Anderson, D. K. (1988). *Cognitive flexibility theory: Advanced knowledge acquisition in ill-structured domains* (Tech. Rep. No. 441). Champaign, IL: University of Illinois, Center for the Study of Reading.

13

Reflections on the Implications of Constructivism for Educational Technology

Charles M. Reigeluth
Indiana University, Bloomington

I applaud this book on the implications of constructivism for educational technology. Constructivism is a valuable perspective that has much to contribute to our understanding of how to facilitate learning, and I think educational technologists will gain some valuable insights from the special issue. The following are comments about each of the first six chapters, by constructivists, of this book. I have chosen not to comment on the chapters by Dick (chapter 7) and Merrill (chapter 8) because they are themselves commentary on the other six chapters.

DUFFY AND JONASSEN

My major concern with the Duffy and Jonassen chapter (1)—and the Cunningham chapter (3)—is that the authors advocate an extreme view of constructivism, with an ideological fervor that borders on evangelism, rejecting all other perspectives as "heresy." In their chapter (2), Bednar, Cunningham, Duffy, and Perry talk more like evangelists trying to sell educators on a new religion, than like educators trying to identify the best ways to facilitate learning. Constructivism has much that is of value to educators, but so do other perspectives. And what constructivism has to offer is not equally useful for all learning situations.

For example, a major thesis of Duffy and Jonassen is that "There are many ways to structure the world and there are many meanings or perspectives for any event or concept. Thus, there is not a correct meaning that we are striving for" (chapter 1). I agree with that—*sometimes*. There are also instructional situations where there *is* a correct meaning that we are striving for. There *are* situations where learners want and/or need to acquire the understandings and skills of an "expert" as defined by "objectivist cognitive psychology." It concerns me that such an open-minded, pragmatic approach doesn't seem to be a part of the authors' "holy writ." Educational practitioners, who are looking for the best means to facilitate a diversity of kinds of learning, can't afford the luxury of being so ideological, dogmatic, and exclusionary in their view of education. As such, educational technologists need to be more pragmatic and eclectic, drawing from diverse theoretical perspectives as each proves useful in facilitating different kinds of learning. It was encouraging to see Spiro and his colleagues supporting this notion in their chapter (chapter 5; see my comments later).

Similarly, I have concerns about the authors' statement that "there is no ultimate, shared reality, but rather, reality is the outcome of a constructive process." And "...each [person] has their own construction, their own understanding, rather than both encompassing some common reality." Again, this seems like an extremist, ideological view of the world. Can't the constructive process result in a shared reality? Aren't there any objective, verifiable realities in the world? Can't some constructions be right and others wrong? I agree that many views are not a matter of right or wrong; there are equally plausible views. And I agree that all knowledge we have is the outcome of a constructive process. But let's be reasonable. We couldn't even have language without *some* shared reality. And it seems to me that the purpose of learning is to increase the extent to which we share the more plausible realities.

It is also helpful to keep in mind that educational technologists have long espoused some of the major tenets of constructivism. They have for some time advocated "situating" learning experiences in authentic activities. For example, in 1975, Merrill advocated making examples and practice consistent with the postinstructional requirements (Merrill & Wood, 1975). And I don't think any would deny that a learner's experience influences her or his understanding of an event or concept. Also, educational technologists have long decried that schools have decontextualized learning.

Much of what is advocated under the rubric of these authors' extreme view of constructivism seems to me to be more relevant to curriculum theory rather than to instructional theory, for it is more concerned with decisions about *what* to teach than with *how* to teach it. Although the two are highly interrelated, very different considerations are used to make decisions for each. Decisions about *what* to teach are made primarily on the basis of pragmatism (e.g., through a needs analysis) or philosophy and values (e.g., through a democratic process). Decisions about *how* to teach are made on the basis of what works best for different kinds of learning, learners and situations, which is what instructional theory attempts to prescribe. When Duffy and Jonassen (chapter 1) say, "Instruction should not focus on transmitting plans to the learner...," they are stating a philosophical position that may contradict the pragmatic requirements in a given training situation. For example, certain employees in the ABC company may only need to use plans to perform a task. But, on the other hand, I also believe that in many situations it is better to "...develop the skills of the learner to construct plans...."

I have two additional concerns with the chapter by Duffy and Jonassen. First, they hold that our instructional designs are "an implicit expression of our theory of learning." But, not all instructional designs are based on a theory of learning. Some were developed inductively by trial and error: teachers found that certain instructional strategies worked better than others. Those teachers may have no inkling as to why, or what learning processes are involved. In fact, theories of learning have been invented to explain why instructional strategies work, as well as instructional strategies being invented to implement a theory of learning.

Second, Duffy and Jonassen refer to "goals for learning" and a "concept of what it means to 'understand' the subject matter" as synonymous with "theory of learning." But these are both outcomes, ends. Theory, on the other hand, is concerned with change relationships: how learning occurs, in the case of learning theory, or how to best facilitate learning, in the case of instructional theory.

Finally, there is a minor inaccuracy I would like to clarify. Duffy and Jonassen advocate an integration of learning theory and instructional theory, and contrast that goal with "Reigeluth's call for a distinction" between the two. I didn't *call* for such a distinction; I tried to *clarify* some distinctions between the two. They *are* different, though related, phenomena, as Herbert Simon (1969), a Nobel laureate, pointed out so well in his book, *The Sciences of the Artificial*. I don't believe learning theory and instructional theory should be divorced from each other, any more than theory and practice (which are also two different things) should be divorced. But it is still useful to understand the differences between the two. Like all descriptive and prescriptive bodies of knowledge, both learning theory and instructional theory have much to contribute to the other. Hence, I support the authors' thesis that it is beneficial to "integrate" learning theory and instructional theory, but I also feel it is important to recognize the differences between the two.

CUNNINGHAM

The Cunningham chapter (3) also seems to me to take an extremist, exclusionary, and somewhat evangelical, view of cognitivism. I agree that

> ...when instruction is embedded in situations where students are involved in realistic or actual tasks, assessment arises naturally from those situations.... (chapter 3)

Sometimes, I also think that there are times when formal tests or "objective measurements" are needed, such as when you want to make sure that someone like a surgeon who is going to perform an operation on you has acquired specific skills. It's not sufficient to know that the doctor was on a team of medical students that performed the operation successfully; you want to know if that doctor can do it without that team. Cunningham, in the voice of Sagredo, also says:

> If the purpose of the group is to promote the attainment of the same objective by every member, then your criticism may be justified.... If, however, the objective of the group is a collective one—that is, to solve the problem at hand.... (chapter 3)

If the objective of the group is only to solve the problem at hand, then it is a performance objective, not an instructional objective, and you need performance technology, not educational technology. But just as importantly, you could well have a team-learning situation where the purpose is not for all members to learn the same objective. Each team member may well need to learn a different role from the others. That is a separate issue from whether one needs to make sure that the necessary learning has occurred. The point is that there *are* some situations in which it is important to confirm that certain learning has occurred, and successful completion of the task by the team will not, in *some* situations, be enough to make that confirmation.

The author, again in the voice of Sagredo, also says:

> Objective measurement is a fiction or at best a degenerative case where knowledge is so decontextualized that only one context (the school context) is relevant. (chapter 3)

I'm sure that in some cases this is true, but certainly not all. There are also cases where performance-based testing in context can—and should—be done objectively. Even the author's prescription that "learning should occur in realistic settings" is not always true; cost-effectiveness considerations may occasionally favor the use of a not-so-realistic setting. Such sweeping ideological pronouncements do little to help practitioners make wise, professional, effective decisions.

Like Duffy and Jonassen, Cunningham offers a number of prescriptions that are more relevant to curriculum theory than to instructional theory, such as:

> The role of education in a constructivist view is to show students how to construct knowledge, to promote collaboration..., and to arrive at self-chosen positions.... (chapter 3)

Again, these objectives will be very appropriate for some situations but will not be appropriate for others.

I have two other concerns, which may be more of a philosophical nature, although research may also prove illuminative. Cunningham indicates that the teacher should be the judge as to whether a task has been successfully completed (learned). Putting the teacher in the role of judge is an industrial-age mindset that establishes an adversarial relationship between the teacher and the learner. Many who are interested in restructuring education to meet the needs of learners in the information age are calling for outside evaluators—often a panel of evaluators that includes community members and other students, as well as teachers—so that the teacher assumes the role of coach or facilitator, someone who is on the learner's side.

Finally, Cunningham says that higher level skills cannot be "conceived independent of the problems to which they are applied." This is in direct conflict with what most other constructivists emphasize as the importance of promoting transfer of higher level skills. In fact, the Cognition and Technology Group (chapter 6) advocates "pairs of related adventures" to help students to "analyze exactly what they are able to carry over from one context to another and what is specific to each context but not generalizable." The latter is the kind of rational, nonideological approach that educational practitioners need to most facilitate learning.

PERKINS

In contrast to the previous three chapters, I found this one (chapter 4, and all the remaining ones) to be a much more reasoned and pragmatic view of the application of constructivism to education. The five facets of a learning environment, the BIG-WIG distinction (along with the author's viewpoint that the important issue is to find the appropriate balance of the two), and the morals for front-end analysis, instructional strategies, and assessment were all valuable insights that all educational technologists would do well to incorporate into their instructional design repertoires.

SPIRO, FELTOVICH, JACOBSON, AND COULSON

I found the chapter by Spiro, Feltovich, Jacobson, and Coulson (5) to be insightful and informative. I could not find a single point of disagreement, and I came away with many valuable new insights. I was impressed by their delimitation of boundaries for the generalizability of their Cognitive Flexibility Theory and Random Access Instruction:

> We will be concerned only with learning objectives important to *advanced (post-introductory) knowledge acquisition*: to attain an understanding of important elements of conceptual complexity, to be able to use acquired concepts for reasoning and inference, and to be able to flexibly apply conceptual knowledge to novel situations. (chapter 5)

And in introducing their hypertext approach:

> The omission of other varieties of computer-based instruction from our discussion does not imply any negative evaluation of their merits. Indeed, in other instructional contexts the kinds of hypertexts we will discuss would be inappropriate (e.g., computer-based drill would be better suited to the instructional objective of memorizing the multiplication tables.... (chapter 5)

And the acknowledgment that

> ...*compartmentalization* of knowledge components is an effective strategy in well-structured domains, but blocks effective learning in more intertwined, ill-structured domains which require high degrees of knowledge interconnectedness. (chapter 5)

I am particularly impressed with the analysis of kinds of learning deficiencies (actually, kinds of oversimplification, or "reductive bias"): additivity bias, discreteness bias, and compartmentalization bias. I also like the notion of the "new constructivism" as "doubly constructive":

> (1) understandings are constructed by using prior knowledge to go beyond the information given; and (2) the prior knowledge that is brought to bear is itself constructed, rather than retrieved intact from memory, on a case-by-case basis [in ill-structured domains]. (chapter 5)

I am concerned by something Duffy and Jonassen (chapter 1) said in their two paragraphs about this chapter: "We cannot simplify the context by removing the complex features, for example, as is done in forming an epitome (Reigeluth & Stein, 1983)." This is a misleading statement, first because it does not accurately characterize the Elaboration Theory, and second because it does not accurately characterize what Spiro and his colleagues say in chapter 5. An epitome does not simplify the *context* at all; it utilizes a class of simple *real-world* cases, complete with all their real-world context. I was surprised to find that Spiro and his colleagues make no reference to epitomes at all in their chapter, and none of their three kinds of oversimplification (additivity bias, discreteness bias, and compartmentalization bias) is prescribed by the elaboration theory. It surprises me that Duffy and Jonassen would make such an inaccurate characterization.

I was also particularly impressed with the discussion of oversimplification by Spiro and his colleagues:

> The common denominator in the majority of advanced learning failures that we have observed is *oversimplification*, and one serious kind of oversimplification is looking at a concept or phenomenon or case from just one perspective. In an ill-structured domain, that single perspective will *miss* important aspects of conceptual understanding, may actually mislead with regard to some of the fuller aspects of understanding, and will account for too little of the variability in the way knowledge must be applied to new cases. (chapter 5)

Perhaps this statement also applies to those who only view learning and instruction from an extreme and exclusionary constructivist perspective.

COGNITION AND TECHNOLOGY GROUP

Like the previous two chapters, I found chapter 6 to be a very reasoned and pragmatic view of the application of constructivism to education. The seven design principles (or more accurately strategies) are ones that educational technologists either have already incorporated or should incorporate into their instructional design repertoires. My only concern is that it was not made very clear as to when each of the seven strategies should—and should not—be used. Clearly, a video-based presentation format is not always most appropriate. And the same is true of each of the other six strategies. Nevertheless, the strategies are all important ones for practitioners to call upon when appropriate.

CONCLUSION

Overall, I found these chapters to be a useful contribution to our professional dialogue. I applaud the editors for putting it together. And I encourage educational technologists to continue to explore the most appropriate application of constructivist insights.

ACKNOWLEDGMENT

I extend my appreciation to Mike Molenda for his valuable comments on an early draft of this chapter. However, Molenda deserves no abuse for any of the opinions expressed herein; I deserve the exclusive right thereto.

REFERENCES

Merrill, M. D., & Wood, N. D. (1975). An instructional strategy taxonomy: Theory and applications. *Journal for Research in Mathematics Education, 6,* 195-201.

Reigeluth, C. M., & Stein, F. S. (1983). The elaboration theory of instruction. In C. M. Reigeluth (Ed.), *Instructional-design theories and models: An overview of their current status.* Hillsdale, NJ: Lawrence Erlbaum Associates.

Simon, H. A. (1969). *Sciences of the artificial.* Cambridge, MA: MIT Press.

14

In Defense of Extremism

Donald J. Cunningham
Indiana University, Bloomington

Perhaps the most distinguishing feature of constructivism, as I view it, is its emphasis on argument, discussion, and debate. The first eight chapters of this text, upon which these remarks are based, (and the remaining chapters) are perfect examples of the value of this emphasis. It is very clear that we so-called experts have different perspectives on the type and role of theory in the instructional design process. Even under a common theoretical heading, the readers of the special issue were treated to divergent viewpoints: Within constructivism, for example, the articles ranged from "moderate" to "extreme," to use Merrill's (chapter 8) characterization. This sort of diversity characterizes all knowledge domains, and the extent to which we can accommodate to this fact and avoid the dogmatism associated with any particular position, the healthier a field will be.

This, in fact, was a major reason why I chose the unusual format of a dialogue for my contribution. I have been asked a number of times which character in the dialogue was me. They were *all* me at one point or another in my career. Simplicio raises some of the exact objections to constructivism that I have faced or raised with myself over the course of my epistemological odyssey. Sagredo represents me in my more positive moments about a perspective with which I have become associated. And Salviati represents the little voice in my head saying, "Hold on. This other person has a point which you need to consider. There may be a better position than the one you now hold." At the heart of constructivism is the notion that knowledge is constructed, which in the present instance means that our theoretical views are personal creations, embedded in a social context, within a social community that accepts the assumptions underlying the perspective. There is no right or wrong here in any absolute sense. Holding a theoretical perspective means making a personal commitment to it, while recognizing the potential validity of other positions. The world view created by one theoretical view often cannot accommodate the world view created by another. That is not a cause for anxiety, but, rather, for celebration. A major difference between objectivists and constructivists, I would argue, is that the former expect and encourage acceptance and closure of a world view, while the latter expect and encourage debate. What I urged in the dialogue was simply awareness of the assumptions underlying your chosen world view and of the assumptions underlying others, so that your commitment to one or the other can be deliberate and informed. There were no converts in the dialogue.

I have no objection to Merrill (chapter 8), for example, assuming that knowledge can be represented "outside the mind" and presuming "that there is some correspondence between (this knowledge) and representations in the mind." Given this assumption, his work is a masterful embodiment of the objectivist perspective. But it does concern me that he rejects out of hand the alternative view and fails to recognize the objectivist foundation that underlies his work. I am not asking him to accept my assumptions, but simply to acknowledge that his are different but no more "defensible" (at this point in time, at least) than mine. Just as we can learn much about our culture by studying other cultures, so too can we enrich our theoretical world views by studying others.

Dick (chapter 7), on the other hand, seems much more aware of the foundational assumptions underlying his perspective and raises important questions which emerge from it and about which the constructivist should ponder. Consider the issue, for example, of entry behaviors. From the perspective of objectivism, entry behavior is best dealt with prior to instruction by specifying the depth to which the task analysis should proceed (i.e., what does the student need to be able to do in order to successfully complete the next level task in the learning hierarchy?). For the constructivist, this sort of concern emerges within the *doing* of the task, more of a top down approach (i.e., if we need to know how to construct a graph of the relationship between unemployment and trade tariffs to better understand the causes of unemployment in Detroit, how do we find out how to do that?). This same general tendency is true of most of the issues raised by Dick (e.g., assessment, learner control, learning domains, etc.). We are no less concerned about these issues, but believe that they emerge out of the task at hand and cannot be prespecified, except in a very general sense, independent of that task.

There are two particularly troubling aspects of Merrill's paper about which I must comment. First, he claims that Bednar, Cunningham, Duffy, and Perry (chapter 2) "suggest that IST has deliberately developed instruction which is ineffective because instructional designers believe that this inadequate instruction is better." I have carefully reread Bednar et al. (chapter 2) and cannot find this sentiment stated or implied. And it would be astounding for those authors to hold such a view since they all (except possibly me, who was fired from the IST department at Indiana University) have practiced in the field for many years and would, therefore, be impugning their *own* motives. But the fact of the matter is that Merrill has reached this interpretation and others may as well. If so, let me say clearly that this was not our intention. The principal message of that article was that instructional developers should clearly understand the epistemological and psychological assumptions underlying their perspective and design instruction consistent with that perspective, all the while realizing that there may be alternative, equally defensible perspectives.

Which brings me to the second, and clearly related, point. It is unfortunate that Merrill chose to draw most heavily upon a paper which did not appear in the special issue of *Educational Technology* in which the other chapters in Parts I and II first appeared. I, for one, am willing to let readers of Bednar et al. (chapter 2) judge for themselves whether Merrill's characterization of our position is accurate. It is impossible, in this brief space, to rebut all of his criticisms, but perhaps the most difficult to swallow is his characterization of us as utter solipsists. He wants his heart surgeon "committed to the standard objective view," rather than some idiosyncratic, undoubtedly aberrant one. Merrill seems to have neglected to remember that philosophers of science (e.g., Kuhn, 1970) have, for many years, stressed the process of social negotiation within scientific communities which have brought forth these "standard objective views." And it is truly amazing how quickly these views change. Up until a few years ago, by-pass operations were considered benign and routine; now, I understand, the conventional wisdom is to use nonsurgical methods to clear the blockage, if at all possible. If the "standard objective view" changes so often, what is "objective" about it?

In Bednar et al. (chapter 2) and elsewhere (e.g., Cunningham, in press), we have always stressed the *social* construction of meaning. We live in a world whose form we cannot know in any exhaustive sense, but which undoubtedly places constraints upon the kind of semiosis possible. And we live in communities and cultures that select the aspects of that world to which they will pay attention. In one medical community, for example, the heart may be regarded as a pump and we treat it in order to maximize that function. In another medical community, the heart might be regarded as only one component of an intricate system of balance between dynamic forces, and it is this balance that becomes the focus of our medical interventions. Is one of these views correct and the other incorrect? I don't know, but I *am* sure that both are *constructions* of the world (i.e., world views) that have arisen out of social negotiation within a culture as to what constitutes evidence. And I am sure that both views would reject a view that the heart is an oreo cookie.

I am over the word limit imposed upon me by the editors, so I will make only one final point very briefly. Merrill has characterized my position as "extreme." Let me assure him and the other readers that you ain't seen nuthin yet. In a paper in preparation for a conference in Belgium in May 1991, I will start from the assumption that humans are "structurally closed" (Maturana & Varela, 1987) and that instruction in the usual sense is impossible. What is the role of instructional design under such an assumption? Wait and see (or read Knuth & Cunningham, in press).

ACKNOWLEDGMENT

This response (as well as the dialogue) was written when I was a visiting professor at the University of Ulster, Coleraine, Northern Ireland. My thanks to Harry McMahon for his comments on an earlier draft.

REFERENCES

Cunningham, D. (in press). Beyond educational psychology: Steps toward an education semiotic. *Educational Psychology Review.*

Knuth, R., & Cunningham, D. (in press). Tools for constructivism. In T. Duffy, J. Lowyck, & D. Jonassen (Eds.), *The design of constructivist learning environments: Implications for instructional design and the use of technology.* Heidelberg: Springer-Verlag.

Kuhn, T. (1970). *The structure of scientific revolutions* (2nd ed.). Chicago: University of Chicago Press.

Maturana, H., & Varela, F. (1987). *The tree of knowledge.* Boston: New Science Library.

15

What Constructivism Demands of the Learner

D. N. Perkins
Harvard Graduate School of Education

In his response to the chapters on constructivism and instructional technology, Walter Dick (chapter 7) raised a number of thoughtful issues. Particularly striking to me was his question "Why does there appear to be almost no concern for the entry behaviors of students? Designers use analytic techniques to determine what a student *must know or be able to do* before beginning instruction, because without these skills research shows they will likely not be able to learn new skills. Why are constructivists not concerned that the gap will be too great...?" The response from David Merrill (chapter 8) less directly revealed a similar concern when he emphasized the complexity of authentic situated tasks and the futility of denying simplifying moves that bring the tasks within reach.

These are legitimate concerns. Moreover, they point to a larger class of concerns that might be summed up in the phrase "What constructivism demands of the learner." While constructivism is supposed to be a learner-centered approach, in retrospect I am struck by how little attention chapters 1 through 8 (and mine is no exception) paid to constructivist instruction as learners experience it, how its challenges might look to them.

So let us explore briefly three ways in which a constructivist pedagogy often imposes sharp demands on learners—cognitive complexity, task management, and "buying in."

COGNITIVE COMPLEXITY

Very often, constructivist instruction asks students to cope with very complex situations. In my earlier chapter (4), I emphasized that constructivist instruction commonly confronts learners with a "phenomenarium" (an artificially limited arena where phenomena to investigate occur, such as an aquarium or a computerized Newtonian "microworld") or with a "construction kit" (a set of modular parts with which to make things, as in

TinkerToys with its physical parts or Logo with its computer-command parts). The phenomenaria and construction kits that learners face are calculatedly rich environments—and the complexity comes with the turf. Because it is desirable as a learning opportunity does not mean that it is not a problem so far as cognitive demands are concerned.

The cognitive load seems particularly likely to be high in a favorite context for constructivist pedagogies: science and mathematics concepts prone to misconceptions. Here, students are likely to have prior "naive" models of the phenomena in question (e.g., Aristotelian concepts of motion) that the learning experience tries to replace with better models (e.g., Newtonian concepts of motion) (e.g., Clement, 1982, 1983; McCloskey, 1983).

In conventional instruction, learners often follow a path that might be called "conflict-buried." They choose to ignore or hardly note the conflict between their naive models and the target model. They learn to play "the school game" for the tests and assignments. However, responding to qualitative questions that probe for understanding, they reveal the original naive model intact, typically without any recognition that it is in conflict with the target model (cf. Perkins & Simmons, 1988; Posner, Strike, Hewson, & Gertzog, 1982; Strike & Posner, 1985).

Much constructivist instruction is anomaly driven, in the Piagetian spirit. It aims to confront the learners with situations that make the inherent inconsistencies in the learners' naive model plain and challenge the learners either to construct better models or at least to ponder the merits of alternative models presented by the teacher (Posner et al., 1982; Strike & Posner, 1985). My point is that this "conflict-faced" path has very high cognitive demand. Learners are asked to compare and contrast an entrenched but barely articulated model with a newly sketched model (by themselves or the teacher) with which they have very little working familiarity. No wonder learners often have a hard time with this path.

A third path, which constructivists do not so often talk about, might be called "conflict-deferred." Here learners would be invited to "bracket" their intuitive models for a while and just learn a new way of thinking and talking about the phenomena. When the new way has become somewhat familiar and consolidated, then the instruction turns back to the naive model and explores relationships between the two.

TASK MANAGEMENT

Another key component of an educational setting that I mentioned in chapter 4 was "task managers," elements in the instructional setting that helped to sequence students through the learning experience. Task managers include the teacher, instructions in the text, and of course the learners themselves; that is, task management is distributed in the classroom setting—a facet of "distributed intelligence" (Pea, in press; Perkins, in press a).

Typical constructivist instruction asks learners to play more of the task management role than in conventional instruction. The reason is sensible: Students are not likely to become autonomous thinkers and learners if they lack an opportunity to manage their own learning. In typical teacher/test-controlled settings, whatever students may learn about the content, they are likely to get little experience managing their interactions with the content themselves.

While the aim is laudable, often constructivist learning situations throw students suddenly and almost wholly on their own managerial resources. They either "hack it" or they don't, and many are so unused to managing tasks themselves that they fend poorly. The high cognitive complexity of many constructivist learning settings of course exacerbates the problem.

There is a classic solution that helps with both task management per se and the cognitive complexity problem: "scaffolding" or "coaching," as for instance in the "cognitive apprenticeship" model (Collins, Brown, & Newman, 1989). It is the job of the constructivist teacher (or interactive technology) to hold learners in their "zone of proximal development" by providing just enough help and guidance, but not too much. Exactly this happens in many naturalistic learning situations such as mother-child relationships and apprenticeship settings.

The solution is a good one in principle. Unfortunately, very often appropriate scaffolding is not part of the repertoire of either the teacher or the technology. And it can be difficult for a teacher to scaffold adequately large groups of students.

BUYING IN

Whatever the challenges of cognitive complexity and task management, a rather different kind of challenge concerns learners' attitudes toward the enterprise. When learners are asked to thrash around for themselves to some extent, there are often characteristic reactions such as, "Why don't you just tell me what you want me to know?" Such learners are not "buying in" to the constructivist agenda of the instruction, a problem that inevitably stands in the way of a fully engaged learning experience.

An ardent constructivist might naturally respond, "Well, buying into this sort of thing is part of what they're supposed to learn. They'll come around."

However heartfelt, I am not sure that such a response is entirely reasonable. From the learners' perspective, they are being asked to jump through hoops to discover X for themselves when they could, they think, straightforwardly be told X with some practice to follow to get used to doing things with *X*. They are being charged what they see as a high price in what I have elsewhere called the "cognitive economy" of the classroom (Perkins, in press b).

Of course, the teacher or instructional designer in question believes that it is ineffective simply to tell learners *X* and then provide varied practice. And perhaps they are right (I think sometimes they are and sometimes they are not, depending on X and the learners). But in any case, they embark on the basis of a theory about what it takes to learn *X* which may simply look bizarre to the students.

In such cases, one basically is asking for the students to learn two things at once—*X* (by a route that looks roundabout to them) and a new theory of learning (that says that the route isn't so roundabout after all). This is a lot to ask. It at least seems to recommend that the teacher or instructional designer approach the double agenda as such, engaging students constructively in thinking both about *X* and about the learning process reflectively (with care to keep the cognitive load and task management problem under control).

MORALS FOR THE CONSTRUCTIVIST ENTERPRISE

Perhaps this will be enough to make the argument that, to the learner, a constructivist learning experience may not look welcoming. It may seem—indeed be—dauntingly complex. It may ask the learner to make choices about what to do first and next for which the learner feels ill-prepared. And it may seem a tortuous path toward an end that looks, to the learner at least, as though it might be much more directly addressed.

These remarks could easily be taken as an argument that constructivist pedagogy creates more problems than it solves, and hence should be dismissed. Let me state plainly that I think quite the opposite: Constructivist instruction with such problems should be repaired, not abandoned. I recognize many examples of constructivist practice that have taken care to dodge such pitfalls. The learner-demands highlighted here are not inescapable flaws in the constructivist agenda but common trouble spots that can be evaded by careful instructional design—for instance, providing cognitive supports to reduce cognitive load, perhaps choosing the "conflict deferred" rather than the "conflict faced" path, ensuring fine-tuned scaffolding to help with task management, and acknowledging explicitly as part of the instructional process the double learning agenda inherent in the "buying in" problem.

The larger lesson is that any pedagogy—but especially constructivism, given its commitments—does well to include a vision of how students experience it. They, after all, are the ones who have to try to walk in the shoes we theorists, teachers, and designers cobble together for them.

ACKNOWLEDGMENTS

This chapter was prepared at Project Zero and at the Educational Technology Center of the Harvard Graduate School of Education, operating with support from the Spencer, MacArthur, and Ford Foundations. The ideas presented here are not necessarily those of the supporting agencies.

REFERENCES

Clement, J. (1982). Students' preconceptions in introductory mechanics. *American Journal of Physics, 50,* 66-71.

Clement, J. (1983). A conceptual model discussed by Galileo and used intuitively by physics students. In D. Gentner & A. L. Stevens (Eds.), *Mental models.* Hillsdale, NJ: Lawrence Erlbaum Associates.

Collins, A., Brown, J. S., & Newman, S. F. (1989). Cognitive apprenticeship: Teaching the craft of reading, writing, and mathematics. In L. B. Resnick (Ed.), *Knowing, learning, and instruction: Essays in honor of Robert Glaser* (pp. 453-494). Hillsdale, NJ: Lawrence Erlbaum Associates.

McCloskely, M. (1983). Naive theories of motion. In D. Genter & A. L. Stevens (Eds.), *Mental Models* (pp. 299-324). Hillsdale, NJ: Lawrence Erlbaum Associates.

Pea, R. (in press). Distributed intelligence and education. In D. N. Perkins, J. Schwartz, M. M. West, & M. S. Wiske, (Eds.), *Teaching for understanding in the age of technology,* volume in preparation.

Perkins, D. N. (in press a). Person plus: A distributed view of thinking and learning. In G. Salomon (Ed.), *Distributed cognitions,* New York: Cambridge University Press.

Perkins, D. N. (in press b). *Schools of thought: The necessary shape of education.* New York: The Free Press.

Perkins, D. N., & Simmons, R. (1988). Patterns of misunderstanding: An integrative model of misconceptions in science, mathematics, and programming. *Review of Educational Research, 58*(3), 303-326.

Posner, G. J., Strike, K. A., Hewson, P. W., & Gertzog, W. A. (1982). Accommodation of a scientific conception: Toward a theory of conceptual change. *Science Education, 66*(2), 211-227.

Strike, K., & Posner, G. (1985). A conceptual change view of learning and understanding. In L. H. T. West & A. L. Pines (Eds.), *Cognitive structure and conceptual change.* New York: Academic Press.

V REFLECTIONS ON THE CONVERSATION

16

Constructing Constructivism

Catherine Fosnot
University of Southern Connecticut

In order for instructional designers to find any benefit in constructivism, it is important that the theory be understood for what it is and differentiated from various other learning theories. This will take much discourse on our part because we bring differing understandings to the task of making meaning. Lately, many educators have gotten on the "constructivist bandwagon," offering various definitions, interpretations, and hence applications of the theory to education. The chapters which I have been asked to review make this point very clear.

CONSTRUCTIVISM: KNOWING AND COMING TO KNOW

In my mind, constructivism is at once a theory of "knowing" and a theory about "coming to know." As such, it draws its empirical base from science, philosophy, and psychology (particularly cognitive developmental research).

As a theory of knowing, it purports that organisms actively transform and interpret experience with mental structures—they assimilate (Piaget, 1977), meaning that they literally "make similar," via cognitive structures, the experiences they engage in.

Organisms have an innate need to organize and adapt to their environment simply for survival, thus they also accommodate their structures to their environment. In other words, experience, knowledge, and hence "truth," are always a result of the constructed cognitive structures used in interpreting. On a macrogenesis level this is obvious; the reptile interprets the world very differently than the human, whose mind categorizes and manipulates symbols; a two year old understands objects falling towards the ground differently than the adult physicist who has constructed particle theory. This is not just a case of differing information or accumulated experience; rather, it is a case of differing interpretations given the operational structures used—which themselves are the result of organization and adaptation.

It is also true on the microgenesis level of ideas. Some ideas require cognitive developmental shifts in perspective as they are constructed and thus have an aspect of structure within them. By structure in this sense, I am referring to conceptual structure, an idea having "wholeness" (at least temporarily so) in that it explains how the parts within the system interrelate (see Fosnot, 1988 for a further discussion of structure, or to Schifter and Fosnot, 1992, where we have labeled them and defined them as "big ideas"). For example, the shift from Newtonian mechanics to the relativity theory of Einstein and to theories of quantum mechanics and chaos required structural shifts in perspective; Roman numerals worked fine until the world needed to represent larger quantities—hence place-value systems were constructed; thinking of the world from our own egocentric perspective, as a flat surface, to thinking about it as a living spherical mass of particles and energy requires a new structural understanding. These new understandings cannot be understood simply by transmission of information; first, because even the transmission is interpreted (assimilated), and secondly because it demands a mental reordering, a giving up of the old perspective, at times reintegrating it, in order to construct the new.

Knowledge from this perspective cannot be deemed objective truth, but only an interpretive act. To assume that adult humans know the "truth" is not only arrogant, it foolishly misses the point that we, as humans, are in the process of construction. This point is very aptly made by Cunningham (chapter 3) and Duffy and Jonassen (chapter 1) and needs little further elaboration. For Dick (chapter 7), who had never heard of objectivism, I refer him to Descartes, who, with the pronouncement of "I think, therefore I am," set off the whole rational thought movement upon which objective truth is based—the idea that variables could be isolated and controlled, that objects could be studied separate from the self's effect on them. These ideas, embedded in objectivism, formed the basis for Newton's mechanics. Heisenberg's work and Bohr's work in quantum mechanics, as well as the more contemporary "bootstrap" and "S-Matrix" theories have shown the fallacies in objectivism, pointing out that the question determines the answer, the questioner affects the results, and the universe needs to be understood as simply "a dynamic web of interrelated events. None of the properties of any part of this web [previously thought by Newton to be isolable] are fundamental; they all follow from the properties of the other parts, and the overall consistency of their mutual interrelations determines the structure of the entire web" (Capra, 1982, p. 93).

Should readers begin to think I am merely discussing a structuralist theory, let me assure you that I am not. I view constructivism as a poststructuralist theory, one that also describes how learners "come to know." Piaget (1970, p. 140) wrote, "The subject exists because, to put it very briefly, the being of structures consists in their coming to be, that is, their being 'under construction'...there is no structure apart from construction." As human organisms growing, developing, and evolving, we are constructing (organizing and adapting) both cognitively and physically as we interact in our environment.

Many of the concepts we teach in the schools require construction involving reordering and invention. I use the word "invent" here on purpose so as to differentiate it from discovery learning. Discovery is a more passive process of uncovering to get at the truth (an objective truth which the teacher holds). The process of construction is more like the process of inventing, or at least re-inventing, in that it is akin to the creative process. It requires the reorganization of old "data" and the building of new models for that learner. Thus the development of the idea, the progressive ordering and reordering, is of prime importance—and indeed is the essence of constructivism. The mind is never at any point in development a blank slate, a *tabula rasa*. Reflexes at birth are reorganized into schemes of grasping, into means-end reaching, into mental maps of actions, into understandings of compensatory actions, into concepts of causality. As ideas are tried and presented, they succeed or fail; models are argued and debated—holes, insufficiencies, and contradictions appear as humans negotiate meaning, construct, and reconstruct.

Much research has been accumulated over the past 50 years in developmental psychology circles documenting such progressive restructuring. Certainly Piaget's work on time, speed, the world, number, space, etc., is perhaps the most well known, but contemporary researchers have studied place value and number operations (Kamii, 1987; Labinowicz, 1985), probability (Fosnot, 1990), balance (Fosnot, Forman, Edwards, & Goldhaber, 1988), fractions (Streefland, 1991), reading (Chall, 1983), writing (Calkins, 1986; Graves, 1983), spelling (Henderson, 1985), to name only a few topics.

MAKING THE LEAP TO PEDAGOGY

While constructivism is a well-documented theory of knowing and coming to know, it is not as yet a well-documented theory of teaching. Educators are being asked to make the leap into designing instruction that is aligned with this new view of learning. While this is the needed next step, it is a difficult one. Einstein's theory of relativity explained the universe more completely than Newton's, but Newton's laws and formulae are still used successfully to describe impact at low speeds, or to explain the movement of balls on a billiard table. So too, a constructivist approach to teaching will need to identify what instructional strategies will facilitate concept construction and when they are needed. For example, while Perkins may be correct in stating that even learning someone's name has an aspect of constructivism in it, certainly as a teacher I am not going to put learners in collaborative groups and play a Rumplestiltskin game. Direct transmission strategies are far more efficient. On the other hand if I am working with a 2-year-old who is just beginning to talk, learning my name may require some elaborate construction on his/her part such as understanding the concept of what a name is. Thus being told the names of several people, himself/herself included, may more likely facilitate the needed construction. For a 6-year-old attempting to spell my name, isolating the phonemes *k, a, th, er, i, n* and blending them back into the whole requires a difficult construction. By watching his/her invented spelling attempts, I gain an understanding of her present level of assimilation from which she/he will build. I may use a direct transmission approach naming for him/her the letter sounds s/he can isolate, but may use only probing questions or put him/her with a partner to discuss other sounds they hear in my name in order to stretch his/her towards isolating and blending phonemes further. In the latter case I recognize that part-whole integration is needed and requires construction; whereas, in the former only new labels (letter names) are needed—a simple case of social arbitrary knowledge. With a sixth grader grappling with fractions, I will show the symbolic notation 3/4 (because this is social arbitrary knowledge decided by previous mathematicians) and explain that mathematicians write the solution that way, but only after solving problems such as sharing three yards of rope with four people. And I will encourage him/her to think about why three things shared four ways ended up being 3/4 of a yard each, if that will always happen with fractions, and why or why not. For this investigation I would be apt to use group collaboration and then convene a "math congress" (class meeting) for the "mathematicians" to share their findings. I would be extremely careful here to use WIG constructivism (Perkins, chapter 4) because understanding fractions requires the learners to grapple with the "big idea" of fractions as ratios, and as division, not just as parts of wholes.

PRINCIPLES OF INSTRUCTION

There are some general principles of instruction that I believe can be put forth from an analysis of constructivism. First, cognitive developmental research shows that learners progress from concrete explorations in meaningful contexts, to symbolic representations of these actions, to abstract models (Karmiloff-Smith & Inhelder, 1974; Piaget, 1977). Thus I was particularly disturbed to read Perkins' (chapter 4) description of what he termed "BIG" constructivism. Instruction begins in this model with two symbolic descriptions and learners are asked to discriminate and thereby construct concepts of heat and temperature. This approach seems perfectly well explained to me by using Gagné's discrimination learning model and thus I find no surprise in the fact that Merrill (chapter 8) and Dick (chapter 7) find it so appealing. In my mind it is not constructivist at all.

I was just as disturbed to read the Vanderbilt Group's (chapter 6) description of instruction, in which they use very rich meaningful contexts to engage learners in problem solving--a wonderful start—but then they appear to revert to practice and exercises on "basic skills or concept areas such as decimals, fractions, money, time, etc." Since these concepts require conceptual reorganization, they must be constructed; practice on exercises is an insufficient strategy of instruction here, even when it is embedded in real problems. It took humans years to construct these concepts. As Perkins (chapter 4) so aptly states, "Understanding is not something that comes free with full databanks and thorough practice; it is something won by the struggles of the organism to learn-to conjecture, probe, puzzle out, forecast...."

For conceptual structures—such as decimals and fractions—to be developed, instruction must at some point go beyond the concrete problem experience. Piaget (1977) describes the mechanism of reflective abstraction as the most important process in the construction of structures. He tells the story of the boy who sat counting pebbles, rearranging them, and then recounting. At first puzzled by the fact that the sum was always the same, he kept rearranging them. Eventually he constructed the idea that sum was independent of order (of course the boy didn't put it in those exact words!) by going beyond the problem, or specific case with pebbles, to the general case of all numerical quantities.

A second principle that can be derived from constructivism is that learning is always a case of building with, and from, initial assimilatory structures. Only through challenges to these structures, will gaps, insufficiencies, or contradictions become apparent to learners—thus facilitating reflective abstraction and accommodation. Thus "entry-level understanding" is of utmost importance. The teacher does not need to preassess all learners; in fact, doing this prior to teaching and out of context makes no sense in a constructivist model. Rich generative environments like those suggested by the Vanderbilt Group (Group 6) are excellent starting points of instruction because they are so open. But as the teacher moves around the room listening to strategies being employed, and asking questions to elicit assimilatory structures, she/he must become aware of these entry-level understandings. She/he can then stretch and challenge these notions individually and by facilitating whole group discussions where learners are asked to argue, prove, and explain their ideas.

The constructivist notion of assimilation has often been misconstrued in the literature as a process of "taking in" or of making connections between new knowledge and past knowledge, rather than seeing it as the active process of organizing and transforming the experience. When one reads Piaget closely, it is clear he was not talking about a process of "taking in," but instead "acting on." Previously advanced learning theories, such as associationism (Spence, Herbart) or connectionism (Thorndike) discuss learning as a "taking in." As early as the turn of the century Herbart described the mind as composed of active mental states or ideas and suggested that the basis for transfer was a growing apperceptive mass which consisted of new mental states or ideas added to a store of old ones in the mind.

As Dick (chapter 7) pointed out in his critique of chapters 1 through 6, none of the authors discussed entry levels (assimilatory structures) of learners. Jonassen (chapter 7) makes a point of responding to this criticism, but he concludes that "constructivist learning environments are most appropriate for the second stage [of learning], advanced knowledge acquisition....Because learners have not assembled or integrated adequate knowledge structures during introductory knowledge acquisition, it is likely that introductory knowledge acquisition is better supported by more objectivistic approaches." In the chart he provides (Figure 12.1), he labels these instructional strategies as practice and feedback. In my mind, he has missed the main point of constructivism. Learners are always making meaning, no matter what level of understanding they are on. Constructivism is not a theory to explain only complex, ill-structured domains; it is a theory of how learners make meaning, period! To the young learner trying to crack the phonemic reading code, there is as much complexity as there is for the adult reader reading a passage from multiple perspectives—if one views the task in relation to the learner and his/her assimilatory structure. To assume the learner is a blank slate until presented with information, and to characterize experiences or tasks separate from the learner's meaning of them, is objectivistic—a perspective which in the first chapter Jonassen (& Duffy) so radically opposed!

Spiro, Feltovich, Jacobson, and Coulson (chapter 5) offer a definition of constructivism which they equate with Cognitive Flexibility Theory. They describe this "new constructivism as doubly constructive; (a) understandings are constructed by using prior knowledge to go beyond the information given; and (b) the prior knowledge that is brought to bear is itself constructed." (I agree with this definition wholeheartedly but I can't fathom why these authors found it necessary to call this "new constructivism." Anyone schooled in Piaget's theory has believed this all along—Piaget calls this process "generalized assimilation.") While their definition appears on the surface to take entry level understanding into consideration, their practice of presenting multiple perspectives to develop "multiple knowledge representations" leaves room for question. What kind of meaning are learners making with each of these "revisitings"? Are the authors assuming learners are making the same interpretations of each perspective, as they? What attempts are made by the teacher to ascertain the meanings learners are making; and what attempts are made to challenge through discussion the learner's interpretation? Couldn't what they are doing be explained quite well from an associationist or connectionist theory of learning—transfer is more likely because the connections are strengthened? Why do they assume young learners are not dealing with complex problems? Is a multiple perspective approach appropriate for all learners? Entry level is again an issue here. Chall's work in reading development shows that it is appropriate only in the most advanced stages—again in relation to the learner's scheme. My own work (Fosnot et al., 1988) using stop-action video to focus on various aspects of a problem-solving episode (balancing blocks on a fulcrum) demonstrated that the focus most in line with the learner's scheme was the most beneficial. In fact, for some children, other foci served as distractors, and subjects actually did worse on the posttest (assessing their understanding of the balance principles employed) than they did on the pretest.

A third principle of pedagogy that might be advanced from constructivism is to teach for conceptual understanding. This statement sounds trite; of course we would all agree that understanding is the goal of instruction. But I believe that we have only given this lip service. We talk about reading skills, writing skills, skills in arithmetic computation, spelling skills, problem-solving strategies, and mastery. Understanding is not "mastered"; it can always be deepened as ideas and models are extended to new experiences. Skills and strategies are behaviors that are representative of the conceptual structures employed. I believe we have focused on behaviors because (a) we have used a behaviorist psychology in instructional design and (b) they are easy to assess. I have seen children skillfully doing arithmetic computations but having little understanding of place value, and teachers having to re-explain it with the introduction of each new operation and algorithm for the next five years because learners never understood it in the first place. Practice and reinforcement are appropriate strategies if our goal is to "train for mastery of skills." If our goal is truly to educate, to teach for understanding, then much rethinking is needed. I am not arguing that skills are unnecessary. They do have their place in learning, but too frequently conceptual understanding is given short shrift, with most of the instructional time spent on practice and exercises.

A Scenario

The following scenario provides a window into a third-grade constructivist (in my mind) classroom. The teacher began the lesson with a plexiglas box filled with jellybeans, which she had placed in layers separated by paper, suggesting that the children think of ways to figure out how many beans were in the jar. The children were given unifix cubes to use as tools and were asked to record their solutions. After working in collaborative groups for awhile, they convened a "math congress" to discuss their ideas. A few children began by explaining that they were going to count the top layer, see how many layers there were, and then add them up. Another child suggested that the same strategy could be used to count the top layer if they counted the rows and looked at how many rows there were. Agreeing with this strategy, they began to count the beans in each row but then became confused whether some beans should be counted once or twice—

once as a unit in the row, once to represent the number of the row. (This is a common confusion as children struggle to construct multiplication—entering with a unitary assimilatory structure they must grapple with a grouping structure in order to make sense of the task.) The teacher was non-commital; instead she simply facilitated discussion. After much debate, they resolved that issue explaining and proving their reasoning to the rest of the group, which concurred. For the top layer they produced an answer of 6 rows with 8 beans in each. The teacher recorded 6 x 8 explaining that mathematicians write the expression with an *X* to show groups and to differentiate it from addition and subtraction. Some children argued that from where they were sitting they saw 8 rows of 6. They counted to make sure it was still 48 and discussion ensued over whether the total answer would always be the same when the digits were reversed (the commutative property). After proving to each other that it would, by building several rectangles and recognizing the reciprocal nature of the columns and rows, they began to count the layers and over the next several sessions proposed short-cut addition strategies (involving the distributive and associative properties of multiplication) such as adding up two layers three times. After each session the teacher had the children write in mathematics journals their individual ideas so that she had a clear idea where each child was, and she wrote back, in dialogue fashion, in each journal asking questions. From this one problem, which is certainly in no way as rich as the Jasper problems, the teacher engaged the children in investigating multiplication, its properties, area, and volume.

I share this scenario for several reasons. First, it shows an example of how a constructivist approach can be used with young children. Second, the teacher used no fancy, expensive technology but was able to capitalize on learners' initial conceptions and stretch them, letting learners put forth their own ideas and argue them within their learning community. Third, it suggests an avenue for assessment strategies, an issue that both Cunningham (chapter 3) and Jonassen (chapter 12) address. In a constructivist model it makes more sense (to me) to document learning, rather than to assess it. Perhaps this is just a matter of semantics, but I think not. Just as physicists, when they moved away from objectivism, began to study patterns of movements, shapes, and interactions, we need to do the same. Portfolios of students' writing, mathematics problem solving, or recordings of science investigations can be kept, as well as individual journals and clinical interviews. Patterns of growth can be recorded using a developmental structural analysis. If needed, triangulation measures, ethnographic case studies, and interrater reliability measures can be used to document classroom learning and classroom interactions. Post hoc assessment measures which are conducted out of meaningful learning contexts test only the testers' question, and hence how learners take tests, rather than real learning.

EMPOWERING TEACHERS

I have seen well-designed materials and instructional environments such as LOGO, the *Geometric Supposer*, as well as many of the others mentioned by Perkins (chapter 4), totally misused by teachers who meant well but who held strongly to objectivist and transmission beliefs and thus interpreted the material's use through their model. I've also seen the reverse, like the teacher described previously who taught a very stimulating and enriched unit with simple materials. The key is the teacher.

In 1989, with federal funds, the Center for Constructivist Teaching/Teacher Preparation Project was founded. This is a 2-year 45-credit graduate program connected to five partnership schools. Technology and design issues are woven throughout the program (Fosnot, 1992). To help them understand constructivism, prospective teachers become learners in an institute which is team taught by Liberal Arts and Science and Education faculty using a constructivist pedagogy. In subsequent reflection on their learning, they are asked to look at the strategies that facilitated learning. Every attempt is made to contradict old notions like "teaching is telling."

CONCLUSION

Understanding constructivism requires a structural shift in our world view. As we attempt to understand, we are, ourselves, constructing. The building begins with our initial assimilatory structures which we use to modify, interpret, and transform that which we read, hear about, and discuss. With a child development background, my assimilatory structure is heavily Piagetian. Others approach the building from a behaviorist, objectivist perspective. Through discourse, argument, and debate we will negotiate meaning—differentiating constructivism from other models—and construct new models of pedagogy together.

REFERENCES

Calkins, L. (1986). *The art of teaching writing*. Portsmouth, NH: Heinemann Press.

Capra, F. (1982). *The turning point*. New York: Simon & Schuster.

Chall, J. (1983). *Stages of reading development*. New York: McGraw-Hill.

Fosnot, C. T. (1988). *The dance of education*. Paper presented at the annual conference of the Association for Educational Communications and Technology, New Orleans, LA.

Fosnot, C. T. (1990). *The development of an understanding of probability.* Paper presented at the 20th anniversary symposium of the Jean Piaget Society, Philadelphia, PA.

Fosnot, C. T. (1992). *Center for Constructivist Teaching/Teacher Preparation Project.* Paper presented at the Association for Teacher Educators' Annual Conference in Orlando, FL.

Fosnot, C. T., Forman, G., Edwards, C. P., & Goldhaber, J. (1988). The development of an understanding of balance and the effect of training via stop-action video. *Journal of Applied Developmental Psychology, 9*(1), 1-33.

Graves, D. (1983). *Writing: Teachers and children at work.* Portsmouth, NH: Heinemann Press.

Henderson, E. H. (1985). *Teaching spelling.* Boston: Houghton-Mifflin.

Kamii, C. (1987). *Young children reinvent arithmetic.* New York: Teachers College Press.

Karmiloff-Smith, A., & Inhelder, B. (1974). If you want to get ahead, get a theory. *Cognition, 3,* 195-222.

Labinowicz, E. (1985). *Learning from children.* Menlo Park, CA: Addison-Wesley.

Piaget, J. (1970). *Structuralism.* New York: Basic Books.

Piaget, J. (1977). *The development of thought: Equilibration of cognitive structures.* New York: Viking Press.

Schifter, D., & Fosnot, C. T. (1992). *Reconstructing mathematics education: Stories of teachers meeting the challenge of reform.* New York: Teachers College Press.

Streefland, L. (1991). *Fractions in realistic mathematics education: A paradigm of developmental research.* Dordrecht: Kluwer Academic Publishers.

17

The Assumptions of Constructivism and Instructional Design

William Winn
University of Washington

The idea that knowledge is constructed is not new. The dynamic nature of learning and the mediation of new knowledge by old are now generally accepted (Gagné, 1985; Gagné & Glaser, 1987). Yet the chapters by the "constructivists" (1 through 6) and the replies to them by instructional designers (chapters 7 & 8), suggest that there is something new afoot that promises to generate debate and perhaps even to change the way we go about making instructional decisions. Why this debate should occur now is not serendipitous. Our ability to provide cognitive accounts of skill and knowledge acquisition have led instructional designers to develop cognitive theories of instruction and instructional design (Bonner, 1988; Di-Vesta & Rieber, 1987; Tennyson & Rasch, 1988). However, it seems that instructional designers have been reluctant to abandon their traditional assumptions, and particularly the procedures of instructional design, to accommodate the new ideas about learning. The evident autonomy of learners in knowledge construction makes it difficult (Winn, 1989, 1990) if not impossible (Streibel, 1989) to predict how they will learn or to plan instructional activities. A real accommodation of instructional design to cognitive theory therefore requires a change in the assumptions about how people learn and about how instructional decisions are made.

Chapters 1 through 6 describe projects that are based on a different set of assumptions than those underlying traditional instructional design. For that reason they deserve our careful attention. The purpose of this chapter is to talk about three of these assumptions and to point out how they could lead to a reconceptualization of some aspects of instructional design so as to make it more responsive to constructivist accounts of learning.

AN EMPHASIS ON LEARNING RATHER THAN ON PERFORMANCE AND INSTRUCTION

The behavioral roots of instructional design have led to the assumptions that if you know enough about your students and what it is they have to learn, you can select strategies and build instructional models that bring about predictable changes in students' knowledge and skill (Gagné & Dick, 1983; Reigeluth, 1983); and that the only way you can tell if you have succeeded in this is by observing student performance (Dick & Carey, 1985; Gagné, Briggs, & Wager, 1988).

This emphasis on instruction and performance has served us well for teaching basic knowledge and skill in relatively structured knowledge domains. However, as Spiro, Feltovich, Jacobson and Coulson (chapter 5) pointed out, a great deal of what is taught requires the mastery of advanced knowledge in ill-structured domains. Here, the complexity of what has to be learned precludes the prediction of student behavior and makes it difficult to determine, a priori, what will be judged acceptable performance. It also requires a different conception of instructional strategy.

Traditionally, goals and objectives are set by curriculum developers and instructional designers. Instructional strategies are selected by the designer that are expected to teach the objectives to the student. Both content and strategy are therefore imposed on the student from the outside. Under constructivism, however, students select or develop their own learning strategies, and often their own goals and objectives. Rather than prescribing instructional strategies for the student, the designer now uses a different kind of strategy that guides or perhaps coaches the student as the need arises, but does not impose a particular way to learn. The result is that instruction and performance are de-emphasized by constructivists. The student is given much of the responsibility for deciding what to learn and how to learn it. The function of the teacher or instructional system is to support what the student decides to do.

The emphasis on learning that this approach promotes capitalizes on students' extensive and largely ignored ability to create interpretations for themselves (Cunningham, chapter 3), to actively grapple with things until they make sense (Perkins, chapter 4). Also, it requires designers to reason from their knowledge of how people think and learn rather than mechanically to apply procedures laid out in an instructional design model. I have argued elsewhere (Winn, 1989) that reasoning thus from basic learning theory can make it easier for designers to deal with problems that occur when the prescriptions of instructional theory do not work.

A DIFFERENT ROLE FOR TECHNOLOGY

Instruction, once designed, has to be delivered. The roots of instructional design in Educational Technology have meant that instruction is often designed with a view to delivery via some technology (claims and admonitions to the contrary! See AECT [1977]; Clark [1983, 1985]). Also, the task-oriented nature of instructional design has meant that it is always directed towards some specific content. It is obvious that this is not the way constructivists operate. Instruction is not designed in specific content areas, and computer programs are not written to teach. Hypertext systems of the kind described by Spiro et al. (chapter 5) have been used in domains as diverse as literary criticism, cardio-vascular medicine (Spiro, Coulson, Feltovich, & Anderson, 1988), and military strategy. The Cognition and Technology Group at Vanderbilt University (chapter 6) have produced the Jasper videodiscs that tell stories in which are embedded rich and complex mathematics problems inviting creative and varied solutions. Students are not taught algorithms for solving specific problems. The same research group (Bransford, Sherwood, Hasselbring, Kinzer, & Williams, 1990) describes similar projects in social studies, science and a variety of areas in the humanities.

The distinction between the use of technology for teaching content and its use to promote learning has been made very clearly by Zucchermaglia (1991). She distinguishes between "full" and "empty" technologies. The former are "full" because they contain information to be transferred to the student. They are exemplified by computer-assisted instruction and intelligent tutoring systems. The latter are "shells" that can accept any content designed to allow students to explore and to construct meaning for themselves. They function not as instructional systems, but as tools (see Olson, 1985; Salomon, 1988) that students use to develop cognitive skills. Perkins' (chapter 4) "Information banks, symbol pads, construction kits, and phenomenaria" are examples of such tools.

DOING DESIGN DIFFERENTLY

With little emphasis on instruction and performance, and with delivery systems that do not deliver content, what is there left for the designer to design? I believe there are two roles which the designer still needs to play. The first is to continue to design instruction in basic knowledge of well-structured domains. I am not yet convinced that all knowledge can be constructed by students. The student has to have some knowledge from which to start construction. And that knowledge needs to be explicitly taught. Constructivists may well disagree with this. However, it seems that the systems we have looked at deal with complex, ill-structured, advanced knowledge. It remains to be seen just how much of what is taught in public education (rather than in training) falls into this category.

Second, while instructional design by constructivists may seem to be a contradiction in terms, there is still a lot of designing to do. The "shells" have to be designed. The work of the Cognition and Technology Group (chapter 6) required the design of the videodiscs and programs that provide access to them. This activity might more properly be construed as "message design" (Fleming & Levie, 1978; Fleming, in press). It suggests that more attention needs to be given to the message itself than to the results of students interacting with it.

Then there is the matter of imbuing the "shells" with the ability to support students in their construction of meaning. This means that the selection of strategies, and even of content, is now shifted to the moment a student learns and is not decided ahead of time by a designer. I have suggested elsewhere (Winn, 1987) that this might be the province of highly "intelligent" systems, which would be so adaptive as to develop relevant strategies "on the fly." Within the constructivist model, however, this becomes the province of the student rather than the designer or the system. Again, we must acknowledge the ability of students to make sensible decisions about their own learning. The ability of students to do this, of course, will vary. The teacher or other delivery system must therefore be flexible enough to provide varying amounts of guidance to students as the need arises.

The effect of shifting instructional decisions to the time of delivery is to re-integrate the design of instruction with its implementation. This is consistent with positions that claim that thinking cannot be separated from doing (Nunan, 1983; Schon, 1983). It is also a reasonable reaction against the assumptions of traditional instructional design that the effects of instructional prescriptions are predictable, and that Education is a deterministic (or probabilistic [Reigeluth, 1983]) enterprise.

CONSTRUCTIVISM AND INSTRUCTIONAL DESIGN

It would be nice to write a concluding statement about constructivism and instructional design. However, it is premature for conclusions. To begin with, constructivism, in its present guise, remains to be defined. Chapters 1 through 6 merely describe activities that have in common a belief in and a reliance on the ability of students to learn a great deal on their own. Second, as Merrill (chapter 8) points out, instructional design, as ID_2, has made significant adaptations to developments in cognitive theory.

The issue raised here is whether these adaptations are enough to allow the application of the traditional procedures and assumptions of instructional design to more advanced and complex levels of learning. Personally, I do not think so. There is a point where the complexity of learning makes prediction of performance and prescription of instruction impossible. While not providing a clear definition of constructivism, the chapters have nonetheless given us an idea of where that point is.

REFERENCES

Association for Educational Communication and Technology (1977). *Educational Technology: Definition and glossary of terms.* Washington, DC: Association for Educational Communication and Technology.

Bonner, J. Implications of cognitive theory for instructional design: Revisited. (1988). *Educational Communication and Technology Journal, 36,* 3-14.

Bransford, J. D., Sherwood, R. D., Hasselbring, T. S., Kinzer, C. K., & Williams, S. M. (1990). Anchored instruction: Why we need it and how technology can help. In D. Nix & R. Spiro (Eds.), *Cognition, education and multimedia.* Hillsdale, NJ: Lawrence Erlbaum Associates, 115-141.

Clark, R. E. (1983). Reconsidering research on learning from media. *Review of Educational Research, 53,* 445-460.

Clark, R. E. (1985). Confounding in educational computing research. *Journal of Educational Computing Research, 1,* 137-148.

Dick, W., & Carey, L. (1985). *The systematic design of instruction.* 2nd ed. Glenview, IL: Scott Foresman.

DiVesta, F. J., & Rieber, L. P. (1987). Characteristics of cognitive instructional design: The next generation. *Educational Communication and Technology Journal, 35,* 213-230.

Fleming, M. L. (Ed.) (in press). *Instructional message design.* Hillsdale, NJ: Educational Technology Publications.

Fleming, M. L., & Levie, W. H. (1978). *Instructional message design: Principles from the behavioral sciences.* Hillsdale, NJ: Educational Technology Publications.

Gagné, E. D. (1985). *The cognitive psychology of school learning.* Boston: Little Brown.

Gagné, R. M., Briggs, L., & Wager, W. (1988). *Principles of instructional design* (third edition). New York: Holt, Rinehart & Winston.

Gagné, R. M., & Dick, W. (1983). Instructional psychology. *Annual Review of Psychology, 34,* 261-295.

Gagné, R. M., & Glaser, R. (1987). Foundations in learning research. In R. M. Gagné (Ed.), *Instructional Technology: Foundations.* Hillsdale, NJ: Lawrence Erlbaum Associates.

Nunan, T. (1983). *Countering educational design.* New York: Nichols Publishing Company.

Olson, D. (1985). Computers as tools for the intellect *Educational Researcher, 14* (5), 5-8.

Reigeluth, C. M. (1983). Instructional design: What is it and why is it? In C. M. Reigeluth (Ed.), *Instructional-design theories and models*. Hillsdale, NJ: Lawrence Erlbaum Associates.

Salomon, G. (1988). Artificial intelligence in reverse: Computer tools that turn cognitive. *Journal of Educational Computing Research, 4,* 123-140.

Schon, D. A. (1983). *The reflective practitioner*. New York: Basic Books.

Spiro, R. J., Coulson, R. L., Feltovich, P. L., & Anderson, D. K. (1988). Cognitive flexibility theory: Advanced knowledge acquisition in ill-structured domains. In V. Patel (Ed.), *Tenth annual conference of the Cognitive Science Society* (pp. 375-383). Hillsdale, NJ: Lawrence Erlbaum Associates.

Streibel, M. J. (1989, February). *Instructional plans and situated learning: The challenge of Suchman's theory of situated action for instructional designers and instructional systems.* Paper presented at the annual meeting of the Association for Educational Communication and Technology, Dallas, Texas.

Tennyson, R. D., & Rasch, M. (1988). Linking cognitive learning theory to instructional prescriptions. *Instructional Science, 17,* 369-385.

Winn, W. D. (1987). Instructional design and intelligent systems: Shifts in the designer's decision-making role. *Instructional Science, 16,* 59-77.

Winn, W. D. (1989). Towards a rationale and theoretical basis for educational technology. *Educational Technology Research & Development, 37,* 35-46.

Winn, W. D. (1990). Some implications of cognitive theory for instructional design. *Instructional Science, 19,* 53-69.

Zucchermaglia, C. (1991, May). *Toward a cognitive ergonomics of educational technology.* Paper presented at the NATO Advanced Research Workshop on The Design of Constructivist Learning Environments. Leuven, Belgium.

18

Constructive Criticisms

Brockenbrough S. Allen
San Diego State University

My purpose in this chapter is to broadly examine the ideas in this book against the general background of change that has overtaken instructional development during the last decade. After a year of reflection, I have come to the conclusion that I was basically a constructivist in my earlier experience as an educator and that I am returning from a long trip through what I shall refer to in this essay as "classical instructional design."

I don't regret my journey through classical methods and theories. Much of what I have learned along the way will still be useful. We are in transition; the conversations in this book are just the beginning of an inquiry. It will take a long time to test the assumptions and proposals laid out in these pages and many years to develop robust methods. I still have doubts, but it is good to be home.

INSTRUCTIONAL INTENTIONS

Comments in this book by Merrill (chapter 8), Reigeluth (chapter 13), and Dick (chapter 7) express concern that constructivism will lead to a failure to define what will be taught and a failure to measure what has been learned. While acknowledging the importance of individual differences in prior knowledge and experience, these defenders of classical instructional design (and derivatives such as ID_2 and elaboration theory) argue that some prespecification of learning outcomes and of knowledge is required for application of systematic approaches to instructional design (see especially Dick, chapter 7).

Most of the constructivists in this book take positions that are not inconsistent with the view that *instruction* implies:

1. *intentions* to promote development of certain capacities and skills in learners,
2. *assessment* of some type of outcomes or results and,
3. *methods* which are believed to increase the probability that the intentions will be fulfilled.

For example, an explicit but general goal in most constructivist proposals is to promote flexibility in understanding—the ability to adopt multiple perspectives of a domain and to use this ability to negotiate with others about alternative interpretations. Not one of the classicists expresses frank disagreement with this goal, but it is not always clear how they view its importance relative to other instructional goals such as meeting "the pragmatic requirements in a given training situation" (Reigeluth, chapter 13); ensuring that children and adults "earn a living and function in society" (Merrill, chapter, 8); or promoting the "mastery of pre-determined skills" (Dick, chapter 7).

However, as Duffy and Bednar (chapter 11) note, Merrill has been emphatic in other writings: that developers of most instruction, especially automated instruction, "explicitly [desire] that the learner adopt the meaning intended by the developer, and not reach a separate and personal interpretation of that meaning." Many constructivists would argue that this is a serious, though unintentional, indictment of classical approaches to design.

The assertive constructivists[1] frequently express opposition to *prespecification* of learning outcomes, and they explicitly argue for negotiable learning outcomes. A central concern in their critique of classical instructional design is that its formal descriptions of outcomes tend to emphasize execution of predetermined responses and action sequences. They emphasize instead, a capacity to engage in *construction* of purposeful actions or "plans" (Suchman, 1987) in response to a variety of situations (Duffy & Jonassen, chapter 1; Spiro et al., chapter 5). Similar criticisms have long been part of debates about instruction. Opponents of instructional objectives in particular, and of classical design in general, have often argued that indexing measures of achievement to performance-oriented objectives promotes development of narrow and inflexible "skill sets" which are not easily transferred to new situations.

Merrill has argued that "most instruction, particularly most uses of automated instruction, concerns transferring, as effectively and efficiently as possible, previously determined interpretations" (cited in Duffy & Bednar, chapter 11). This is probably true, but it may also partly explain why, as Dick (chapter 7) notes, classical design has played such a paltry role in shaping the American public school system. It also helps explain why, for reasons well described by Spiro et al. (chapter 5), classical design has had relatively little impact on education in the professions, and why it is resisted in the arts and humanities. Classical design is still workable in many situations, but it may have a declining range of utility in a future where flexible thinking and openness to multiple interpretations will be perceived, more than ever, as critical faculties.

Like Dick (chapter 7), I was surprised by a dearth in the "ID" literature of formal definitions for *instruction*. My dictionary of etymology (Onions, 1966) was more illuminating. It traces the verb *to instruct* to Latin for *instruere*: to set up, furnish, fit out, teach. However, reading more closely, I found what I thought was an ancient and useful metaphor: the root *struere* means to pile up, to build—while the prefix can apparently be taken to signify *inside*, thus to *build within*. To remember this meaning would be to remember that, ultimately, instruction cannot occur unless it occurs inside people's heads and that no amount of external activity or material can substitute for the existential fact that knowledge must be (re)created by each individual.

INTEGRATION OF CONSTRUCTIVIST AND OBJECTIVIST APPROACHES

Can objectivist and constructivist methods be reconciled or integrated? I believe that they can, to some extent. Let me illustrate briefly with a case study from personal experience.

As a teacher, I experimented with adoption of techniques from the open classroom movement, transplanted from England. I studied Piaget and Montessori, and as a graduate student I developed science curriculum materials in both the BIG and WIG traditions described by Perkins (chapter 4). But like many classrooms, mine was outrageously disrespectful of ideological camps—guided by pragmatism and serendipity. My pedagogy was eclectic (I prefer the term *ecological*) because my allegiance was not to educational methods per se but to a learning community whose population just happened to be (mostly) children. Let me illustrate this approach with a brief case study that describes how constructivist learning can be supported by mastery-oriented instruction and coaching.

From Behaviorist Beginnings to Negotiable Solutions

One year in the early 1970s, my fifth-grade students and I developed a micro-economy that seems similar to the one cited by Duffy and Jonassen in chapter 1. I initiated opportunities for basic experience with money by way of a token reinforcement regime (Sulzer-Azaroff & Mayer, 1977): Students could earn "razzels" (or whatever name we agreed to adopt for that year) by reading books, by completing a quota of math assignments, or by simply working quietly during study sessions. They could spend razzels on relatively scarce privileges or resources, such as visiting another class, going to the library, having lunch with the teacher, or buying the right to be team captain during PE. I used behaviorist methods, but I also was conscientious in working with the students to shift the focus of reinforcement from *extrinsic* to *intrinsic*. In the early phases, students *earned* money for silent reading. Eventually, after reading became a preferred activity, it was shifted to status as *purchasable* privilege—an application of the principle that contingent access to preferred activities can be used to reinforce less-preferred activities (Premack, 1959).

Eventually this quasi-feudal regime (with me as a sort of lord of the manor) developed into a complex, vibrant, and *real* economy driven mostly by activities during recess, after school, and during brief periods of designated class time. As problems arose, I advised students and they conducted research on how to borrow possible solutions from the "real world." Loss and theft of razzels led to a kind of bank box where students could deposit their money. From the inconvenience of cash withdrawals grew a checking system. From the desire to exchange goods and services with students in another micro-economy came bi-weekly auctions in which one currency could be bought with the other. And so arose a fairly wide range of social, economic, and even ethical phenomena: stores, advertising, weekly auctions of "junk" from home; taxes and bankruptcy; the rise and fall of syndicates and partnerships; systems for dealing with embezzlement, counterfeiting, and black markets. (We had to engrave the tokens to discourage counterfeiting.)

This was primarily a problem-oriented social enterprise in which the perception of the students was that the outcome of the enterprise really *did* matter and that the outcome was dependent on their developing the knowledge and skill to solve problems at hand. There were possibilities of "real" failure (not having enough money to buy supplies), even catastrophic failure (losing a business), and there were possibilities for real triumph. The enterprise became an enormous dynamo of skill development for most of the children involved; the level of passion often ran very high. There was sustained effort and real sacrifice. In my experience, many children in our culture only experience this type of commitment to learning in the context of sports and video games.

One of my goals in managing the mini-economy was to provide opportunities for students to practice arithmetical operations in the context of realistic problems. However, I felt I could not safely assume that adequate practice would occur without formal regimes for tutoring and coaching. I adopted a technique for training students based on arithmetical "movements per minute" to track the development of speed and accuracy in arithmetic facts and the "debugging" and "compiling" of various algorithms.

We charted the number of discrete operations each student could correctly perform in one minute daily using semi-log graphs (to emphasize progress during the early phase of the students' learning curve). While students worked at their own pace in individualized math workbooks to prepare for the next day's test, I spent my time scoring the daily "mpm" results and tutoring students with individual problems. Periodically I went over the graphs (kept in a private folder with daily test items) with individual students, and we reviewed their past performance and goals for improvement.

I think the mini-economy was meaningful to students not so much because of a correspondence with the larger (grown-up) world, or from a promised advancement of skills, or even from extrinsic rewards. The ground of authenticity lay in a coherent environment that presented a range of opportunities and challenges in which members of a community could assume different roles and learn through interaction and negotiation about how others perform *their* roles.

One way in which this type of collaboration (and competition) affords opportunities for learning is that children become aware that others are learning something *different* and that the social enterprise *demands* that they understand that other perspectives exist. Contrast this with individualized project-based assignments in which students each work separately on different projects (collections, art, science experiments); the need to understand what others know is hardly compelling.

Ensuring Mastery

Reigeluth (chapter 13) points out that collaborative learning as described by Cunningham does not ensure that everyone will achieve the same level or type of mastery because the unit of analysis for assessment is the group rather than the individual. Mastery-oriented regimes, which are usually designed to ensure convergence in performance, rely on prespecified samples of the knowledge domain developed by the designer. Such sampling may balance broad summaries with in-depth elaborations, but the trade-off between depth and breadth can never be avoided in learning; mastery regimes merely ensure that it will be fixed by designers. Since the regime controls encounters with the domain, the children's experience of learning based on situational necessity (requirements of the social enterprise) is restricted.

These historic limitations of classical design have been partly addressed by learner control regimes, personalized systems of instruction (Keller, 1968), and other strategies for individualizing learning. Often the undesirable side-effect of such techniques is to teach that knowledge of a domain is fundamentally asocial rather than an emergent property of communities in which no single individual possesses comprehensive understanding. "The practices of contemporary schooling deny students the chance to engage the relevant domain culture, because the culture is not in evidence" (Brown, Collins, & Duguid, 1989, p. 34). Thus, it is not surprising that many Americans are apathetic towards lifelong participation in learning communities.

The token economy illustrates one way to build constructivist environments. The reinforcement regime established a basic level of meaning for money, but it was only an initiator for much more complex understandings determined by negotiation and experimentation and through formal rules and algorithms. Understanding evolved from simple to complex as the number of variables in the economy increased. Rieber (1991) has described a somewhat different approach for using "variable stepping" to adjust the complexity of computer-based microworlds to learner capabilities.

Although the students performed thousands of arithmetic operations in the context of natural interactions of the economic community, the system supported them through systematic drills, individual assessment, and remediation. Some constructivists might consider the "mpm" rehearsals to be another example of behaviorist zeal. I prefer to view them as exercises in automaticity (Shiffrin & Dumais, 1981) which freed attention for more complex and contextualized activity.

Classroom enterprises such as I have described are complex and require teacher-manager-coaches who can be bold, take risks, and above all commit themselves to use immediate context for the advancement of larger educational goals. They are, in other words, highly dependent on the personal characteristics of the teacher and probably difficult to replicate without the support of systems such as the Jasper series (Cognition and Technology Group, chapter 6).

Without appropriate expertise, constructivist enterprises tend to degrade into activity that does not promote generalizable or transferable skills. Degraded constructivist environments can trap learners in menial "apprenticeships" that only serve short-term ends. Whole classes can be condemned to poorly planned experiments that exist primarily to fulfill the creative needs of the teacher. On the other hand, even carefully designed "constructivist" learning environments can revert to objectivism when teaching styles are inappropriate—as when students are systematically led through criterion-based instruction on *LOGO* (Papert, 1980) or when impatient chemistry teachers prematurely prompt students for "correct" answers during hypothesis formation (Savenye & Strand, 1989).

Perkins' (chapter 4) five facets of learning environments are relevant here. Computer-based information banks, symbol pads, construction kits, phenomenaria, and task managers could have greatly increased the effectiveness of the enterprise by reducing tedious and repetitive chores and by affording opportunities for more complex planning, data gathering, experimentation, and documentation. What is more important, such "open tools" (Zucchermaglia, 1991) would have made it easier to introduce formal systems for representing ideas (rules, algorithms, taxonomies, etc.) into the streams of constructive classroom activity. Duffy and Bednar (chapter 11) note that a shift from prespecified instruction to open tools may be one way to provide more resources for the kind of complex enterprise I have described.

Many teacher-managers of constructivist learning environments would also acknowledge the usefulness of learning systems (such as my "mpm" approach) that would help students to master specific skills. Large-scale, "turnkey" instructional systems that require schools to buy into an entire program of predetermined learning sequences are often too inflexible and too difficult adapt to such opportunities. Small, flexible transaction shells (Li & Merrill, 1991) which might be thought of as instructional analogs to Zucchermaglia's, 1991) open tools could be used to quickly author special purpose lessons.

IS "DE CONTEXT" EVERYTHING?

The literature on context-dependent effects in areas such as perception, object classification, language processing is immense. Constructivists and classicists alike acknowledge "context" as an important design variable. They agree that decontextualizing knowledge (teaching abstractions in isolation), especially during early engagement with a domain is likely to be ineffective. However, the classicists express two reservations in particularly urgent terms.

The first is that the development and maintenance of context is often expensive, impractical, and inefficient. The second is that dogmatic insistence on learning in context will prevent learners from applying their knowledge to new settings.

Setting aside the issue of whether meaning is possible without context (it isn't), consider how the "top-down" (Jonassen & Hannum, 1991) methods of classical instructional development work to strip context from content. In classical development regimes, knowledge of a domain is "elicited" from experts and other sources; this information then serves as the basis of a subject matter analysis. Although some sophisticated "knowledge engineering" techniques attempt to capture "implicit knowledge," the most widely used approach is to work at a fairly high level of abstraction in which the "sources" use expert language to describe and explain the domain. (Descriptions are often simplified for the benefit of designers.)

Later, often much later, the corpus of generalities (frequently simplified) drives the development (or selection) of instructional devices such as exemplars, problems, cases, epitomes, and analogies. These are then rationalized to correspond to the generalities and ordered by various prescriptions. Context is often "wrapped" around the devices only as lesson specifications are finalized, often in consultation with writers, artists, and production specialists who contribute their own pragmatic and aesthetic knowledge.

If the development team is alert to the likelihood of "top-down bias" (i.e., selection of a set of examples that conforms to a particular generality), they may leaven the results of this process by backtracking and exploring with experts the possibility of incorporating additional, more authentic elements from case studies and scenarios. However, in my experience this is often a neglected option and one that is difficult to exercise as development moves downstream toward design freeze, prototype construction, and product development.

I present this description not as an idealized example or a worst-case scenario, but to call attention to biases of classical design in actual practice. I have seen, taught, and supervised hundreds of projects (both commercial and academic) based on this approach, and I think that its chief drawback is that it depends on the reconstitution of detailed exemplars from high-level abstractions. It often results in oversimplified instruction that is either lean to the point of near impoverishment or coated with irrelevant ornamentation (and sometimes both).

Many important instructional problems (such as described by Spiro et al., chapter 5) are simply ignored by classically trained designers because the difficulty of representing "implicit" and "tacit" knowledge as well-structured and consistent propositions is just too great. Support for learning in such ill-structured domains may still be developed through documentation of contexts and case studies (by video or audio, for example).

Developers and managers of technology-based learning systems use "top-down" design methods in part because they are well adapted to available tools. The computers of the 1970s and 1980s made it relatively easy to manipulate propositions because propositions are fundamentally compatible with *digital* storage. Older technologies which store information in analog form (video, audio, photos, diagrams, pictures) were in comparison more time-consuming, and less forgiving of errors. Managers therefore placed great emphasis on getting content "right" in its abstract form before moving to more cumbersome representational systems.

The wave of innovations in computer-based control of *analog* representations (diagrams, pictures, kinesthetic models, etc.) is beginning to change the balance so that "bottom-up" approaches to design are more practical. While it is true that most computing technology is ultimately digital, the net effect of recent advances is to make it possible to experience a wide variety of non-propositional representations at the user level, from scientific visualization to multimedia and virtual reality (Allen, 1991). In the future, for example, low-cost video technology and "desk-top" editing will make it easier to capture, store, and manipulate representations of authentic contexts, cases, and problems *in situ* and to use them to check "top-down" bias (see, for example, Hoenbein, Chen, & Brescia, in press). Rapid prototyping (Tripp & Bichelmeyer, 1990)—in which analysis, design, and development are coextensive activities—will become more feasible as an alternative to complete pre-specification of subject matter content.

WHY ISN'T REALITY WHAT IT USED TO BE?

It is not completely clear whether all the classicists would consider themselves "objectivists" if it meant they must subscribe to a kind of Nicene creed:

> The purpose of the mind is to "mirror"...reality and its structure through thought processes that are analyzable and decomposable. The meaning that is produced by these thought processes is external to the understander and is determined by the structure of the real world. Learning therefore consists of assimilating that objective reality (Jonassen, chapter 12).

In any case, I suspect that many readers would be comfortable with some substitutions:

> The ~~purpose~~ **function** of the mind is to "~~mirror~~" "**describe**"...reality and its structure through thought processes that are **in certain respects** analyzable and decomposable. The meaning that is ~~produced~~ **represented in** these thought processes is ~~external to~~ **determined mostly by the physiology, language, and culture of** the understander ~~and is determined by the structure of the real world~~. **Much** learning therefore consists of ~~assimilating that objective~~ **coming to understand consensually validated descriptions** of reality.

If you agree with the above statement, it doesn't *necessarily* mean that you agree with the assertive constructivists. Perhaps you have come to see that knowledge is socially constructed but still agree with Merrill (chapter 8) that it is possible to use propositional logic and a universal syntax to "analyze the organization and elaborations of knowledge outside the mind." Perhaps you also agree that it is possible (in principle at least) to build a "knowledge base that is a representation of all of the knowledge and skills to be taught" in a given domain.

Does it seem to you as it does to Reigeluth (chapter 13) that "the purpose of learning is to increase the extent to which we share the more plausible realities"? If so, how do you reconcile this view with that of the Cognition and Technology Group (chapter 6) that one of the "major goals in instruction is to encourage students to develop socially acceptable systems for exploring their ideas and *differences* in opinion" (italics added)?

Constructivism and Realism

Although several authors in this book have offered brief accounts of constructivist epistemology, I will examine the arguments of two important constructivist thinkers—George Lakoff (1987) and Mark Johnson (1987)—because I think it is possible to clarify certain misconceptions that have arisen about *shared reality*. There are many constructivist views on this issue, but Lakoff and Johnson have explored it in ways that may be very useful in future efforts to develop instruction systematically.

First, Lakoff and Johnson do not argue that there is *no* shared understanding of reality. Rather, they argue that human physiology and bodily experience results in a basic level of perception and bodily imagery that is experienced by billions of people.

Second, they do not argue in favor of abandoning propositional systems of knowledge representation, only that such systems are incomplete unless they acknowledge that the *meaning* of all propositions is based on forms of human experience.

Third, they do not deny the importance or utility of what Bernstein (1975) calls "meta-languages of control and innovation" but they insist that such languages are ultimately based on metaphorical and metonymic extension of bodily meaning.

Reality: It's Basic

As do our fellow mammals, we depend on active experimentation and exploration for the development of our internal representations of the world. "Constructivism" isn't merely or only a tactic for advanced learning. It is a powerful strategy for on-going "self-organization" of advanced life forms at all stages of their development. This strategy requires a constant adjustment of internal functions to the external world and it is the means of adaptation to circumstances that cannot be exactly anticipated by any prior genetic code.

> A few days after birth, a newborn baby has enough control over his neck muscles to move his head as well as his eyes toward a source of sound. If the sound continues as he does so, his head movement will change the very time-difference between the ears that initiated it. When he as turned far enough to face the sounding object, the difference will have become zero. In this way, he effectively localizes the sound....In effect, he can "calibrate" his own head size. When he has done so, his ability to localize sounds will be much more satisfactory. The same activities will serve to keep his localization accurate in spite of changing head size as he grows older....Perception is always an interaction between a particular object or event and a more general schemata. It can be regarded as a process of generalizing the object or of particularizing the schema depending on one's theoretical inclination. (Neisser, 1976, pp. 64-65)

Here, Neisser anticipates the terms of later debate on realism although it remained for others such as Lakoff to synthesize a comprehensive argument from anthropological and linguistic evidence. The issue according to Lakoff is not whether most humans share similar perceptions of reality at the "basic level" of colors, rabbits, or chairs. On the contrary, he and other "basic-level realists" believe our built-in "tuning" mechanisms ensure that for practical purposes there is not much difference between individuals and cultures where basic perception of objects is concerned.

"Basic-level" categories are characterized by distinctive actions (smelling a flower, bouncing a ball, listening to a barking dog). Basic-level distinctions are "...generally the most useful distinctions to make in the world" (Rosch, & Lloyd, cited in Lakoff, 1987, p. 49). The *basic level* is the level at which things are first named and the level at which names are shortest and most frequently used. According to Brown (cited in Lakoff, p. 32), it is the "natural level" of "kinds": pigs, cats, trees, gold, silver, and water.

One of the hallmarks of constructivist philosophers and psychologists is their assertion that systems for categorization beyond the basic level are "achievements of the imagination." They view "superordinate classes" and "attributes" as products of culture rather than properties of the natural world.

In science and mathematics, these "achievements of imagination" form the basis for systems of interrelated propositions: theories, hypotheses, principals, laws. Such systems derive their power, according to Lakoff, not from conveyance of any ultimate "meaning" but from the ease with which they can be evaluated and tested. Nevertheless, they are widely believed by many scientists and lay people to represent a kind of objective truth and to provide affordances through which the human mind can know the truth.

However, Lakoff cites evidence that basic-level categories are also the foundation for "folk" classification systems and furthermore that basic-level realism led to Linnaeus' choice of the *genus* as the heart of his scientific system for classifying plants. He argues that Linneaus' decision to use the *fruits* of plants as the basis for generic classification decisions was primarily an accommodation of the perceptual capabilities of human beings rather than a reflection of any "natural" order. Thus, according to Lakoff, even highly organized scientific systems are shaped by basic-level perceptions.

Lakoff presents compelling evidence that systems for classifying objects beyond the basic level vary radically by language and culture. This variation results from differences in *syntax* (structure) as well as differences in semantics (content). Design theorists such as Merrill and Reigeluth assume a universal syntax.

As one of many examples of radical variation in syntax, Lakoff describes how the Dyirbal people of Australia group all objects into four fundamental categories. The Dyirbal use a single and perfectly reasonable principle of classification:

> If there is a basic domain of experience associated with *A*, then it is natural for entities in that domain to be in the same category as *A*. For example, fish are in Class I [*Bayi*, human males, animals] since they are animate. [Therefore] fishing implements (fishing spears, fishing lines, etc.) are also in Class I.... (Lakoff, 1987, p. 93)

It is tempting to think that such a system is somehow more primitive or less rational than formal Western systems of classification which are based on logical propositions and set theory. However, the same "domain-of-experience" principle used by the Dyirbal is the basis for a special section at my local supermarket that groups implements of entirely different fabrication and function: plastic utensils, napkins, paper plates, Styrofoam coolers, beer, and "Frisbees." It is not possible to understand this arrangement through any system of "set-theoretic" logic involving superordinate classes and defining attributes. You have to go on a picnic.

We are not talking about a philosopher's tea party here. The assault on objectivist notions of logic, meaning, and reality has brought theories and paradigms crashing down in disciplines ranging from mathematics (Gödel, 1962), to music, literature, and the arts (Cantor, 1988), and now, finally, to education and instructional design. The arguments are powerful and far too extensive to be even summarized here, but in my opinion they are well represented by Hilary Putnam's humbling expression of the human condition.

> The perspective I shall defend has no unambiguous name. It is a late arrival in the history of philosophy, and even today it keeps being confused with other points of view of a quite different sort. I shall refer to it as the *internalist* perspective, because it is characteristic of this view to hold that *what objects does the world consist of?* is a question that it only makes sense to ask within a theory of description....There is no God's Eye view that we can know or usefully imagine; there are only various points of view of actual persons reflecting various interests and purposes that their descriptions and theories subserve. (Putnam, 1981, pp. 49-50)

The internalist perspective does not necessarily imply an indulgence of solipsism, or an unwillingness to adopt or even promote formal, axiomatic systems (including the set-theoretic method that some assertive constructivists denigrate). It simply adds the caveat that no consistent system of propositions can be validated in terms of its own axioms.

Can Humans Agree on What is Real?

If the search for a "God's Eye view" is no longer tenable, does constructivism offer useful accounts of "shared" reality? The answer is a qualified "yes." Consider the following list of ideas (Johnson, 1987, p. 126) without which technical or folk understanding of most phenomena would be difficult and without which scientific understanding would be impossible (some are flagged for later discussion):

container*	balance	compulsion
blockage	counterforce	restraint*
enablement	attraction*	mass-count*
path*	link	center-periphery
cycle	near-far	scale
part-whole	merging	splitting
full-empty	matching	superimposition
iteration	contact	process
surface	object*	collection

What is the ultimate source of knowledge such as this? Scientific investigation? Work in labs and technical training facilities? State curriculum frameworks? Dictionaries and encyclopedias? Sandboxes and playrooms? Explanations from adults?

Johnson argues that the meaning of these *image schemata* must be traced back to our experience of our own bodies. In our earliest moments we begin to develop our understanding of reality from the inside out. Thus, newborn infants are already constructing the image schema Johnson calls *container* as they breathe, take in nourishment, expel wastes, and explore the boundaries of their own bodies. Babies develop a schema for *object* through interactions similar to those described in the earlier quote from Neisser. They develop the *path* schema by crawling and walking, and so on.

Ultimately a child uses words to represent these image schemata and so engages in discourse in which public meaning is possible because the image schemata are "pervasive, well-defined, and full of sufficient internal structure to constrain our understanding and reasoning...They structure our "mode of being-in-the-world or our way of having-a-world" (Johnson, 1987, p. 126).

Johnson's use of the word *schema* differs from the current meaning in cognitive science and is derived from Kant's meaning of schemata as *non-propositional structures of imagination*. Conventional schema theory (e.g.,

Rumelhart, 1977; Shank & Abelson, 1977; Thorndyke, 1984) is based on general knowledge structures which are then instantiated or filled in with the detailed properties of a particular instance. Although he does not deny the existence or importance of general knowledge structures, Johnson argues that *image schemata* are not amenable to propositional representation because they represent experience that is fundamentally *analog* in nature (continuous, not subject to discretization).

Johnson considers the image schemata level of representation as distinct from the *basic* level because it gives *form* to our understanding. However, he argues that both levels are *real* because they are motivated by interactions with our environment.

> The concepts that result from these interactions must have been, and continue to be, tested constantly, instant by instant, by billions of people over our history as a species. They work pretty well or we wouldn't be here to talk about them. Different kinds of organisms might well have developed different levels of organization to insure their survival and flourishing by giving them a hold on reality. But because we are the kind of organisms we are, living in the kinds of environments that shape our being in countless ways, it is *our* basic-level and image-schematic structures that mesh with our experience. (Johnson, 1987, pp. 208-209)

According to Lakoff and Johnson, cultures and languages build on basic-level and image-level understanding through a process of *metaphorical extension.* Metaphors are of course notoriously resistant to cross-cultural understanding and therefore cannot be considered "real" in the sense that they are understood by all humans.

Most readers of this book are familiar with the important role that metaphors play in advanced levels of discourse and thinking. But Johnson helped me understand how profoundly metaphorical extensions of image schemata influence even the simplest uses of language.

Space limitations prevent additional discussion of Johnson's ideas, but they afford an attractive line of inquiry for instructional design theorists. Consider the previous sentence (proposition) in terms of image schemata:

> container restrains growing mass;
> objects attract objects along path.

Lakoff's and Johnson's interest in metaphors goes far beyond simple comparisons such as one finds on the Miller Analogies Test (Psychological Corporation, 1970). Rather, they emphasize *metaphorical extensions* as the primary means by which humans represent individual experience in the form of language. Thus *propositions* that describe emotions frequently use *metaphors* to represent image schemata which in turn convey bodily processes and states. This, in my mind, is a very human way to "convert" analog data to "digital" form. Lakoff argues that the proposition, "He boiled with anger," is not meaningful except as a metaphor for experience (hot fluid in a container). In our culture, *anger* is also thought of as

fire,
heat,
a dangerous animal,
an opponent,
a burden,
insanity. (Lakoff, 1987, pp. 396-406)

Beyond communication of extreme emotions, Lakoff describes many ways in which culturally determined metaphorical extension is the stuff of complex ideas:

seeing is touching,
percepts are entities,
non-visual perceptual space is physical space,
physical appearance is a physical force,
activation is motion,
activity is a container,
more is up,
lack of control is down,
existence is here,
non-existence is location away,
realized is distal,
soon-to-be realized is proximal,
purposes are destinations. (Lakoff, 1987, pp. 396-538)

OF METAPHORS AND MENTAL MODELS: ON THE ROAD TO *ID3* ?

It is not necessary to subscribe to Merrill's (chapter 8) objectivist epistemology to believe that there is some value in the approach he advocates. Members of a linguistic or cultural community *do* share similar models, systems for classification, and so on. Many disciplines employ highly formalized and consistent systems of propositions that describe relations between entities, classes, attributes, functions, and so on. These can *at some useful level* be represented and taught using generalized knowledge structures and instantiation. This is the approach Merrill and his associates have used in their pioneering efforts to improve the cost-effectiveness and utility of computer-aided instructional design (Merrill, Li, & Jones, 1990).

Merrill's approach can be applied in very useful ways *when it is applicable.* My reservations—which also apply to some arguments of the assertive constructivists—can be summed up this way: Be cautious about claims to universality. Designers are usually more interested in understanding what personal construct psychologists (Kelly, 1955) refer to as the "range of convenience" of a theory than in determining its absolute truth.

This said, let me close with a few brief examples of how selected constructivist ideas might illuminate new possibilities for Merrill's work. I claim this privilege because Merrill and his associates have been explicit in promoting ID_2 as a basis for developing instructional theory (Merrill, Li, & Jones, 1990) and because I deeply respect the skill Merrill has shown in the past in adapting instructional theory to advances in the cognitive sciences.

In consideration of the evidence that Lakoff and others have marshaled, Merrill might want to modify some of the assumptions for ID_2. For example:

> We assume that the semantics or content of cognitive structure is unique to each individual, but that the syntax or structure is not....The content of each individual's mental models may be different but ID_2 assumes that ~~the~~ **similarity in** structure ~~is the same~~ **is a function of commonality in linguistic, cultural, and personal experience**. (Modified from Merrill, chapter 8.)

And also:

> A given learned performance ~~results~~ can result from ~~a given~~ one of several organized and elaborated cognitive structures, which we call mental models; several models that are inconsistent in content or formal syntax can be usefully employed by the same learner during the same performance. (Modified from Merrill, chapter 8.)

The insights of constructivists such as Lakoff and Johnson are particularly relevant to the design of learning environments based on computing technologies such as multimedia, hypermedia, and virtual reality. Although these technologies rely on machine architectures that are ultimately digital in nature, it is now clear that the worlds they will present to users will offer profound possibilities for integrating propositional, metaphoric, imaginal, and kinesthetic understanding (Allen, 1991). The fundamental challenge facing educational computing is that since "analogical message material...is highly antithetical; it lends itself to very different and often quite incompatible digital [verbal, logical, propositional] interpretations" (Watzlawick, Beavin, & Jackson, 1967).

Lakoff's ideas may very well offer a better bridge between these two forms of representation than we have had in the past. Like Merrill, Lakoff proposes to explain how we organize our knowledge by means of mental structures which Lakoff calls *idealized cognitive models* (ICMs). However, in contrast to Merrill's approach, categories are merely by-products of ICMs. "Each ICM is a complex, structured whole, a gestalt, which uses four kinds of structuring principles: propositional structure,...image schematic structure,...metaphoric mappings,...[and] metonymic mappings" (Lakoff, 1987, p. 68).

I believe that the over-dependence of classical design (including ID_2) on propositional representation helps to explain why it has never evolved any proven, systematic, or widely adopted methods for designing and using metaphor-rich and imagery-rich instruction. I also believe it helps to explain why attempts to apply classical instructional design to fields such as art, music, and literature have met with such limited success. In my experience, when classical design has succeeded in these domains it has been because the required learning outcomes have been simple and technical (e.g., identifying poems with iambic pentameter) or because designers have "damned the rules"—exercising artistic and intuitive judgments that are beyond classical theory or methods.

POST-SOMETHING

The concerns and claims of constructivist educators are not necessarily new, but they take on additional relevance and urgency when considered in the light of post-industrial realities (Bell, 1976) and post-modernist perspectives (Cantor, 1988). Although the paradigm shifts reflected in post-industrial and post-modernist thinking are both heavily influenced by the advance of global communications and industrialization, they are expressed in different schools of advocacy and criticism and driven, perhaps, by different constituencies. Nevertheless, these two "shifted paradigms" underlie much current discussion about education, especially in this book.

Post-Industrialism

The post-industrial world is one in which the influence of smart machines is radically transforming the nature of work. In post-industrial enclaves, the rigidness of organization and the automaticity of activity associated with older means of production have given way to complex ecologies of intelligent work (Zuboff, 1988). These new communities require that workers collaborate across disciplines, assess the relevance of information for a given purpose, construct plans in response to novel situations, and engage in self-directed learning in furtherance of their own capacities and those of the "enterprise." Post-industrial enclaves depend on active, flexible, self-generating knowledge—mobile and adaptable to rapidly changing requirements.

The idea that knowledge is some*thing* that can be objectively validated and prioritized, transmitted, and acquired—as if it was a commodity apart from individual understanding, experience, and needs—is the folk metaphor of our age. But as replication of information becomes ever more precise and voluminous, it may be useful to retain a special meaning of *knowledge* as an integrated set of understandings that ultimately can only be constructed by and reside in the mind of a *knower*.

In many post-industrial settings, situated-cognition (Brown, Collins, & Duguid, 1989) and problem-oriented understanding are valued over inert knowledge that is merely descriptive and recitative. In part, this is because the planetary corpus of "knowledge" is growing exponentially and the methods for storing and accessing it "outside the head" are advancing rapidly. The biology of our brain, however, is basically the same as it was 30,000 years ago: 1,500 cc of cranial capacity is about all we're going to get in the immediate future. So the most valued kind of thinking in post-industrial organizations is quite different from the white-collar paper factories of the past, which emphasized fragmentation of mental work and which placed more emphasis on remembrance, repetition, and automaticity.

Leaders of post-industrial enclaves like to speak of "empowering" citizens and workers to solve local problems because allocating authority and responsibility to do so decreases the need for the members of a community to communicate with centralized authority, encourages development of expertise at the site where it will be used, and improves organizational responsiveness and efficiency. Thus management expert Peter Drucker (1992) argues that:

> ...everyone in the information-based organization needs constantly to be thinking through what information he or she needs to make a valuable contribution to his or her own job. This may well be the most radical break with the present conventions of work. (p. 347)

"Empowering" employees involves reallocating authority and responsibility for decisions not only about information, but about development of competence. The two are, of course, tightly intertwined: In "industrial" organizations, "top-down" systems for developing employee training and education are based on training needs assessment (Rossett, 1987), which is then used by central planners who in turn pre-specify required training outcomes/content and oversee development of the methods and materials.

The utility of this approach is limited in post-industrial organizations for the same reason that hierarchical, authority-based management schemes are limited: They cannot keep up with rapid change. They also tend to waste resources on inefficient cascades of information between top and lower levels instead of focusing it on the "sharp end" of the organization where services and products are actually developed and marketed. In an era of flatter organizational hierarchies and "distributed" management, human resource development will also become a distributed function.

Under such conditions it is often more convenient to help worker-learners to construct knowledge that is specifically relevant to problems as they occur rather than to anticipate all possible learning needs and to make provisions for instruction or training in advance. This paradigm is the basis for "just-in-time" learning systems that are being adopted by a number of leading corporations and which are making their way into computer systems. The benefits of just-in-time learning are analogous to those of just-in-time inventory control: Investments of "intellectual capital" are committed to learning activities near the time when they will yield a return through productive activity. Knowledge doesn't "depreciate" between the day of construction and day of use. What is learned is integrated with what is done.

A persistent and underlying theme in most debates over national educational and industrial policy is that the United States is failing to make the transition to a post-industrial order. A recent government report (SCANS, 1991) advocated realignment of school practices to prepare workers for post-industrial settings. But it remains to be seen to what extent the rhetoric of "empowerment" will be realized by implemented policy. There is room for caution about calls for education in context. The power elite of the industrial age will undoubtedly resist encroachment on its privileges and authority by any rising tide of knowledgeable workers (Toffler, 1990). One way to do so—by tradition, intent, neglect, naiveté—is to minimize access to generalizable knowledge.

> We can see that the class system has affected the distribution of knowledge. Historically, and now, only a tiny percentage of the population has been socialized in knowledge at the level of the meta-languages of control and innovation, whereas the mass of the population has been socialized into knowledge at the level of context-tied operations. A tiny percentage of the population has been given access to the principles of intellectual change....If orders of meaning are universalistic, then...meanings are less tied to a given context....Where meanings have this characteristic then individuals have access to the grounds of their experience and can change the grounds. Where orders of meaning are particularistic...such meanings are...more context bound, that is, tied to a local relationship and to a local structure. (Bernstein, cited in Zuboff, 1988, p. 444)

Post-Modernism

The post-modern world is populated by hundreds of millions of people who now, with varying allegiance, hold the view that all descriptions of reality are socially constructed—rather than manifestations of absolute truth. Coexisting with this world are the many traditions and philosophies which assert that their description is the one true and objective description. One measure of the pervasiveness of post-modern influence is that many educated and informed adherents of one tradition or another now at least recognize that they have a choice and can adopt one of many competing reality description systems.

Before this century, lack of education and communications minimized awareness of other cultures. Only small fractions of humanity, which had traveled extensively and been subjected to transcultural turmoil, were able to entertain the hypothesis that all descriptions of reality are constructed by and for the people who use them. Increasing acceptance of this hypothesis has lead to cultural confusion and artistic angst:

> We are not in the midst of a great moment in the arts and literature. We are in a period after the fall, a period of fragmentation and reconsideration, perhaps of the beginning of a comprehensive new movement in literature and the arts but it is still too early to tell what the coalescing shape of this new movement will be. On the other hand, we may be in a time of frustration, doubling back, of essentially standing still....Modernism is paradise lost. We cannot return to it as a cultural entity, as a thing for today. (Cantor, 1988, pp. 380-401)

The same can be said of contemporary education. Essentially we live in an era where our most conscientious efforts to evaluate propositions in terms of truth or falsity do not yield answers about *meaning*. The question isn't simply whether Columbus was a heroic discoverer who, in the name of God, initiated unparalleled opportunities for trade and development or whether he was an egocentric leader of the invaders who brought death and slavery to native peoples. The question is also who were the Europeans and who were the Native Americans and how did they represent their knowledge of the world and of each other? Post-modernists would argue that there is no single "correct answer" to this question—only different viewpoints. New doubts about interpretations of the past can be taken on as a burdened search for blame or adopted as a quest for historically and culturally unique insights that might, like some exotic plant in a distant jungle, contain the chemistry that could cure the ills in our thinking and our values.

Thus, the debate over constructivism (and the post-modern crisis which it reflects) is not merely about cognition but about morality. Multiculturalists argue, for instance, that systems which assume (and *teach*) one determinable, consistent, and objective set of standards for representing reality have long been used to justify economic oppression, cultural hegemonism, and ecological exploitation. The issue can be expressed more forcefully this way: Insisting that our view is in fact a "God's Eye view" is not merely a matter of hubris. It is a potentially immoral claim because it can so easily lead to actions against "unbelievers" and "aliens," because it can be used to rationalize our dominion over nature (Capra, 1983), and because it impedes the development of human consciousness (Barrett, 1987) and therefore of spiritual liberation (Torbert, 1972). There is, of course, a conservative view that expresses concern about the dangers of moral relativism (Bellah, Madsen, Sullivan, Swindler, & Tipton, 1986; Bloom, 1987). While moral issues are hardly unrelated to education, they will not be explored here. However, they may underlie the tone of zeal and evangelism that colors some of the commentaries in this book.

I think that America's tradition of accommodating diverse immigrant populations, its looming demographic shifts, its *relative* tolerance for diversity of opinion and belief, its flexible legal and political systems, and its openness to new ideas offer some hope that we can play a constructive role in a world struggling to define new terms of cultural interaction. The potential is particularly great where rapidly developing technologies for information, communication, and learning are concerned.

As we look back over a history in which the meaning of fundamental concepts such as self-determination, liberty, economic justice, spiritual commitment, and conservation have changed radically, how can we not agree with the Cognition and Technology Group (chapter 6) that instruction should help students to understand that "ideas of goodness" are subject to change?

ACKNOWLEDGMENT

Development of this chapter was partially supported by LARC, the National Foreign Language Resource Center at SDSU. I express my appreciation to Barbara E. Allen and Robert P. Hoffman for their assistance in manuscript preparation.

NOTE

1. I include Bednar, Cunningham, Duffy, and Jonassen in this group because of their outspoken criticism of the epistemological foundations of classical design.

REFERENCES

Allen, B. S. (1991). Virtualities. In B. Branyan-Broadbent & R. K. Wood (Eds.), *Educational media and technology yearbook* (Vol. 17). Englewood, CO: Libraries Unlimited.

Barrett, W. (1987). *Death of the soul: From Descartes to the computer.* New York: Doubleday.

Bell, D. (1976). *The coming of post-industrial society: A venture in social forecasting* (rev. ed.). New York: Basic Books.

Bellah, R. N., Madsen, R., Sullivan, W. M., Swindler, A., & Tipton, S. M. (1986). *Habits of the heart.* New York: Harper Row.

Bernstein, B. (1975). *Class, codes, and control: Theoretical studies towards a sociology of language.* New York: Schocken Books.

Bloom, A. (1987). *The closing of the American mind: How higher education has failed democracy and impoverished the souls of today's students.* New York: Simon & Shuster.

Brown, J. S., Collins, A., & Duguid, P. (1989). Situated cognition and the culture of learning. *Educational Researcher, 18*, 32-42.

Cantor, N. (1988). *Twentieth-century culture: Modernism to deconstruction.* New York: Peter Lang.

Capra, F. (1983). *The turning point.* New York: Bantam.

Drucker, P. F. (1992). *Managing for the future.* New York: Dutton.

Gödel, K. (1962). *On formally undecided propositions.* New York: Basic Books.

Hoenbein, P. C., Chen, P., & Brescia, W. (in press). Hypermedia and sociology: A simulation for developing research skills. *Liberal Arts Computing.*

Johnson, M. (1987). *The body in the mind: The bodily basis of meaning, imagination, and reason.* Chicago: University of Chicago Press.

Jonassen, D. H., & Hannum, W. H. (1991). Analysis of task analysis procedures. In G. J. Anglin (Ed.), *Instructional technology: Past, present, and future.* Englewood, CO: Libraries Unlimited.

Keller, F. S. (1968). Good-bye teacher! *Journal of Applied Behavioral Analysis, 1*, 79-84.

Kelly, G. A. (1955). *The psychology of personal constructs: Vol.1: A theory of personality.* New York: W. W. Norton.

Lakoff, G. (1987). *Women, fire, and dangerous things: What categories reveal about the mind.* Chicago: University of Chicago Press.

Li, Z. & Merrill, M. D. (1991). Transaction shells: A new approach to courseware authoring. *Journal of Research on Computing in Education, 23(1), 72-86.*

Merrill, M. D., Li, Z., & Jones, M. K. (1990). The second generation instructional design research program. *Educational Technology, 30*(3), 26-30.

Neisser, U. (1976). *Cognition and reality.* San Francisco: W. H. Freeman.

Onions, C. T. (Ed.). (1966). *The Oxford dictionary of English etymology.* New York: Oxford University Press.

Papert, S. (1980). *Mindstorms: Children, computers, and powerful ideas.* New York: Basic Books.

Premack, D. (1959). Toward empirical behavior laws: 1. Positive reinforcement. *Psychological Review, 66*, 219-233.

Psychological Corporation, The. (1970). *Miller analogies test manual.* New York.

Putnam, H. (1981). *Reason, truth, and history.* New York: Cambridge University Press.

Rieber, L. P. (1991). Computer-based microworlds: A bridge between constructivism and direct instruction (ERIC No. ED 335007). *Proceedings of Selected Research Paper Presentations at the 1991 Annual Convention of the Association for Educational Communications and Technology,* 12, 692-707.

Rossett, A. (1987). *Training needs assessment.* Englewood Cliffs, NJ: Educational Technology Publications.

Rumelhart, D. (1977). *Introduction to human information processing.* New York: Wiley.

Savenye, W. C., & Strand, E. (1989, April). Teaching science using interactive videodisc: Results of the pilot year evaluation of the Texas Learning Technology Group Project (ERIC No. ED308838). *Proceedings of Selected Research*

Papers Presented at the Annual Meeting of the Association for Educational Research.

SCANS. (1991, June). *What work requires of schools: A SCANS report for America 2000.* The Secretary's Commission on Achieving Necessary Skills, US Department of Labor, Washington, DC.

Schank, R., & Abelson, R. (1977). *Scripts, plans, goals, and understanding.* Hillsdale, NJ: Lawrence Erlbaum Associates.

Shiffrin, R. M., & Dumais, S. T. (1981). The development of automatism. In J. R. Anderson (Ed.), *Cognitive skills and their acquisition.* Hillsdale, NJ: Lawrence Erlbaum Associates.

Suchman, L. A. (1987). *Plans and situated actions.* New York: Cambridge University Press.

Sulzer-Azaroff, B., & Mayer, G. R. (1977). *Applying behavioral analysis procedures with children and youth.* New York: Holt, Rinehart & Winston.

Thorndyke, P. W. (1984). Application of schema theory in cognitive research. In J. R. Anderson & S. Kosslyn (Eds.), *Tutorials in learning and memory: Essays in honor of Gordon Bower.* San Francisco: W. H. Freeman.

Toffler, A. (1990). *Powershift: Knowledge, wealth, and violence at the edge of the 21st century.* New York: Bantam.

Torbert, W. R. (1972). *Learning from experience: Toward consciousness.* New York: Columbia University Press.

Tripp, S. D. & Bichelmeyer, B. (1990). Rapid prototyping: An alternative instructional design strategy. *Educational Technology Research and Development, 38*(1), 31-44.

Watzlawick, P., Beavin, J. H., & Jackson, D. D. (1967). *Pragmatics of human communication: A study of interactional patterns, pathologies, and paradoxes.* New York: W. W. Norton.

Zuboff, S. (1988). *In the age of the smart machine: The future of work and power.* New York: Basic Books.

Zucchermaglia, C. (1991). *Toward a cognitive ergonomics of educational technology.* Paper presented at the NATO Advanced Research Workshop on the Design of Constructivist Learning Environments, Leuven, Belgium.

19

An Eclectic Examination of Some Issues in the Constructivist-ISD Controversy

Sigmund Tobias
City College, City University of New York

This book, focusing on constructivism, also contains a spirited disagreement between Merrill (chapter 8), speaking for the instructional design (ISD) community, and the constructivists. Interestingly enough, the controversy does not appear to be between Merrill and the chapters he claimed to be commenting on, but rather between his views and those by Bednar, Cunningham, Duffy, and Perry (chapter 2). Time and time again Merrill references that chapter for his sharpest disagreement, rather than any of the chapters he was discussing. Scientific controversy is probably as motivating an event as any of the alternatives proposed by the constructivists, or the Jasper discs discussed by the Cognition and Technology Group at Vanderbilt University (chapter 6). I would guess that participants in these controversies are even more aroused than readers, so I am grateful to the editors for pulling me in from the sidelines to give an eclectic's comments on the issues raised by the constructivist-ISD controversy.

I must confess to an incredible sense of *deja vu* in reading some of the constructivist chapters generally, particularly the one by the Vanderbilt Group describing the video discs containing authentic tasks. The Jasper discs sound much like *Passion for Life,* a wonderful French film made more than 40 years ago (Le Chanois, 1949). The movie tells of a new teacher who comes to a French village and excites his students, some of whom were perennial non-achievers in school even though they function very effectively while performing different tasks in their environment. In the film, the teacher energizes the students by abandoning the boring traditional curriculum and using the environment as the student's laboratory. He enlightens a number of environmental problems by bringing different bodies of knowledge to bear to solve real problems. Of course, there was no mention of "situated cognition," "inert knowledge," or even "authentic problems," in the film, but the issues raised were surprisingly similar to those cited by the constructivists.

Some controversies have a way of reappearing in slightly different disguises every few decades. Generally, the intervening years equip the changing casts of participants on all sides of such issues with newer tools for enlightening the issues discussed. In the present case, behaviorism has run its course and the cognitive paradigm is in command of most psychological provinces, save for a few hamlets here or there. (It is hard to foresee specifically what the reaction to the predominance of the cognitive paradigm is likely to be eventually, but it is less difficult to predict that there will be such a reaction and that a new wave will then brush aside cognitive constructs which they find to be tired for failing to clarify a multitude of intractable phenomena.) Constructivism can be seen as an end product of the cognitive psychologists' emphasis on students' internal representations of external phenomena, and the pivotal role assigned to the cognitive processing of those phenomena.

The present debate is an example of a perennial controversy between advocates of the notion that instruction should be tailored either to individuals' unique attributes or to the curriculum's standards. As usual in such recurring controversies, the present protagonists approach the debate with new experiences, fresh concepts, and one would hope new data (though I will return to that point later) in order to clarify educators' and researchers' continuing concern with developing optimal instructional methods.

As someone interested in individual differences, I share Dick's (chapter 7) concern that the constructivists pay too little attention to the experiences students bring to school with them. Prior knowledge may be less than ideal for creating a truly adaptive instruction, but not dealing with it explicitly is clearly a major problem. As Dick also noted, the constructivists apparently let student preference be the principal factor in determining the approach taken to problems. Unfortunately, Clark (1982) has pointed out that students often choose unwisely since they tend to prefer less effective instructional methods than those that might be prescribed for them. Clearly, this issue has to be re-examined by the constructivist camp.

A careful reading of the constructivist papers suggests that depth of coverage is being substituted for breadth. Whether we are dealing with Spiro et al.'s (chapter 5) repeated exposures to material in different contexts, or with the Vanderbilt Group's (chapter 6) Jasper materials, it becomes clear that content is being covered in a very "deep" way at the expense of "breadth." One can imagine that students taught the first term of American history, for example, from a constructivist perspective might have a very profound understanding of the injustices imposed by taxation without representation and of the many ramifications such taxation has. However, would they learn anything about the war of 1812, Shay's rebellion, the whiskey rebellion, or the Monroe Doctrine? Presumably, constructivists would respond by saying that once students have a profound grasp of the basic generalizations, they can infer—or teach themselves—some of the content not "covered" in experiential instruction. Fortunately, these are empirical questions and they should be investigated.

Merrill (chapter 8) seems most concerned that the constructivist position would make the development of prepackaged instructional materials by any procedure, including ID_2—the design and delivery system Merrill's group is developing (Merrill, Li, & Jones, 1990)—impossible. That may not be the case. According to Merrill et al. (1990), a component of ID_2 has provisions for information gathering regarding "attributes of the learner population, and attributes and constraints of the environment and delivery system in which the instruction will be administered" (p. 10). Such a component should then be able to adapt instruction to individual difference and context parameters of different trainees. If well done, that component has much to recommend it irrespective of the constructivists-ISD controversy. It could be predicted that instructional materials developed from any framework would be enhanced by including provisions for relating the materials to relevant segments of students' prior learning and to the contexts in which that learning is most likely to be applied. The evidence on this issue will be in the quality of both the "main line" instruction and the adaptations generated by ID_2 as determined by succeeding empirical evaluations of its effectiveness.

The heart of the Merrill-Constructivists controversy revolves around the issue of transfer. Merrill holds that "To insist on context never being separated from use is to deny the teaching of abstractions....[A]t some point in the instruction these abstractions not only can, but must, be decontextualized if the student is to gain the maximum benefit and ability to transfer" (chapter 8). The constructivist position assumes that transfer can be facilitated by involvement in authentic tasks anchored in meaningful contexts. The transfer issue has been and is a thorny one about which there is a great deal of dispute, irrespective of the constructivist-ISD controversy (Detterman & Sternberg, in press). It is interesting, to note that the Vanderbilt Group finds that even good sixth-grade students showed little transfer from school to real life problems. Paradoxically, Saxe (1988) reported that child candy sellers in Brazil showed little transfer from the mathematical operations they practiced in their work on the street to the mathematics taught in school.

Thoughtful researchers are puzzled by the difficulties of demonstrating transfer experimentally, since a lot of anecdotal evidence indicates that people solve novel problems by the application of prior learning. Perhaps, as suggested elsewhere (Tobias, 1989), all models of learning and instruction will have to pay more attention to the energizing effects of affective factors on cognition generally, and motivational variables specifically, to unravel these and other puzzling situations in which intuition and research findings are in apparent conflict. Preliminary research attempting to relate such variables suggests that these are also likely to be difficult problems (Tobias & Kauffman, 1991). It should be noted that neither the constructivist nor ISD positions devote much attention to the specific impact of motivational variables on cognitive processes. Assuming that one presentation or another has more positive motivational attributes is unlikely to enlighten these, or any other, instructional puzzles.

The questions about transfer will not yield to spirited polemics—neither will any of the other thorny issues raised by the controversy. It is troubling to see so few references to research results on all sides of this controversy, and when such references are made they are usually parenthetical. While the format of the chapters and the journal in which they originally appeared are inappropriate for the presentation of detailed research findings, the fact that data are referred to only in passing is a cause for concern. The fact that there may be disagreements about the type of research needed to support any of the positions, should not prevent either camp from utilizing the energy generated by such a controversy to conduct investigations examining their assumptions. Nothing will stimulate a new shift away from contemporary paradigms more rapidly than reliance on ever more esoteric jargon which is unsubstantiated by research findings. Perhaps the time has come for a respite from polemics in order to devote more attention to the conduct of research.

ACKNOWLEDGMENT

This chapter was prepared while serving as a Summer Faculty Fellow at the Naval Personnel Research and Development Center in San Diego, in a program sponsored by the American Society for Engineering Education and the United States Navy.

REFERENCES

Clark, R. E. (1982). Antagonism between achievement and enjoyment in ATI studies. *Educational Psychologist, 17,* 92-101.

Detterman, D. K., & Sternberg, R. J. (in press). *Transfer on trial: Intelligence, cognition and instruction.* Norwood, NJ: Ablex.

Le Chanois, J. P. (1949). *L'Ecole buissonni 'ere* (Passion for life). Paris: Cooperative Generale du Cinema Française.

Merrill, M. D. (1991). Constructivism and instructional design. *Educational Technology, 31*(5), 45-53.

Merrill, M. D., Li, Z., & Jones, M. K. (1990). The second generation instructional design research program. *Educational Technology, 30*(3), 26-30.

Saxe, G. B. (1988). Candy selling and math learning. *Educational Researcher ,17*(6),14-21.

Tobias, S. (1989). Another look at research on the adaptation of instruction to student characteristics. *Educational Psychologist, 24,* 213-227.

Tobias, S., & Kaufman, C. J. (1991, April). *Incentives and problem solving*. Paper presented at the annual convention of the American Educational Research Association, Chicago, IL.

Author Index

Subject Index